THE HISTORY OF
THE WOOLLEN AND WORSTED
INDUSTRIES

PROCESSES OF THE WOOLLEN AND WORSTED INDUSTRIES.

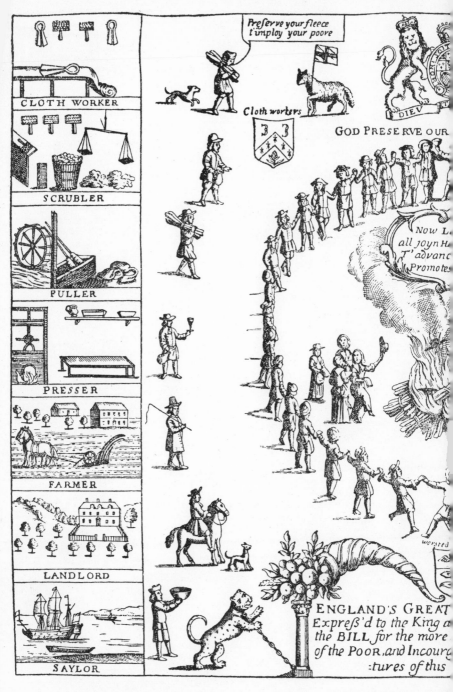

A SEVENTEENTH-CENTURY BROADSIDE ILLUSTRATING THE

THE HISTORY OF
THE WOOLLEN AND
WORSTED INDUSTRIES

E. LIPSON

FRANK CASS & CO. LTD.
1965

First published by
A. & C. Black Ltd., in 1921
and now reprinted by their
kind permission.

This edition published by Frank Cass & Co. Ltd.,
10 Woburn Walk, London W.C.1.

First edition   1921
Second impression 1965

Printed by Charles Birchall & Sons Ltd.
London and Liverpool.

AUTHOR'S PREFACE

THE sources from which the materials for this History have been drawn are given in a Bibliographical Note in the Appendix. While the book is based on the original authorities, detailed references have been omitted in view of the nature of the Series to which it belongs.

The chapter on the mediæval woollen industry in Vol. I. of *The Economic History of England* has been rewritten (with the exception of a few paragraphs) and extended. I hope in Vol. II.—now in preparation—to treat, in full detail and with complete references, several of the topics dealt with in the present book, together with other aspects of English Economic History in the seventeenth and eighteenth centuries.

The reader who is unacquainted with the processes of the woollen industry may find it convenient to read first the account given on pp. 128-142.

I have to thank Professor C. H. Firth for the broadside reproduced in this book. My thanks are also due to my pupil, Mr. F. Miller, Oriel College, Oxford, for his assistance in reading the proofs.

E. LIPSON.

OXFORD,
February, 1921.

CONTENTS

ILLUSTRATIONS

THE WOOLLEN AND WORSTED INDUSTRIES

CHAPTER I

THE ORIGIN AND GROWTH OF THE WOOLLEN AND WORSTED INDUSTRIES

IN the nineteenth century the English woollen industry[1] Prestige of the English woollen industry. was eclipsed in importance by the cotton industry, but in former ages it was pre-eminently the staple manufacture of the country. At the opening of the eighteenth century the value of our cotton exports was scarcely more than £20,000,[2] whereas the exports of woollen manufacture are said to have exceeded three million pounds, or nearly one-half of the entire export trade. Nothing is more remarkable than the prestige enjoyed by the woollen industry in remoter times. As early as 1454 Parliament declared that " the making of cloth within all parts of the realm is the greatest occupation and living of the poor commons of this land." Camden (1607) described English cloth as " one of the pillars of the State "; Coke termed it " the worthiest and richest commodity of this kingdom "; Bacon called it " this great wheel " of the realm; and the Venetian Ambassador wrote home in 1610 that it formed " the chief wealth of this nation." A writer during the Civil War asserted that " the most substantial and staple commodity that our country affords for the maintenance of trade is cloth," and he explained the origin of the woolsack as intended

---

[1] For the sake of brevity the term "woollen industry " will be used to include "worsted," except where they are specially distinguished.

[2] In 1697 the value of the cotton exports was approximately £5,920; in 1701, £23,250; in 1710, £5,700; in 1741, £17,910.

" to put our judges in the House of Lords in mind of preserving and advancing the trade and manufactory of wool."
Chief Justice Hale, writing after the Restoration, considered
the woollen manufacture the " basis of all commerce ";
William Carter (1672) extolled it as " the flower, strength,
and sinew of this nation "; James II. spoke of it, in a proclamation of 1688, as " the staple manufacture in this our
kingdom "; and a statute of William III. (1698) pronounced
it to be " the greatest and most profitable commodity of
this kingdom on which the value of lands and the trade of
the nation do chiefly depend." The volume of praise continued, in the following century, with unabated force.
In the eyes of John Haynes (1715) English cloth was still
" the glory of our kingdom," while Daniel Defoe (1724)
praised it as " the richest and most valuable manufacture
in the world." " Nothing can answer all the ends of dress,"
he wrote, " but good English broad cloth, fine camblets,
druggets, serges, and such like. These " other countries
" must have, and with these none but England can supply
them. Be their country hot or cold, torrid or frigid, 'tis
the same thing, near the Equinox or near the Pole, the
English woollen manufacturer clothes them all; here it
covers them warm from the freezing breath of the northern
bear, and there it shades them and keeps them cool from
the searching beams of a perpendicular sun. Let no man
wonder that the woollen manufacture is arrived to such
a magnitude when in a word it may be said to clothe the
world." Even as late as 1782 a writer is found to protest
against the cotton mills " lately erected in the neighbourhood of Manchester," and to utter the warning that if these
mills were " suffered to destroy our woollen and stuff[1]
manufactures, they will prove the most fatal discoveries ever
made in Old England." Half a century later (1833), however, the cloth manufacture had been completely out-
distanced by its younger but more vigorous rival. The
woollen exports now totalled six and a half million pounds,
or twice the value of the exports of 1700, but cotton exports
totalled over eighteen million pounds, or nine hundred

[1] *I.e.*, worsted.

times the value of the exports of 1700. In 1828 William Radcliffe, a cotton manufacturer, was able to affirm with justice that "cotton by the magnitude of its manufacture must now justly rank as the staple trade of this kingdom."[1]

Among the industries of England the woollen manufacture occupies a unique position. In the first place, it was the premier English industry from the twelfth to the nineteenth centuries. To quote a petition laid before Parliament in 1800, it was "our earliest, most extensive and most valuable manufacture." "There are many more people employed," said a writer in 1683, "and more profit made, and money imported, by this manufactory" of cloth "alone than by all the other manufactories of England joined together." A Parliamentary Report on Trade drawn up in the reign of William III. estimated that, after the Restoration, the woollen manufacture accounted for "near two-thirds" of the general exports. It was, therefore, justly described as "the master-wheel of trade," and Englishmen proudly boasted that we clothed "half of Europe by our English cloth," making the Continent England's "servant" since it wore England's "livery." *Its unique position: (i.) England's premier industry down to the nineteenth century.*

In the second place, the raw material for the woollen industry was mostly raised at home, the importation of foreign wool being inconsiderable down to the nineteenth century. Native wool held pride of place since it was universally reputed the best in Europe. Lambard, an Elizabethan antiquary, records with satisfaction that the sheep of this realm "be now (God be thanked therefor) worthy of great estimation both for the exceeding fineness of the fleece, which passeth all other in Europe at this day, and for the abundant store of flocks so increasing everywhere that the whole realm might rightly be called Sheppey." And Dryden boasted with truth: *(ii.) Its fortunes interwoven with those of English agriculture.*

---

[1] In 1907, according to the Returns received under the Census of Production Act, the total value of the output of woollen and worsted factories in the United Kingdom was £70,331,000, and the number of persons employed was 257,017. The corresponding figures for cotton were £176,940,000, and 572,869 persons.

" Though Jason's Fleece was fam'd of old,
The British wool is growing gold;
No mines can more of wealth supply:
It keeps the peasant from the cold,
And takes for kings the Tyrian dye."[1]

The mutual dependence of industry and tillage inspired
the prayer of Fuller that " the plough may go along and
the wheel around, so that being fed by the one and clothed
by the other there may be, by God's blessing, no danger of
starvation in our nation"; but his vision of an ordered
commonwealth, in which the manufacturer and the farmer
co-operated harmoniously, was not fulfilled. The English
manufacturers enjoyed untold advantage over their foreign
competitors in their ability to draw freely upon native
sources for their raw material, but when they sought to
exclude them completely from the English wool-market
they came into sharp collision with the English graziers.
Thus the fortunes of the textile manufacture were closely
interwoven with those of agriculture, and the rivalry of
these two great industries fills an important chapter in
English Economic History.   In the nineteenth century the
conflict between the landed and commercial interests was
fought out over the question of cheap food; in the seventeenth and eighteenth centuries the conflict was over cheap
raw material.   The free importation of foreign wool and the
prohibition of the export of native wool—these were the
cardinal problems of economic controversy debated in
innumerable pamphlets and broadsheets.   Even more
fundamental was the conflict of interests arising from the fact
that the progress of the woollen industry seemed to divert
the national energies from tillage into other and more
unstable channels: a trend viewed with apprehension by
those early economists who preferred to see the prosperity
of England broad-based on land rather than on the shifting
foundations of industry.   " We have too great a clothing
commonwealth," said a member of Parliament in 1614, and
Thomas Mun, in *England's Treasure by Forraign Trade*,

---

[1] *King Arthur.*
[2] Published in 1664, but written before the Civil War.

voiced the general uneasiness when he wrote: Clothing " is the greatest wealth and best employment of the poor of this kingdom, yet nevertheless we may peradventure employ ourselves with better safety, plenty, and profit in using more tillage and fishing than to trust so wholly to the making of cloth; for in times of war, or by other occasions, if some foreign Princes should prohibit the use thereof in their dominions, it might suddenly cause much poverty and dangerous uproars, especially by our poor people, when they should be deprived of their ordinary maintenance."

In the third place, the history of the woollen industry illustrates with peculiar clearness the different phases of English industrial development. No other industry affords better material for studying the growth and decay of the various economic organisms which have taken root in English soil at one period or another—the " gild " system, where the worker owned both the material and the instruments of production; the " domestic " system, where he owned the instruments but not the material; and the " factory " system, where he owns neither the instruments nor the material.[1] The earliest craft gilds in this country were the weavers' gilds, and the subsequent disintegration of the gild system, and the rise of other forms of industrial organisation, find in the cloth manufacture their clearest and most notable expression. We shall observe, in particular, that the Industrial Revolution did not give birth to the capitalist system. Capitalism existed in the English woollen industry four centuries before the introduction of machinery, although it assumed different forms in the " domestic " and " factory " stages of its evolution. *(iii.) Illustrates the phases of English industrial development.*

In the fourth place, the cloth manufacture was the first branch of industry to be subjected to national control and a uniform system of regulation. The favourite child of the Legislature, it was hedged round on every side with innumerable statutes " by way of guards and fences." As Adam Smith remarked: " Our woollen manufacturers have been more successful than any other class of workmen in persuading the Legislature that the prosperity of the nation *(iv.) The favourite child of the Legislature.*

[1] See below, Chapter II.

depends upon the success and extension of their particular business." Towards the end of the eighteenth century an abstract was published of " laws relating to the growers of wool and to the manufacturers of, and dealers in, all sorts of woollen commodities." It contained the titles of over three hundred laws then on the statute book. These laws regulated the clipping of sheep, the packing of wool, the length, breadth, weight, and " true making " of cloth, the use of materials in dyeing, the methods of fulling and " tentering," and the nature of the instruments for rowing and shearing.[1] It is not surprising, therefore, to find a Commission reporting, as early as 1622, that " the laws now in force concerning the making and dressing of cloth are so many and by the multitude of them are so intricate that it is very hard to resolve what the law is." Not only did the Government create for the protection of the woollen industry an elaborate code of restrictive legislation, but its foreign policy—and especially the encouragement of voyages of discovery—was largely inspired by the desire to open up new markets abroad.[2]

(v.) Its geographical distribution.
In the fifth place, the woollen industry was the most widespread of all English industries. A chapter in this book is devoted to its geographical distribution from the twelfth to the nineteenth centuries, but, although certain parts of the kingdom were pre-eminently the " manufacturing districts " of England, there was probably not a town, village, or hamlet throughout the length and breadth of the country which was not connected at some time or other with the manufacture of cloth. Spinning was a cottage industry everywhere carried on by women and children, nothing more being required than a spindle and distaff or wheel; and weaving, similarly, was a household occupation. It was the universal character of the woollen industry which gave it its peculiar significance, since in its progress and development were bound up the national fortunes and the interests of every section of the community.

The influence of the woollen industry is shown, finally, in the extent to which the English language has been en-

---

[1] See below, p. 141.   [2] See below, p. 102.

riched by words and phrases connected in their origin with (vi.) Its influence on litera- ture and popular speech. the manufacture of cloth. No industry has left more traces in popular literature and on popular speech. Such phrases as " to spin a yarn," " weavers of long tales," " the thread of a discourse," " a web of sophistry," " unravelling a mystery," " tangled skein," betray at once their source. Shakespeare uses frequent metaphors from spinning and weaving: " The web of our life is of a mingled yarn, good and ill together "; " life is a shuttle "; " their thread of life is spun "; " ill-weav'd ambition, how much art thou shrunk !" Scott makes a similar use in *Marmion* :

> " Oh, what a tangled web we weave
> When first we practise to deceive !"

We still speak of " fine-drawn " theories and " home-spun " youths; and life may still be described as a " web " of which the " thread " is cut short by the fates with their abhorred shears. There are several proverbial expressions, such as, " weave in faith, and God will find thread "; " to have tow on one's distaff " (to have work in hand); " he goes far to warp and the mill so near " (corresponding to: " carrying coals to Newcastle "); " to have neither reed nor gears, shuttle nor shears " (applied to a destitute person). Many personal names betoken the original occupation of some ancestor—for example, Dyer, Fuller, Lister, Tailor, Tucker, Walker, Weaver, and Webster; and local nomen-clature has preserved names like " Rack-closes," " East-Stretch," " Tucking-Mill Field," which refer to fulling and tentering cloth. Lastly, the close identification of women with the spinning industry is reflected in the use of the word " spinster " to denote an unmarried woman.

The arts of spinning and weaving rank among the most Origin of the woollen industry. primitive of the industrial arts. The fancy of a later age ascribed their origin to our primæval parents. " Drapery " is unquestionably so ancient as to have the honour of being the immediate successor of the fig-leaves. And though we are not quite certain that our great first father began it within his fair Eden, yet we are assured that Eve's spinistry

and Adam's spade set to work together." The tradition
of the weavers connected them with Naamah:

> " That Naamah sister was to Tubal Cain,
> First us'd this Art, the Scripture doth make plain."

We find occasional references to spinning and weaving
in this country even in the earliest times. An edict of
Diocletian[1] makes mention of British cloth; remains of
dyeing works have been found at Silchester; traces of
fulling in rural dwellings in Kent, Surrey, and Gloucestershire; and the Romans are said to have had an " imperial
weaving manufactory " at Winchester for the use of the
Emperors—the wool being spun so fine, according to
Dionysius Periegetes,[2] that it was " comparable to a spider's
web." In Anglo-Saxon England the mother of King Alfred
is represented as skilled in spinning wool, and the chronicler
Fabyan tells us that Edward the Elder " sette his sonnes
to scole and his doughters he sette to woll werke, takyng
example of Charlys the Conquestour." It is even possible
that English woollen fabrics were being exported to the
Continent as early as the eighth century, for our earliest
commercial treaty—the famous letter of Charles the Great
to Offa, King of Mercia (796)—contains this passage: " Our
subjects make request concerning the size of the cloaks:
that you will have them made of the same pattern as used
to come to us in old times." The authentic history of
the English woollen industry does not begin, however,
until after the Norman Conquest, when we find gilds of
weavers established under Henry I. in London, Winchester,
Oxford, Lincoln, and Huntingdon. This shows that an
organised weaving industry was carried on in the twelfth
century as a trade, and not merely as a family or domestic
occupation. About the same time large quantities of
woad were imported for purposes of dyeing. Not only
was cloth manufactured for the home market in numerous
parts of the country during the twelfth and thirteenth
centuries, but many local varieties were also exported.

---

[1] Third century A.D.
[2] A geographer of the third or fourth century.

The cloths of Stamford found a market at Venice as early as 1265, and they even gained a European reputation, since it was considered worth while to imitate them at Milan. Other varieties exported to Spain and elsewhere were those of York, Beverley, Lincoln, Coggeshall, Colchester, Maldon, and Sudbury. These finer English cloths were also bought for the King's wardrobe, and the purchases made on the royal behalf furnish information as to the relative values of the different fabrics. Thus in 1182 the Sheriff of Lincolnshire purchased cloth at the rate of 6s. 8d. for an ell[1] of scarlet, 3s. for green say, 1s. 8d. for grey say, and 3s. for an ell of blanket—erroneously supposed to have been " named after its first maker, Thomas Blanket," who actually lived a century and a half later.

The year 1258 affords the first important landmark in the history of the English woollen industry. Henry III. was on the throne, and his attachment to foreign favourites had awakened the lively resentment of his English subjects. Under the leadership of Simon de Montfort a Great Council of the barons was held at Oxford and took in hand the reform of the country. One of its measures showed the growing desire of Englishmen to foster the native industry. It forbade the export of wool, and ordered that " the wool of the country should be worked up in England and not sold to foreigners, and that everyone should use woollen cloth made within the country." Those who wished to wear the more delicate fabrics woven in the looms of Flanders were bidden " not to seek over-precious garments." This appeal to the patriotism of the nation does not seem to have been very successful. The Government found it impossible for any length of time to prevent the export of wool, for it was anxious on political grounds to keep on friendly terms with the Flemish people. In the Middle Ages England was the great enemy of France, and Flanders, which was the gate into France, could be a valuable ally to this country as well as a dangerous foe, since her coast was immediately opposite our own. Accordingly, another scheme was set on foot. The attempt to starve out the

Attempts to foster a native industry in the thirteenth century.

---

[1] An ell is 45 inches.

competition of the Flemish manufacturers by refusing to supply them with raw material was bound to fail, not only because it excited intense ill-feeling against us, but because the Flemings endeavoured to secure supplies of wool from other countries. It seemed a better plan to meet the rivalry of Flanders by improving the quality of the native cloth. If English manufacturers were to gain possession of the home market and oust their foreign rivals, they must first learn the secrets of their craft, and improve their standard of workmanship, instead of trying to force inferior substitutes upon an unwilling nation. How was this to be done ? To-day a manufacturer who seeks to capture the market endeavours, first of all, to improve his machi nery and commercial success now depends, among other factors, upon inventive genius. In the Middle Ages the basis of industrial life was not machinery but craftsmanship, and skilled labour was therefore the most important asset in building up a mediæval industry.[1] Now England was certainly not entirely destitute of skilled cloth-workers—for we have already seen how English cloths had gained a reputation in markets abroad, and were not disdained even for the King's own wardrobe—but they showed a narrow spirit in their attempts to keep the cloth trade in their own hands as their private monopoly. Hence the only way in which a native cloth manufacture could be successfully fostered was by inducing foreign craftsmen to settle in the country and impart their technical knowledge and skill to English artisans. One step in this direction was taken at the end of Henry III.'s reign (1271) when the Government declared that " all workers of woollen cloths, male and female, as well of Flanders as of other lands, may safely come into our realm, there to make cloths, upon the understanding that those who shall so come and make such cloths shall be quit of toll and tallage and of payment of other customs for their work until the end of five years."

Decay of the woollen industry.
This invitation serves to show that the design of introducing foreign weavers into England was already present to the minds of English rulers in the thirteenth century;

[1] This is still true in the case of dyeing.

nevertheless for the moment nothing was done. Two
generations were to elapse before the project bore fruit;
and during these two generations the condition of the native
woollen manufacture steadily deteriorated. We shall cite
a few examples in order to show its impoverished state on
the eve of the great experiment which was destined to
transform the economic life of England. In the time of
King John the weavers of Oxford were sixty " and more "
in number; half a century later they were reduced to fifteen,
and a century later all the Oxford weavers were dead and
none had taken their place. The weavers of York, once
the chief seat of the cloth trade in the North of England,
were in a similar plight; they now numbered scarcely more
than a dozen. The weavers of Lincoln had counted more
than two hundred in the twelfth century, whereas in the
early part of the fourteenth century there were no weavers
left either in the city or its suburbs. Under Henry III.
Northampton is said to have contained as many as three
hundred cloth-workers; but in the next reign they were too
poor to support the taxes, and fled from the town. Even in
London, already the foremost city in England by reason of
its wealth, dignity, and commercial pre-eminence, the
number of weaving looms had fallen from three hundred and
eighty to eighty. On every hand, in fact, we meet with
evidence of a general decline of industry in which all towns
alike shared.

These symptoms of decay naturally excited great alarm.
It was necessary to take prompt and vigorous steps if the
woollen industry, which had been in so flourishing a condition in the twelfth century, was to be saved from extinction.
Edward II. has been styled " the first king since the Norman
Conquest who was not a man of business," but the industrial policy of his reign, at any rate, does credit to the
good intentions of his Government. He ordered (1326)
that no cloth which was not made in England, Wales, or
Ireland, should be bought in this country except by the
" king, queen, earls, barons, knights, and ladies, and their
children born in wedlock, archbishops, bishops, and other
persons and people of Holy Church, and seculars who can

The industrial policy of Edward II.

spend forty pounds sterling a year of their rents "; the
latter alone were allowed to purchase the finer fabrics
imported from abroad. More important was the promise
to grant suitable " franchises "—that is, privileges—to the
weavers, dyers, fullers, and others who worked upon cloths.
It would seem that Edward II. had definitely planned the
settlement of alien artisans in England; and the alarm of
foreign manufacturers was shown in their attempts to buy
up all the teasels and burs[1] they could find throughout the
land, as well as the materials used in dyeing, madder and
woad, fuller's earth,[2] " and all other things which pertain
to the working of cloth," in order to prevent a revival of
the woollen industry in this country.

The immigration of Flemish weavers.

Edward II.'s schemes were cut short by his deposition,
and it was reserved for his successor to carry out the design
which he had set on foot. The reign of Edward III. marks
a great epoch in the history of the English cloth trade, but
to understand his work aright, we must bear in mind that
Edward was not the founder of the English woollen industry. The art of weaving woollen cloth was well established in this country as far back as the twelfth century,
and Edward's work was not to create a new industry, but
to revive an old one which was fast decaying. This was
accomplished by bringing over Flemish weavers into
England. There was great unrest in the Low Countries
owing to various political and economic causes, and the
Flemings therefore lent a ready ear to the solicitations of
English agents who invited them to settle here. In 1331
Edward granted letters of protection to John Kempe of
Flanders, " weaver of woollen cloths," and to " the men,
servants and apprentices," whom he was bringing with him
to exercise his craft in England; at the same time he offered
similar letters to all weavers and other workers of cloth
who came from over the sea to carry on their trade or
" mistery " within the realm. In 1337 a statute promised
the most liberal franchises and " fair treating." " All the

---

[1] Burs are the prickly seed-vessels or flower-heads of plants, used
in connection with teasling cloth. For teasels, see below, p. 141.

[2] " Fuller's earth," which Fuller, the Church historian, termed
" a precious treasure," was used for cleansing cloth.

cloth-workers of strange lands," recited the Act, " of what-soever country they be, which will come into England, Ireland, Wales, and Scotland, within the King's power, shall come safely and surely, and shall be in the King's protection and safe-conduct, to dwell in the same lands choosing where they will; and to the intent that the said cloth-workers shall have the greater will to come and dwell here, our sovereign lord the King will grant them franchises as many and such as may suffice them." As a result of this invitation there was a large influx of alien weavers, dyers, and fullers, who took up their residence in the large towns—London, York, Winchester, Norwich, Bristol, and Abingdon—and also scattered themselves over the countryside.

An old historian, the " worthy " Fuller, describes the Fuller's account. coming of the alien weavers in quaint and exaggerated terms. " The King and State began now to grow sensible of the great gain the Netherlands got by our English wool; in memory whereof the Duke of Burgundy, not long after, instituted the Order of the Golden Fleece; wherein, indeed, the fleece was ours, the golden theirs—so vast their emolu-ment by the trade of clothing. Our King, therefore, resolved, if possible, to reduce the trade of his own country who as yet were ignorant of that art, as knowing no more what to do with their wool than the sheep that wear it, as to any artificial and curious drapery; their best clothes then being no better than friezes, such their coarseness for want of skill in the making. . . . The intercourse now being great betwixt the English and the Netherlands . . . unsuspected emissaries were employed by our King into those countries, who brought themselves into familiarity with those Dutch-men as were absolute masters of their trade, but not masters of themselves; as either journeymen or apprentices. These bemoaned the slavishness of these poor servants whom their masters used rather like heathen than Christians; yea, rather like horses than men. Early up and late in bed, and all day hard work and harder fare (a few herrings and mouldy cheese), and all to enrich the churls their masters, without any profit to themselves. But how happy these should be if they would but come into England, bringing their mistery with them and which would provide them welcome in all places. Here they should feed on beef and mutton. . . . Happy the yeoman's house into which one of these Dutchmen did enter, bringing industry and wealth along with them. Such who came in strangers within their doors soon after went out bridegrooms, and returned sons-in-law, having married the daughters of their landlords who first entertained them; yea, the yeomen in whose houses they harboured soon proceeded gentlemen, gaining great worship to themselves, arms and worship to their estates." Fuller adds that the strangers were " sprinkled .everywhere," giving as the reason the King's apprehension " lest on discontent they might embrace a general resolution to return." However welcome the immigrant weavers may have been in country districts, their presence in towns was very distasteful to their industrial competitors; for while they proved amenable to the civic authorities, they refused to submit to the control of the native weavers or enter their gild. The English artisans resented the rivalry of the newcomers, who set at defiance their monopoly and refused to contribute towards the annual dues which the weavers' gilds owed the Crown. The King intervened on behalf of the alien craftsmen and ordered that they should not be compelled to join the weavers' gild, but the friction between denizens and aliens did not die down, and as late as 1421 the foreign weavers complained that they were " grievously persecuted and harassed" by the native weavers, who would not allow them to ply their craft in London and other towns.

State protection of industry.
Edward's experiment was attended with complete success, and in 1613 an old writer was able to say that the English cloth-makers had grown so " perfect in this mistery that it is at this instant the glory of our traffic and maintenance of our poor, many hundred thousands depending wholly on the same, chief pillar to our prince's revenue, the life of our merchant, the living of our clothier." Not only did Edward encourage the settlement of alien craftsmen, he also took steps to protect the native industry from foreign competition, and to ensure an adequate supply of raw material.

On the one hand, he forbade the importation of manufactured cloth; on the other, he prohibited the export of English wool.[1] It is true that neither Edward nor his successors adhered very strictly to a protectionist policy. They were too deeply engrossed in their foreign schemes to pursue a consistent economic policy, and their industrial schemes were easily sacrificed to their political ambitions and dreams of aggrandisement on the Continent. One of the charges against the Lancastrian Government was that wool had " course and passage out of the realm, wherefore all strangers take but little reward to buy our English cloth, but make it themselves "; and the Yorkist dynasty sought to gain popularity by reverting to a policy of protection. Thus in the Middle Ages the policy of protection was only fitfully maintained, and we have to wait until the seventeenth century for the definite adoption of an industrial protective policy. Whether State protection is needed in the case of a well-established industry has often been debated, but at least the justification for it is more apparent in the case of an infant industry which is too weak to be exposed to the full rigour of an unrestricted competition. In so far as the Government was actuated, not by the desire for revenue but by the desire to establish the cloth trade on a sound basis, its measures seem to have been acceptable to the nation at large.

The industrial policy of Edward III., whether or not it *Progress of the cloth trade.* was consciously inspired by the desire to foster a native cloth manufacture,[2] revealed to England her true destiny, and helped to prepare the day for her transformation from a land of agricultural labourers into a land of industrial artisans. Even in his own lifetime his measures were rewarded with surprising success. One proof of the progress made during his reign is that woollen cloth was being exported in sufficient quantity to make it worth while to impose customs duties upon it. This raised some protest at

---

[1] " These statutes," wrote a chronicler (Adam Murimuth), " had no effect, nor did anyone take the trouble to observe them."

[2] Edward's industrial measures were closely connected with his political schemes, and the question how far they were the product of diplomatic exigencies is difficult to determine.

first, but the exporters of cloth had little ground for complaint in comparison with the exporters of wool, for the latter paid the enormous duty of 33 per cent., while the former paid less than 2. The evidence of statistics serves to show how abundantly this progress was maintained during the fifteenth and sixteenth centuries. In Edward III.'s reign about 30,000 sacks of wool were sent abroad year by year; but a century and a half later this number, so far from increasing, had fallen to a quarter, and afterwards it fell to a sixth. Nor was this extraordinary shrinkage due to any shortage of wool. On the contrary, we shall presently see how the supply of wool was growing by leaps and bounds owing to a revolution in agriculture, which covered England with sheepfarms in place of cornfields. But wool was now being supplied to the home market; it went to meet the demands of the native clothing industry. The figures which illustrate the expansion of the cloth trade are in remarkable contrast with those of the wool trade. In the middle of the fourteenth century, the number of cloths exported was about 5,000. In the reign of Henry VIII. (1509–47) the average number of cloths sent abroad annually had multiplied twenty-fold, apart from the increase in the number of kersies and worsted cloths. These figures afford eloquent testimony to the progress of a revolution which was converting England into an industrial country, whose staple export was no longer raw material, but manufactured goods. Evidence of the growth of the woollen industry is also revealed very strikingly in the fate which overtook the towns of Flanders, once the workshops of the mediæval world. The Flemings were sorely pressed by the competition of the English cloth-makers, and no longer enjoyed the monopoly of the weaving craft. Bruges, which in the thirteenth century boasted of 40,000 looms, was declining in numbers and making desperate but ineffectual efforts to recover its prosperity. Ypres, with a population in 1408 of over 80,000 inhabitants and 3,000 to 4,000 cloth-workers—this was a great figure for a mediæval town—had sunk in 1486 to less than 6,000 inhabitants and barely

a score or two cloth factories. Thus England was fast
outstripping her industrial rivals. Her cloth was finding
a market in every known quarter of the globe. She had
obtained control of her own market, and she was ousting
her competitors from the markets of other countries. The
romance of trade records, indeed, no achievement more
astonishing than this industrial revolution of the fifteenth
century.

A new class emerged into prominence—a manufacturing Prosperity
class.[1] Hitherto society had consisted mainly of two of the towns.
separate and distinct communities: landlords and labourers,
knights and husbandmen; to these was now added an artisan
class, composed of men who pursued the " art " or " mistery "
of manufactures. This appearance of a manufacturing
class was a momentous event. It naturally brought in its
train new social problems, but for the moment we are content to notice how it meant for England an enormous
accession of wealth. The prosperity of the country was writ
large over all the manufacturing districts; it was reflected
especially in a great development of town life. Before the
fifteenth century most English towns were in a wretched,
squalid condition, mean and poor, sparsely inhabited,
scarcely more than large-sized villages. In 1414 the
inhabitants of Rye mustered only a few shillings between
them, while before the century had closed the town could
boast of no less than five burgesses worth £400 each. This
is only one example among many, and there is abundant
evidence to show the marked advance which the towns
were making in prosperity. Of the growing wealth of
the country there is striking testimony in the words of
a Venetian who wrote at the end of the fifteenth century.
" In one single street named the Strand leading to St.
Paul's," he tells us, " there are fifty-two goldsmiths' shops
so rich and full of silver vessels, great and small, that in
all the shops in Milan, Rome, Venice, and Florence put
together I do not think there would be found so many of
the magnificence that are to be seen in London." His

[1] *I.e.*, a class engaged in industry. On the use of the term "manufacturer," see below, p. 41.

words confirm the observations made by Manuel, the Emperor of the Byzantine Empire, who visited England in the year 1400: " in populousness and power, in riches and luxury, London, the metropolis of the isle, may claim a pre-eminence over all the cities of the West." Of the country as a whole he remarks: " The land is overspread with towns and villages; though destitute of wines and not abounding in fruit trees, it is fertile in wheat and barley, in honey and wool; *and much cloth is manufactured by the inhabitants.*" Everywhere a class of rich burgesses came into existence, whose houses and plate and tapestry all bore witness to their material progress: who entertained kings at their table as their guests and in the assessment of taxes ranked with earls and barons. Their prosperity was evinced also in a fine display of public spirit, in the foundation of hospitals and schools, the repair of roads and bridges—in the olden days these things were matters of private benevolence—and many other spheres of public utility. Benefactors of the poor bequeathed money to give a start in life to young men who wanted to set up as cloth-makers. The reign of Henry VI. was specially noteworthy for the benefactions of wealthy London citizens. Richard Whittington, the hero of legendary exploits and an abiding witness of the triumph of merit over adversity, devoted his wealth to the erection of the London Guildhall and its library. Other citizens supplied the City with water or built granaries for the storage of corn against times of scarcity. Many magnificent churches, the fruit of the piety of rich clothiers, still cover the country-side, though the prosperity to which they once bore witness has long passed away to other centres of industrial activity. Signs of industrial wealth meet us, in fact, on every hand—in the erection of churches and town halls, market crosses and paved streets, gates, bridges, and harbours. The towns were now in a position also to lend money to the King, though this was a privilege which they would gladly have been spared. It is hardly surprising, therefore, to find that in the fifteenth century industry was proving more attractive than husbandry. It offered a wider scope to men of initiative and enterprise, and opened up a great career where wealth and prestige lay within the grasp of all who could approve themselves worthy by their skill and resources. The cloth trade afforded fresh openings in life, and all the restless and ambitious spirits, who were discontented with their mode of existence and craved for new opportunities of advancement, flocked into the towns to seek more profitable sources of livelihood.

It is a remarkable testimony to the growth of the woollen industry that it was directly responsible for an agrarian revolution—the substitution of wool-growing for corn-growing. This revolution took place during the fifteenth and sixteenth centuries, the movement reaching its height in the reigns of Henry VII., Henry VIII., and Edward VI. The first condition of a flourishing industry is an ample supply of raw material, and the rapidity with which the native cloth manufacture was expanding produced a corresponding demand for wool on the part of the English clothiers. The profit derived by graziers from the growing of wool tempted landlords and farmers to turn their land into pasture. " The foot of the sheep," men said, " turns sand into gold," and sheep were regarded " as the most profitablest cattle any man can have." The development of pasturage at the expense of tillage attracted universal attention. On every side were heard indignant protests at the enormous quantity of sheep. " God gave the earth to men to inhabit," cried Tyndale, " and not unto sheep and wild deer." " Where," cried Latimer in a sermon preached before Edward VI., " have been a great many householders and inhabitants, there is now but a shepherd and his dog." Sir Thomas More, in a famous passage in *Utopia*, denounced sheep as " devourers of men." " They unpeople villages and towns, turning the best inhabited places into solitudes; tenants are turned out of their possessions and either beg or rob. One shepherd can look after a flock which will stock an extent of ground that would require many hands if it were to be ploughed and reaped." A ballad of the time ran:

The Agrarian Revolution.

> " The towns go down, the land decays . . .
>   Great men maketh nowadays
>   a sheep-cote in the church . . .
>   Commons to close and keep;
>   Poor folk for bread cry and weep;
>   Towns pulled down to pasture sheep;
>   this is the new guise !"

Sometimes the woollen manufacturer himself turned sheep-farmer. One famous clothier of the fifteenth century, John Tame, kept large flocks of sheep at Fairford, and the wool produced there was worked up in his weaving sheds at Cirencester. In fact the growth of the textile industries, while it was responsible for the depopulation of the country-side owing to the substitution of pasture land for corn-fields, served to provide openings for many of those who were cut adrift from the soil. In any case the agrarian changes of the sixteenth century afford striking proof of the expansion of the cloth trade, and reveal its influence in diverting the energies of the rural community into channels which might best satisfy the needs and require-ments of the textile industries.

The Glaston-bury weavers.

The Tudor epoch witnessed a renewed immigration of alien craftsmen. At the beginning of his reign Henry VII. authorised the settlement of foreign cloth-makers, and the Protector Somerset in 1551 planted at Glastonbury Abbey a colony of weavers, chiefly Flemings, who are described as " outlandish, learned, and godly men." He undertook to provide them with accommodation and four acres of land for each family, and he advanced them nearly £500. His plans were cut short by his fall, and the settlers soon found themselves in difficulties. The King intervened on their behalf, and a Commission was appointed to investigate their affairs. It reported that the settlement was likely to bring " great commodity to the commonweal ": the strangers being " very godly, honest, poor folk, of quiet and sober conversation, and showing themselves ever willing and ready to instruct and teach young children and others their craft." The housing problem was a serious one, only six houses being available for forty-six families, and building operations were taken in hand. Two dye-houses for dyeing

and calendering worsted were placed at their disposal
within the monastery, and money was advanced them to
buy wool and materials for dyeing—woad, madder, alum—
and to pay loom-makers, spinners, and others. The
Glastonbury weavers became naturalised and claimed to be
treated as Englishmen in respect of taxes, to enjoy freedom
of religious worship, to have a gild with their own warden
and overseers, and a hall where they could examine all
cloths made amongst them and punish offenders, according
to the custom beyond the seas " where the like mistery is
occupied." These projects, however, never materialised,
for on the death of Edward VI. the weavers, bereft of their
protector, left the country.

The most important event in the industrial history of The New
the sixteenth century was the coming of the Dutch and Draperies:
Walloon weavers. Their immigration constitutes the (i.) Norwich.
second great landmark in the history of the English cloth
trade, just as the influx of Flemish weavers in the fourteenth
century was the first. In the reign of Elizabeth the Netherlands formed part of the Spanish Empire, and the Dutch
revolted against the tyrannical rule of Philip II. and his
viceroy Duke Alva, who had set up the " Council of Blood "
in order to stamp out the Reformation. The cruelty of
Alva's administration caused a large exodus of the most
skilful and industrious section of the population—and the
folly of religious persecution was once more revealed in the
most signal fashion. The exiles were welcomed by the
English Government both as religious refugees and as a
valuable accession to the economic resources of the country,
for they established in this country a new branch of the
woollen industry. This was the manufacture of the finer
fabrics, known as the " new draperies," many of which
were either unknown in this country or were beyond the
technical skill of English textile workers. Among other
centres the strangers settled in Norwich, whose prosperity
was declining owing to a succession of epidemics and fires
and the migration of craftsmen into the country districts.
At the opening of the fifteenth century Norwich had been
the second city in the kingdom; a century later it ranked

sixth, and in 1545 grass was growing in the market-place.
Its rulers were anxious, therefore, to attract skilled artisans
to the city in order to revive its prosperity. They complained that the worsted manufacture " by which many
citizens both merchants and artisans before that time had
their whole livings and a great number of poor of the city
were set on work " was greatly depressed and its cloths
" out of estimation and vent (sale)." In response to their
entreaty the authorities obtained licence allowing thirty
alien master - craftsmen to settle in Norwich. They are
described as " divers strangers of the Low Countries," that
" came over for refuge against the persecution then raised
against them by the power of the Duke Alva." The letters
patent granting this permission enumerate the manufactures
which the newcomers were to introduce, and a very curious
list is given: " bays, arras, says, tapestry, mokadoes,
stament, carsays, and other outlandish commodities."[1]
" It surpasseth my skill," confesses Fuller, " to name the
several stuffs " made of worsted; and he quaintly adds:
" The nimble woof, its artificial dancing in several postures
about the standing warp, produceth infinite varieties in this
kind." An old English rhyme ran:

> " Hops, Reformation, *Bays*, and Beer
> Came into England all in a year."

Some interesting letters have been preserved written by
the strangers at Norwich to their kinsfolk at home. One
entreats his father and mother, his brothers and sisters,
to come to England at once without waiting any longer.
He tells his father that his debtors, " Pieter Keerle and
Steven de Mol, are at Norwich, who await you anxiously to
settle up with you;" and he adds: " I and my brother will
supply you with what you require here as weavers, for
there is a great trade doing." " I have a gold coin,"
proceeds the writer, " I would like to send it in the letter,
but when you come to Norwich I will give it you, for then

---

[1] Bays: originally a cloth of fine and light texture; arras: rich
tapestry fabric; says: a cloth of fine texture resembling serge;
mockado: a kind of cloth; stament: a coarse worsted; carsays:
obsolete form of kersey, a coarse cloth.

you may have nothing in your pockets; when you come to Norwich you shall have gold." Another writes to his wife to sell what she has and to come over. " There is a good trade in bays and I will look after a house as quickly as I can to get into business, for then it will be easy to make money. I will get ready the gear for making bays against your coming. Bring all your and your daughter's clothing, for people go well clad here. . . . I let you know that we are merry and happy with each other. . . . It is very dear to hear the word of God peacefully."

As a result of the introduction of Dutch and Walloon The prosperity of Norwich. weavers the prosperity of Norwich increased by leaps and bounds. The revenues of the city were more than doubled. The number of cloths sold by the Company of Russel Weavers rose from 276 to 2,845 in the year 1572; in the same year there were no less than four thousand aliens dwelling in Norwich, and before the plague of 1578 carried off a large number of the inhabitants there were as many as six thousand. The authorities freely admitted that the city had " received no small benefit by her majesty's permission." The strangers, it was said, showed themselves quiet and orderly, and worked diligently to earn their livelihood. A document drawn up about 1575 bears striking testimony to the services conferred by the strangers upon Norwich. " They brought a great commodity thither, namely, the making of bays, mokadoes, etc.—whereby they do not only set on work their own people, but do also set on work our own people within the city, as also a great number of people near twenty miles about the city. By their means our city is well inhabited, and decayed houses re-edified and repaired that were in ruin. They live holy of themselves without charge, and do beg of no man, and do sustain all their own poor people." But in spite of the advantages arising from the presence of aliens at Norwich, much friction ensued owing to the efforts of the authorities to place them under control and compel them to sell their commodities to freemen—that is, citizens—only. The native cloth-workers—the shearers of worsted—also complained that as a result of the new draperies their occupation

was nearly gone. In 1571 a " Book of Orders " was drawn
up for the strangers of Norwich, and among other regulations they were allowed to trade freely with citizens and
foreigners alike.

(ii.)
Colchester.   Norwich was not the only seat of the new draperies.
About 1565 the Dutch immigrants also settled at Colchester,
where twenty years later they numbered nearly thirteen
hundred. The town of Colchester has now suffered eclipse,
a fate which it has shared with many other mediæval towns,
but in the old days it was an important centre of the woollen
industry—in the words of Drayton :

" On all the Essexian shore the town of greatest fame."

The strangers were warmly welcomed by the authorities.
" We cannot but greatly commend the same strangers unto
you," they wrote to the Privy Council, " for sithence their
first coming hither we find them to be very honest, godly,
civil and well-ordered people, not given to any outrage or
excess."   Nor were they mistaken in their expectation that
the newcomers would bring great profit, " to the Common
Estate of the town," for Colchester became one of the chief
centres in England of the new manufactures. The writer
of a letter to Walsingham, the Secretary of State, observes
that before the refugees came to Colchester a great many
houses stood empty, and " tenants could not be gotten for
them at any reasonable rent."   He adds : " For God's cause
I beseech you to pity the poor strangers."   But at Colchester, as at Norwich, despite the benefits conferred by
the Dutch settlers, there was great difficulty in adjusting
the relations between the foreign weavers and the native
inhabitants. Attempts were even made to expel them
from the town, and they were disturbed and troubled by
" the meaner sort " as well as by the native weavers. The
latter were jealous of their foreign competitors, and in
particular they resented the right enjoyed by the Dutch
to examine all the new draperies made in the town, whether
by aliens or denizens, and to put their seal on those which
satisfied their scrutiny. The wrangling between the English
and Dutch weavers at Colchester went on during the
seventeenth century. In 1633 the authorities again bore

testimony to the services rendered by the strangers: they declared that the Colchester bay trade then employed " not only the poor inhabitants of the town, but also most part of the country round about for the space of ten miles there near adjoining, and also sendeth to your majesty's city of London weekly above £3,000 worth of the most staple commodities that is in this kingdom, as (namely) bays and says, besides the great trade it hath by sea." Troubles also arose at Halstead in Essex, where some settled in 1576, on account of the jealousy of the native manufacturers, whose persecution eventually drove them from the town. Their withdrawal ruined the prosperity of Halstead, where at the time of their settlement eight or nine score bays were sent week by week to London, providing much employment for spinners and weavers in the neighbourhood, while now the output mustered a bare " seven or eight single bays in one whole week." This blind attachment of the native weavers to their own narrow interests was an obstacle to the progress of the new manufacture. Their dislike of innovations also made them look with hostile eyes upon the introduction of the new draperies: " slight and vain commodities," as they termed them, " wherein the common people delight." Yet in spite of all resistance the new draperies ousted the old. " For the Hampshire kersies." said the Merchant Adventurers, in 1614, " let Guildford, Godalming, Farnham, Petersfield, Basing, and other towns in Hampshire report: their decays are extant."

Alien weavers settled in other towns—in London and Canterbury, Stamford and Sandwich, Thetford and Yarmouth. At Southampton the Privy Council allowed twenty families to settle in the town, each with ten men-servants, on condition that every household retained and instructed two English apprentices for a period of seven years. This proviso was laid down in order that the secrets of the new manufacture might become the possession of the native cloth-workers. Protestant refugees also found their way to Sussex. Rye, owing to its proximity to the French coast, attracted fugitives from France, where the feuds between the adherents of the new religion and the champions of the old had developed into open warfare. Shortly after

(iii.) Other seats of the new draperies.

the accession of Elizabeth to the throne, the Mayor of Rye informed the Government that there was " daily great resort of Frenchmen insomuch as already is esteemed to be five hundred persons; and we be in great want of corn for their and our sustentation, by reason the country adjoining is barren." The problem of providing for the newcomers was accentuated ten years later (1572) when the massacre of St. Bartholomew caused a great exodus of Huguenots from their country; but in the course of time the refugees were absorbed into the mass of the population, and the national life was enriched and strengthened by the infusion of this new blood. In recounting the various factors which have helped to build up the industrial supremacy of our country, we must not forget the debt of gratitude which England owes to the strangers within her gates, whose technical skill and knowledge of the industrial arts enabled her to wrest the secrets of the woollen manufacture from her rivals and become the workshop of the world.[1]

[1] In the reign of James II. there was an incursion of Huguenot weavers, who fled from France after the Revocation of the Edict of Nantes. The London weavers did not take kindly to their new competitors. Cf. *The Valiant Weaver, or the London Prentices' most sad and dreadful Complaint against the French by reason they under-rate their works* :

> " You weavers all; I pray give ear,
> A story true I will declare.
> Our masters they do much repine,
> Saying the French them undermine
> And gets their Trade away from them. . . .
>
> " Our weaving trade is grown so dead,
> We scarcely can get us bread . . .
> Because the French are grown so ill,
> In selling their work at an under price,
> Which makes the tears run from our eyes.
>   And weavers all may curse their fates
>   Because the French work under rates.
>
> " Have we not cause for to complain
> To serve seven years and all in vain,
> Because of these false-hearted men,
> I wish they were at France agen,
> By reason our work we cannot sell,
> By them we are ruin'd, 'tis known full well.
>   And weavers all may curse their fates,
>   Because the French work under rates."

The verses end with an exhortation to " cast all sorow away and " keep up your rates ":

> " I charge you all, ne'er stand in fear
> Nor be afraid of proud Monsieur."

CHAPTER II

THE ORGANISATION OF THE WOOLLEN AND WORSTED INDUSTRIES

WE have given an account of the origin and growth of the Scope of the Chapter. woollen industry. We have now to speak about the men and women who prepared the wool, wove at the looms, and fulled and dressed and dyed the cloth. The story of the various processes involved in the preparation and manufacture of cloth is reserved for another chapter;[1] here we are concerned with the workers themselves. What was the condition of a textile artisan in the days before machinery ? How does it compare with the situation of his descendant, the factory operative ? It is the purpose of this chapter to attempt an answer to these questions.

The fundamental interest of the English woollen industry The Gild System. lies in the fact that it has passed through every stage of industrial organisation: the stage of the " gild " system, the stage of the " domestic " system, and the stage of the " factory " system. In the order of historical sequence we must describe first the gild system. Under the gild system, as defined in this book, the various classes of textile artisans owned both the material on which they worked and the instruments of production. They were independent craftsmen who sold not their labour, but the product of their labour, a distinction of vital economic significance. Thus the spinners bought the wool and sold the yarn; the weaver bought the yarn and sold the cloth; the fuller bought the cloth raw and sold it fulled;[2] the shearman bought the cloth fulled and sold it dressed; the dyer bought either wool or cloth and sold it dyed. This form of industrial organisation was very rudimentary, but it

---

[1] See below, Chapter IV.

[2] The fuller who bought cloth raw is mentioned in a Statute of 1391.

27

gave birth to the most remarkable institution of mediæval industrial life—namely, the craft gild.

The Craft Gild.   The craft gild may be defined as a body of skilled workers, who dwelt as a rule within the walls of the same town and carried on the same occupation. It was essentially an urban institution adapted to the period, extending from the twelfth to the sixteenth centuries, when the manufacture of cloth was carried on mainly in towns like London, Norwich, York, Beverley, and Nottingham, among other seats of industry. In these towns the different classes of textile workers—weavers, fullers, dyers, and shearmen—were organised in craft gilds, and in their capacity as gildsmen they enjoyed various rights and were burdened with various obligations. We can best understand the nature of these rights and obligations by examining the composition of the craft gild and the functions which it served.

Apprenticeship.   The craft gild comprised three classes of members—the masters, the journeymen, and the apprentices. It was usually necessary to pass through all the three grades of membership: the apprentice became a journeyman, the journeyman rose to the status of a master. Apprenticeship was a system of technical training; its object was to teach the craftsman the secrets of his craft and render him duly qualified to carry on his calling. In the Middle Ages it was not considered right, either in the interests of the public or in the interests of the workers themselves, that an unskilled man should work at a trade without a long period of training; and to obtain the necessary training an apprentice bound himself to a master. In the agreement, or "indenture," between master and apprentice the former undertook to provide bed and board and instruction in his art; sometimes also a small salary; sometimes even his schooling and a knowledge of languages. He was expected to regulate the apparel of the apprentice, and was also responsible for his " good demeaning and bearing "—that is, for his conduct. To enforce his authority he was allowed to chastise an apprentice who proved refractory. If the master neglected his duties the apprentice was at liberty to leave his service. On the part of the apprentice, as his share of the contract, were demanded obedience, self-control, and fidelity to his master's service; he was expected to protect his master from loss, not to steal his master's goods— " not by sixpence in the year "—and not to frequent inns or gaming houses. " He must not," says a sixteenth-century writer, Sir Thomas Smith, " lie forth of his master's doors, he must not occupy any stock of his own, nor marry without his master's licence,[1] and he must do all servile offices about the house and be obedient to all his master's commandments, and shall suffer such correction as his master shall think meet." It was not an easy matter to control apprentices, and the unruly youths of London in particular gained notoriety for their ill-behaviour. One of the ordinances of the London Cloth-workers complains that " there hath been and there is at this time great disorder and abuse as well amongst the apprentices and journeymen of the art or mistery of cloth-workers in haunting and frequenting of taverns, ale-houses, and plays, and such like places of evil rule and disorder, and in using unlawful games and playing in the fields and in their masters' houses upon the Sundays and holy days, for that there be very few that govern their servants as they ought to be governed—the very root of many notable inconveniences in the Common-wealth." It therefore laid down that every householder " shall have and use a diligent care and heed to see his apprentices and journeymen to go to church to hear divine service or to some other place where God's word is . . . and also to spend the rest of the same Sunday and holy day in some honest and lawful exercises with their master's licence and not in haunting of alehouses, taverns, plays, unlawful games, or such like." A favourite theme in early literature was the contrast in the fortunes of the industrious and the idle apprentice—the one marrying his master's daughter and riding in his coach as Lord Mayor of London, the other ending a dissipated career on the gallows at Tyburn. The institution of apprenticeship was thus not merely a system of technical training; first and foremost it

---

[1] In an indenture at Norwich (1405), if the apprentice married without the master's permission his term was to be doubled.

was a system of social discipline. It was intended to
fashion not only good craftsmen but good citizens, inspired
with loyalty to their city, and willing to give active service
on its behalf when summoned to the field or the council
chamber. In mediæval times citizenship involved something more than the payment of rates and taxes; it carried
with it heavy responsibilities, and apprenticeship served as
a period of initiation in the public duties which awaited
the future citizen. The bond between master and apprentice was of the closest description; the master stood in place
of the parent to the apprentice, who lived in his house, sat
at his board, and associated with him in the workshop and
the home on terms of the most personal intimacy. In this
way the apprentice was taught the ideals of fair dealing
and sound workmanship, and from generation to generation
" honest and virtuous " masters were raised up to carry on
the traditions of the gild and maintain its reputation.

Journey-
men.
    The length of apprenticeship varied, but the period of
seven years appears to have been generally recognised as
the proper term in which the apprentice could acquire
" sufficient cunning." Weavers as a rule were not allowed
to receive apprentices under the age of fourteen, for a
younger boy was not considered strong enough to work a
loom. After completing his term of training the apprentice
was free to become a journeyman, or wage-earner, and seek
employment as a hired workman. Usually he remained
with his master for another year, though he was now paid
wages, but every journeyman looked forward to the day
when he would cease to be a journeyman and would take
his place among the masters of the gild as a fully qualified
craftsman. Two or three years at least, however, necessarily elapsed before the journeyman was in a position to
claim entry into the inner circle of the gild, and the interval
afforded a breathing-space in which he could accumulate
sufficient capital to set up in his own workshop. But
capital played as a rule a subordinate part in mediæval
industry, and his tools and technical skill were the resources
upon which the master-craftsman was content to rely to
gain a livelihood. His wooden loom could be made with

his own hands, and he had no difficulty in obtaining a supply of wool on credit.[1] In the early days of the woollen industry—and in the West Riding of Yorkshire down to the nineteenth century—no impassable gulf separated the master from the workman, and the masters were themselves artisans recruited from the ranks of the labouring classes.

The functions of the craft gild were in the main fourfold: the control of industry; the performance of religious and social duties; the relief of the poor; and the maintenance of good relations between the gild-brethren.

Functions of the Craft Gild.

The technical ordinances of the gild were intended to protect the consumer against defective wares, and the producer against the competition of untrained workmen. The rules in force among the Weavers of Bristol will serve as an illustration: they fixed the width of the cloth, and directed that " if the threads are deficient in the cloth or are too far apart, which the weavers called *tosed*, that cloth and the instrument on which it is worked ought to be burnt." The same penalty was inflicted when the cloth was made of woollen thread called *thrums*,[2] or if it were " worse in the middle than at the ends." Nowadays a manufacturer may sell his cloth good or bad as he pleases, but in the Middle Ages the gild was responsible for the work turned out by its members, and the main function of the gild authorities was the inspection of workshops. Defective wares were confiscated, and the maker was fined or placed in the pillory, or even, as a last resource, expelled from the gild. In mediæval times men conceived industry in the light of a public service carried on " for the common profit " in the interests of the community as a whole; and the ordinances of the gilds repeatedly insisted that dishonest workmanship brought discredit upon the industry and those engaged in it. Anyone who suffered from the incompetency of a workman sought redress from the gild authorities. At Nottingham " one Robert Mellers, bellfounder, at the feast of Christmas gave to William Nicholson a piece of white kersey to be fulled, sheared, and scoured,

(i.) Control of industry.

---

[1] See below, p. 78.
[2] " Thrums " were the unwoven ends of the warp.

and redelivered to the same Robert Mellers within three weeks then next following; in which piece of kersey a fault of workmanship was discovered; whereupon John Sainton and Robert Strelley, then being Wardens and Masters of the whole craft of Fullers within the town of Nottingham, surveyed that fault, and thereupon decided that the aforesaid William Nicholson should lose his whole work upon the aforesaid piece of kersey and should receive nothing for his labour." Another feature of the gild system was the regulation of wages and prices. Instead of allowing a master to pay what wages he pleased, and to charge what prices he liked, many gilds fixed the remuneration of the artisan and determined the prices of commodities. Among the London Shearmen, for example, whenever a master employed a stranger, it was the duty of the gild authorities to " see the ' foreigner ' work and conscientiously set his salary between his master and him and there to be bound four years in covenant." Wages here depended upon the capacity of the wage-earner; and we also observe the long period of engagement. The gildsman who set the brethren at defiance was roughly handled. The Dyers' gild at Coventry undertook to work only at certain rates; and when a number of dyers refused to be bound by these rates the gild hired Welshmen and Irishmen to waylay and kill them. This drastic treatment of "blacklegs" represents the mediæval form of picketing.

(ii.) Religious and social duties.

In the Middle Ages religion played a very considerable part in the lives of the people. Every gild had a patron saint upon whose altars it was wont to maintain lights: the tutelary saint of the wool-combers was Bishop Blaize, the reputed founder of their craft, in whose honour processions were held even in the nineteenth century. In addition to the performance of their religious duties, the gilds exhibited plays and pageants as part of their contribution to the social life of the community. In these pageants were portrayed biblical incidents; at Norwich, for example, the Mercers, Drapers, and Haberdashers presented the Creation of the World, the Shearmen, Fullers, and Woollen Weavers depicted Abel and Cain, the Worsted Weavers the Holy

Ghost. The importance of the pageant was that it served as a symbol of the communal life of the gild-brethren. It revealed how closely interwoven were the social activities of the gild with its industrial functions. Bound together by their common calling in the pursuit of common aims, the mediæval craftsmen developed an ideal of co-operation and joint effort which affords a wholesome contrast to many aspects of present-day individualism.

In the capacity of friendly societies, the craft gilds con- (iii.) The tributed to the support of their poorer members. In old the Poor. age or sickness the poverty-stricken brethren received an allowance from the common box; and gildmen were expected to leave legacies for the purpose. The Weavers of Gloucester, for example, received a bequest of forty pounds to be distributed annually among the poor, who were to return the loan at the end of the year. Money was also bequeathed to " succour young men that were minded to cloth-making," and philanthropists thus used their wealth to give a start in life to poor young men, who were lent sums of money—often without interest. The most notable was Sir Thomas White, founder of St. John's College, Oxford, who owed his fortune to the cloth trade, and perpetuated his memory in twenty-four towns by his endowments. Side by side with provisions for the sick and the poor went a due regard for the interests of the young. Many free grammar schools were founded and maintained by the gilds, and in this way the voluntary efforts of artisans helped to kindle the lamp of knowledge.

Another purpose of the craft gild was to settle all disputes (iv.) The maintenance between its members, and no craftsman was allowed to sue ance of a fellow-gildsman in a court of law without leave of the solidarity. gild authorities. The rule was intended to strengthen the feeling of solidarity among the workers, to promote " perfect love and charity " among those who were bound together by ties of social and economic interests. The same principle is seen in the injunction that no one must seek an unfair advantage over his fellows; it was strictly forbidden to entice a servant away from his master or a customer from a dealer. The aim of the gild system was, in short, to establish as nearly as possible a condition of absolute equality; and the gild ordinances seem inspired almost by a spirit of communism. Thus the London Shear-men ordered that if one master had three journeymen and another had none, " the wardens shall go to him that hath the said journeymen and shall take of them such as the goodman of the house may best forbear, and deliver him to him that hath none and hath need to have."

Women in industry. Membership of the craft gilds was compulsory on all engaged in a particular industry, and this rule extended to women. The employment of women workers has always been a marked feature of the woollen industry. They served as wool-sorters and wool-wrappers, carders and spinners, dyers and weavers. One-fourth of the cloth woven in York at the end of the fourteenth century was the work of women, and they were enrolled as apprentices and admitted to the membership of the crafts. A large portion of the cloth made at Wakefield in 1396 was manu-factured in " Emma Earle's weaving sheds," whilst among the pilgrims in Chaucer's *Prologue* was a " wife of Bath," who made cloths:

> " Of cloth-making she had such an haunt
> She passed them of Ypres and of Ghent."[1]

The wool-packers of Southampton, whose duty it was to pack the wool for transport, seem to have been entirely women, and they afford a unique example of a women's industrial gild. They were organised as a company of women artisans, and were governed by two wardens elected by the women from their own ranks. Among their ordin-ances was the amusing injunction that the members were " not to bawle nor scold oon with anither." As regards wool-sorting, a Statute of 1554 declared that " the experi-ence thereof consisteth only in women, as clothiers' wives and their women servants." Women are found, in fact, in every branch of the woollen industry. At the end of the sixteenth century one Rachel Thierry applied for the monopoly of pressing all serges made in Hampshire. The

[1] Haunt = use, practice. Passed = surpassed.

application was strongly resisted by the townsmen of Southampton, who asserted that " the woman Thierry is very poor and beggarly, very idle, a prattling gossip unfit to undertake a matter of so great charge. She is very untrustworthy, and we should hold them worse than mad that would hazard or commit their goods unto her hands. And to conclude: she is generally held amongst us as an unfit woman to dwell in a well-governed commonwealth." In course of time an agitation sprang up against the employment of women workers. It was attacked in the fifteenth century on the ground that they competed with men, who were said to deserve the chief consideration since they did " the King service in his wars and in the defence of this his land "; it was also alleged that women were " not of sufficient power " to weave certain kinds of cloth. Weavers were forbidden, therefore, to employ women, except those who were now getting their livelihood from weaving. As a rule a woman was allowed to exercise her husband's craft after his death, and even employ journeymen and apprentices.

We are now in a position to understand the many striking differences between mediæval and modern textile workers. The modern artisan works in a factory; he is usually a wage-earner all his life; sometimes he is a member of a trade union, which is composed exclusively of manual workers who have combined to protect their economic interests. In mediæval industry capital did not play the predominant part which it does to-day; and every wage-earner had reasonable prospects of achieving his independence. There were no permanent classes of employers and employees, the one rigidly divided from the other by the barrier of wealth and social status; hence there was little occasion for antagonism between " Capital " and " Labour." Observe, further, the differences between mediæval and modern employers. The master-craftsman of the gild system played in his time many parts: he was an " artisan " working with his own hands, but he was also an " employer of labour "; he was a " manufacturer " who made commodities, and a " capitalist " who provided

Comparison of mediæval and modern artisans.

tools and material, but he was also a " trader " or " middle-man " who disposed of his goods directly to the consumer. Corresponding to these differences between mediæval craftsmen and their successors are the differences between craft gilds and trade unions. The craft gilds embraced all grades of producers—masters as well as men—and they established complete industrial control over all who were associated together in the pursuit of a common calling. They showed care not only for the worker but also for the customer, reconciling as far as possible the interests of producer and consumer, and insisting on good quality, sound workmanship, and a just price reasonable to buyer and seller. In their ideals we can still find inspiration, and the problem to-day is how to realise the spirit of these ideals in the altered conditions of modern life.

The Domestic System.

The second form of industrial organisation is the domestic system, in which the material was owned not by the workers themselves, but by a class of employers, who united all the different branches of the industry under a single control. The master-craftsman of the gild system, who combined trading and handicraft functions and disposed freely of his wares to consumers, yielded place to the small master of the domestic system, who was confined to the purely manual functions, and depended henceforth on the employer for the provision of materials. He was, in fact, transformed into a wage-earner paid by the piece, although the work was still carried on at home—as under the gild system—and he was employed by more than one master. The domestic system must be distinguished from the factory system—the third form of industrial organisation—since factory workers own neither the material, as under the gild system, nor the instruments of production, as under the domestic system; and they are assembled under an employer's roof, subjected to the discipline of the factory, and confined to the service of one master. The domestic system, however, resembled the factory system in one vital respect: it was organised on a capitalist basis, and the control of industry was vested in the hands of the em-

ployers of labour who stood (except in Yorkshire) outside
the ranks of the manual craftsmen. In the gild system,
on the other hand, the control of industry lay in the hands
of the manual workers themselves, who exercised it through
the medium of their own elected officials.

It is a popular error to date capitalism from the era of Reasons
the Industrial Revolution. Capitalism existed in the growth of
woollen industry four centuries prior to the introduction of capitalism.
machinery, and there was a wage-earning class in the cloth
manufacture as far back as the fourteenth century. The
growth of Capitalism in any industry depends upon the
operation of two factors: the extent of the market and the
division of labour. A local market may easily be supplied
by independent bodies of craftsmen, but a national or
international market demands a more complex organisation; again, where the division of labour is small, the possi-
bilities of co-operation among the different classes of artisans
are correspondingly greater. The working of these two
factors explains the evolution of the woollen industry on
capitalistic lines. On the one hand, an ever-widening
market and a corresponding increase in production made
the investment of capital a profitable venture; on the other
hand, the variety of processes involved in the preparation
and manufacture of cloth seemed to require that the woollen
industry should be organised on a capitalist basis. The
cloth trade passed through many hands, and it was therefore inevitable that the weavers, fullers, dyers, and shearmen should be grouped together in a condition of economic
dependency upon the " clothiers," as the capitalist employers were called. One writer asserts that " from the
wool-grower to the consumer a piece of broad cloth passes
through a hundred different hands, and there are near the
same number of hands dependent on the woollen manufacturer, though not actually concerned in it." These
figures seem rhetorical. A more sober estimate gives the
number of persons employed on a single piece of cloth as
fourteen; this includes the spinners, weavers, burlers, and
cloth-finishers (fullers and shearmen), but not wool-growers,
dyers, makers of looms and spinning wheels, transport

4

workers, and others connected directly or indirectly with
the cloth trade. Without attempting any precise calcula-
tions it is enough to state that the division of labour in the
woollen industry was very considerable. Now it is manifest that the best results in any industry are attained where
the different bodies of artisans concerned in it are brought
to devote themselves to particular processes under the
guidance of a controlling authority. Division of labour is
the indispensable basis of economic progress, for technical
perfection is only achieved by concentration on details—
doing one thing at a time and doing it well. The author
of *Considerations on the East India Trade* (1701) anticipated
Adam Smith in the stress which he laid upon the importance
of the division of labour in industry: " The more variety
of artists to every manufacture, the less is left to the skill of
single persons; the greater the order and regularity of every
work, the same must needs be done in less time, the labour
must be less, and consequently the price of labour less,
though wages should not be abated. Thus a piece of cloth
is made by many artists; one cards and spins, another
makes the loom, another weaves, another dyes, another
dresses the cloth; and thus to proper artists proper parts
of the work are still assigned; the weaver must needs be
more skilful and expeditious at weaving if that shall be his
constant and whole employment, than if the same weaver
is also to card and spin, and make the loom, and weave and
dress and dye the cloth. So the spinner, the fuller, the
dyer, or cloth-worker, must needs be more skilful and
expeditious at his proper business which shall be his whole
and constant employment, than any man can be at the
same work whose skill shall be puzzled and confounded
with variety of other business." The Parliamentary Committee which framed the famous *Report on the State of the
Woollen Industry of England* (1806) attributed " the acknowledged excellence, and till of late, superiority of the cloths
of the West of England " to the great skill which each class
of workmen in the West Country acquired in keeping to
its " proper line," and performing its own particular
operations.

Capitalism did not achieve its conquest of the woollen industry in one stride, nor did the domestic system easily supplant the gild system. It was possible for the two systems to continue side by side; indeed, evidence of the survival of the gild system is found in the sixteenth and even the seventeenth century. Contemporary opinion clearly favoured the maintenance of the system under which the worker owned the materials. In 1532, for example, the butchers of Norwich were ordered to bring their wool-fells into the market and " there make sale " of them to women who lived by spinning. Again, in one of the State Papers, dated 1615, it is explained how " yarn is weekly brought into the market by a great number of poor people that will not spin to the clothier for small wages, but have stock enough to set themselves on work, and do weekly buy their wool in the market by very small parcels according to their use, and weekly return it in yarn, and *make good profit having the benefit both of their labour and of their merchandise, and live exceeding well.* . . . So many that it is supposed that more than half the cloth of Wiltshire, Gloucester, and Somersetshire is made by means of these yarn-makers and poor clothiers that depend wholly on the wool chapman which serves them weekly for wools either for money or credit." Even in the eighteenth century it was not unknown for " poor people to get forty or fifty pounds of wool at a time to employ their wives and children at home in carding and spinning, of which when they have ten or twenty pounds ready for the clothier they go to market with it, and there sell it." Nor is the evidence confined to spinners. Thus Westcote, whose *View of Devonshire* was written in 1630, sets before us the essential features of primitive industry in Devonshire, where " the gentleman farmer or the husbandman sends his wool to the market, which is bought either by the comber or the spinster, and they, next week, bring it thither again in yarn which the weaver buys; and the market following brings that thither again in cloth." And even cloth-finishers in the seventeenth century sometimes purchased raw cloth for resale in a finished condition.

Transition from the Gild to the Domestic System.

Although some of the textile workers managed to retain their economic independence, the great majority gradually lost their independent status. The craftsman, while still a " gild " artisan in the sense that he worked on his own material, would undertake work for a customer, and the dividing-line between " customer " and " employer " became extremely shadowy. When we are told, for example (1364), that dyers, weavers, and fullers " will not work on the cloths of others except at an excessive wage," and " what is worse, the dyers often change the wool and the weavers the yarn, and the fullers the whole cloth," it is evident that these various classes of artisans, while they still sold their own goods, were also working on material given out to them by " customers." The mysterious class of burellers, who apparently made *burel* cloth, are definitely known to have kept weavers in their employment; and the drapers, whose primary function was the sale of cloth which they bought at Blackwell Hall or at fairs, or imported from abroad, sometimes assumed responsibility for the finishing processes and gave out work to shearmen and dyers. Nor was this development confined to London, for in 1415 the dyers of Coventry were accused of dyeing their own cloths with better materials than they used for their customers' cloths. In short, the gild system gradually merged into the domestic system by an easy and natural process of evolution.

Two phases of the Domestic System.

We have indicated in general terms the essential characteristics of the domestic system, and its historical relation to the gild system.[1] We have now to attempt a more detailed analysis. At the outset it is necessary to observe that there are two phases of the domestic system: the phase where the influence of capital is negligible and there is no conflict of capital and labour; and the phase where the influence of capital is considerable, though not as yet completely predominant. The best example of the more primitive phase is to be found in the North of England,[1] and the best example of the more advanced phase in the

[1] On the question whether the " domestic system " of the North ought to be regarded as a form of the gild system, see below, p. 72, *n*. I.

West of England. We shall examine first industrial conditions in the West Country, though some of our illustrations will be drawn from other parts of the kingdom where the structure of industrial society was essentially similar. In the foreground of the picture stands the capitalist.

The capitalist, or clothier as he was called, was the pivot The clothier. of industrial organisation, and in his hands was concentrated the whole control of the woollen industry. One writer even compared him with the sun, inasmuch as " he scattered life and its supports to everyone around him." Another described his occupation as one of " surpassing charity, for clothing not only our own nation, but foreign countries, and above all getting so many poor folks on work in carding, spinning, and such like handmaids of their trade, as they surmount those who relieve beggars at their gates." The position of the clothier at the very centre of the cloth trade enabled him to supervise and direct every stage of the manufacture. He was responsible, in fact, for the whole series of processes from the time when the wool was picked, washed, carded, and spun, until it was woven, fulled, and " perfected " into cloth.[1]

What were the functions of the clothier? The West Functions of the Country clothier, unlike the Yorkshire clothier, was not a clothier. manufacturer in the literal sense in which the word was used before the Industrial Revolution—namely, a man who works with his own hands. The actual manufacturers were the weavers and cloth-finishers, while the clothiers assumed the functions of the *entrepreneur*—that is, they directed the industry and left to others the execution of its details. Most clothiers probably never learnt the regular trade of a weaver; indeed, we find men entering the occupation late in life, after essaying other callings—for example, even law. The West Country clothier was in short an employer, not a manual worker. Nor was he a manufacturer in the modern

[1] The clothier, although the most important, was not the only capitalist employer in the woollen industry. There was a class of " market spinners," who " set many spinners on work " and sold the yarn without working it up into cloth. Similarly in the worsted trade there was a class of " master wool-combers," who owned the wool and employed combers and spinners to convert it into thread, which they afterwards sold.

sense. The modern manufacturer is first and foremost an industrial capitalist. He carries on the industry under his own roof, and makes it his function to study and perfect in detail the whole business of manufacturing. The clothier was a trading rather than an industrial capitalist; he was primarily concerned with buying and selling; he bought the raw material and he sold the finished product; the actual details of the manufacture were left to spinners, weavers, and cloth-finishers. Whether the weaver did the work himself or employed assistants, whether he used one kind of loom or another, did not matter to the clothier. He did not go round the weavers' homes and see how the work was being done; he examined the work only when it was brought home. On the other hand, we cannot describe the clothier as merely a merchant whose province was nothing more than the sale of goods, for he was also an employer of the various classes of artisans engaged in the industry. In short, we must avoid the use of modern terms and modern analogies.

Beginnings of capitalism.   The advent of a capitalist class in the woollen industry dates as far back as the fourteenth century, and it developed in importance as the Middle Ages drew to a close. We cannot assert that cloth-making was the earliest industry to be run on capitalist lines; in the tin-making industry, for example, the wage system existed from very early times. But the conditions of the English cloth trade, as we have seen, facilitated the growth of capitalism on a large scale, and opened up a new stage in the evolution of industrial organisation. The " captains of industry," whom Edward III. invited to England, were clearly not simple artisans but capitalists. John Kempe brought with him from Flanders " men, servants, and apprentices "; and " the workers of wools and cloths " who came from Zeeland had also their men and their servants. At Bristol we even get glimpses of the beginnings of a factory system. Thomas Blanket, afterwards bailiff of the town, and other burgesses set up looms for weaving cloth and employed in their own houses " weavers and other workmen." This was in the year 1339; but the attempt to concentrate hired workmen

under one roof was doubtless exceptional at this early
period.

Our knowledge of the clothiers who existed at the end of
the fourteenth century is derived from the aulnagers'
accounts[1] for the year 1395, which show that capitalism
had already established a footing in the cloth trade. In
Suffolk 733 whole cloths[2] were divided among 120 manufacturers, among whom only 7 or 8 reached a score; but
in addition 15 makers returned 120 to 160 narrow cloths[3]
apiece. In Essex production was on a larger scale: 1,200
narrow cloths were made at Coggeshall by 9 manufacturers
(one alone made 400), and 2,400 at Braintree by 8 manufacturers (two made 600 each and one 480). The most
striking evidence of capitalist enterprise is found among
the West-Country clothiers: at Barnstaple one maker paid
aulnage on 1,080 narrow cloths, another on 1,005, and
9 others on 1,600; and at Salisbury 158 persons returned
6,600 whole cloths. On the other hand, Cornwall produced
only 90 cloths among 13 clothiers; Kent had but 1 clothier
who owned more than 50 narrow cloths; and Winchester
but 3 clothiers who possessed more than 100 whole cloths.
The average number of whole cloths assigned to the Yorkshire manufacturers was as low as 10, though 7 makers
produced 173½ between them, the principal clothier of
Wakefield, Emma Earle, paying subsidy on 48.[4] A seventeenth-century writer (1618) computed that the clothier
" who maketh ordinarily 20 broad cloths every week cannot
set as few awork as 500 persons, for by the time his wool
is come home and is sorted, what with breakers, dyers,
wood-setters, wringers, spinners, weavers, burlers, shearmen, and carriers, besides his own large family, the number
will soon be accomplished." This estimate is doubtless
exaggerated, but in any case none of the makers in the
fourteenth century had so large an output as twenty whole
cloths a week.

Capitalism in the fourteenth century.

---

[1] For the aulnager, see below, p. 113.
[2] Whole cloths were 24 yards by (about) 1¾ yards, when shrunk.
[3] Narrow cloths were 12 yards by 1 yard, when shrunk.
[4] This was in 1396-7.

Origin of the clothiers.   In the closing years of Richard II.'s reign the large manufacturers were apparently restricted to a few centres, but the rapid extension of the woollen industry soon brought in its wake a growing body of capitalist employers. The class of clothiers originated in various ways. Some were probably dealers in wool who caused the raw material to be worked up into cloth and then disposed of it in the market. Others were shearmen or cloth-finishers, who employed workmen in all the earlier processes of carding, spinning, weaving, fulling, and dyeing. Others were recruited from artisans engaged in the more subordinate branches of the woollen industry—for example, weavers, fullers, and dyers. As a rule the clothiers must have been men of substantial position in command of capital. It is evident, at any rate, that the business of cloth-making was not considered to involve social inferiority, for we read of a Mayor of Canterbury who " took upon him the occupation of making of cloths and lived like a gentleman "; and in the West Country the clothier was called the " gentleman clothier."

Dependence of artisans upon the capitalist.   The extent to which those engaged in the different branches of the woollen industry had become dependent upon the clothier was signally shown in 1525, when Cardinal Wolsey endeavoured to raise war taxes. The clothiers of Suffolk, under pressure from the minister, submitted to the imposition, but were left without money to pay the wages of their men. They were forced to dismiss the carders and spinners, weavers and fullers whom they employed, and a revolt against the Government was only narrowly averted. The story is told in Holinshed: " The Duke of Suffolk, sitting in commission about the subsidy in Suffolk, persuaded by courteous means the rich clothiers to assent thereto; but when they came home and went about to discharge and put from them their spinners, carders, fullers, weavers, and other artificers which they kept in work afore time, the people began to assemble in companies." Shakespeare introduces this famous incident into *King Henry VIII*.:

" Upon these taxations,
The clothiers all, not able to maintain
The many to them longing, have put off
The spinsters, carders, fullers, weavers, who,
Unfit for other life, compell'd by hunger
And lack of other means, in desperate manner
Daring the event to the teeth, are all in uproar,
And danger serves among them."

This incident serves, in part at any rate, to explain why the Tudors opposed the development of the capitalist system. Upon the discretion and foresight of a limited group of men had now come to depend the welfare and even the existence of the great body of industrial workers.

Many rich clothiers worked their way up in life from very small beginnings. One of the greatest clothiers of the sixteenth century was Peter Blundell, who deserves to rank as one of the " Worthies of Devon." He was born at Tiverton in the year 1520, and his parents were so poor that as a boy " he was obliged to run on errands and do other little services for the common carriers " in order to support himself. As he grew older he tended their horses, and the care and fidelity with which he performed his duties gained him the esteem and regard of his employers. " With much care he saved a little money, bought a piece of kersey cloth, and sent it to London by one of the carriers, who charged him nothing for the carriage, sold it to great advantage, and made him a faithful return. The profits from this kersey and other savings enabled him to purchase others which he sent and sold in like manner." In a short time he was able to buy " as many kersies as would load one horse, with which he went himself to London, where he was employed some time by the agents in the kersey trade." He remained in London till he had acquired a fortune sufficient to start his own manufacture of kersies, when he returned to Tiverton and established a business. In this way he built up a large enterprise, and when he died, eighty-one years old, he left a fortune of £40,000, the equivalent of over a quarter of a million of modern money. A great part of his fortune was devoted to charitable bequests. He remembered the saying of William of Wyke-

Peter Blundell.

ham, who founded a school at Winchester and a college at Oxford in the fourteenth century: " Though I am not myself a scholar, I will be the means of making more scholars than any scholar in England "; and in emulation of his great predecessor he founded the famous Free Grammar School, which Defoe a century later described as " the beauty of Tiverton."[1]

John Winchcombe.

The most famous clothier of the sixteenth century was John Winchcombe, familiarly known as Jack of Newbury, who is described by Fuller as " the most considerable clothier (without fancy and fiction) England ever beheld." Many legends have gathered round his name, but he was un- doubtedly an historical figure. His will is still preserved in which he bequeathed forty pounds to Newbury Parish Church and legacies to his servants, and his epitaph is shown in Newbury Church, of which he built the tower. In the *Journal to Stella* the author of *Gulliver's Travels* describes a visit to the famous St. John, afterwards Lord Boling- broke, who had married one of Winchcombe's descendants. " His lady is descended from Jack Newbury, of whom books and ballads are written; and there is an old picture of him in the house." The tradition runs that he entertained King Henry VIII. and his Court, and he is said to have marched to Flodden Field at the head of a hundred of his own men. It is likely enough that he furnished a con- tingent of men to meet the Scottish invaders, and the pride of their exploits rings through the lines of the old ballad:

> " The Cheshire lads were brisk and brave
>   And the Kendal lads as free,
> But none surpass'd or I'm a knave
>   The lads of Newberrie."

In *The Pleasant History of John Winchcombe* the pros- perity of the great clothier is depicted by Thomas Deloney in glowing terms:

> " Within one room being large and long
>   There stood two hundred Looms full strong:

[1] Another example of the endowment of learning by woollen manufacturers is Thomas Crispin, a fuller, who founded the principal public school at Kingsbridge.

Two hundred men the truth is so
Wrought in these Looms all in a row.
By every one a pretty boy
Sate making quills with mickle joy.
And in another place hard by,
An hundred women merrily
Were carding hard with joyful cheer
Who singing sate with voices clear.
And in a chamber close beside,
Two hundred maidens did abide,
In petticoats of Stammell red,
And milk-white kerchers on their head. . . .
These pretty maids did never lin[1]
But in that place all day did spin. . . .
Then to another room came they
Where children were in poor array:
And everyone sate picking wool,
The finest from the coarse to cull. . . .
Within another place likewise
Full fifty proper men he spies,
And these were Shearmen everyone,
Whose skill and cunning there was shown:
And hard by them there did remain
Full fourscore Rowers taking pain.
A Dye-house likewise had he then,
Wherein he kept full forty men:
And likewise in his Fulling Mill
Full twenty persons kept he still."

The reputation which his cloth obtained may be gauged
from the advice of the English envoy at Antwerp to the
Protector Somerset to send over " a thousand of Winchcombe's kersies " in discharge of a debt. Even at the end
of the seventeenth century Jack of Newbury was the chief
figure in the pageant of the Cloth-workers of London.

John Winchcombe was not the only clothier in the William Stumpe.
sixteenth century who set up a manufactory and gathered
servants and looms under one roof. It is probable that
the agrarian changes,[2] which turned vast numbers of
labourers adrift from the soil, furnished the labour which
clothiers with some capital at their command were able to
utilise in the woollen industry. Even the monasteries were
occasionally converted into factories. William Stumpe,

---

[1] *I.e.*, cease work.   [2] See above, p. 19.

a clothier of Malmesbury, rented Osney Abbey in 1546, and undertook to employ as many as two thousand workmen who were to labour " continually in cloth-making for the succour of the city of Oxford." Stumpe had also taken over Malmesbury Abbey, and Leland, the antiquary, gives the following description: " The whole lodgings of the Abbey be now longing to one Stumpe, an exceeding rich clothier, that bought them of the King. At this present time every corner of the vast houses of office that belonged to the Abbey be full of looms to weave cloth in. There be made now every year in the town three thousand cloths." Another clothier, who sought to obtain possession of the Abbey of Abingdon, was Tuckar, a cloth-maker of Burford. One of Cromwell's agents wrote to his master in 1538 that the town of Abingdon was likely to decay unless the people were set to work to " drape cloth." Tuckar had promised that he would expend a hundred marks[1] a week in wages to cloth-makers of the town during his life, on condition that he was allowed to rent the lands and fulling mills of the Abbey. " He is a just man both in word and deed, and *daily employs* 500 *of the King's subjects*. If he had carding and spinning he would employ many more. With Cromwell's favour he would set the inhabitants of Abingdon to work, if they will work, so that they would gain more wages in a few years coming than in twenty years past. Weekly need constrains him to send to Abingdon his cart laden with wool to be carded and spun, and likewise he sends to Stroudwater (Gloucestershire)." Thomas Cromwell was doubtless well disposed towards the woollen industry: his father was a fuller and shearman; he himself was married to the daughter of a shearman; and at one time he even carried on the business of finishing cloths.

Other famous clothiers were the Springs of Lavenham, the Tames of Fairford, and Thomas Dolman of Newbury. When Dolman gave up cloth-making, the weavers of Newbury lamented:

" Lord, have mercy upon us, miserable sinners,
Thomas Dolman has built a new house, and turned away
all his spinners."

Tuckar.

Other great clothiers.

[1] A mark is 13s. 4d.

Thomas Spring, surnamed the rich clothier, bequeathed
£200 to finish Lavenham steeple and money for a thousand
masses—he died on the eve of the Reformation—and his
daughter married a son of the Earl of Oxford. John Tame,
who lived in the reign of Edward IV., built up a large
cloth manufacture at Cirencester and kept vast flocks of
sheep at Fairford, prospering so well that he became owner
of several landed estates. His son, Edmund Tame, received a visit from Henry VIII., by whom he was knighted;
he became lord of the manor of Fairford and was three
times high sheriff of Gloucestershire. Fairford, observes
Leland, " never flourished before the coming of the Tames
unto it." His remarks on Bath are worth quoting to
show the influence which the clothiers were exercising
upon the destinies of the towns in which they were established. " The town hath of a long time since been continually most maintained by making of cloth. There were "
within living memory " three clothiers at one time, thus
named, Style, Kent, and Chapman, by whom the town of
Bath then flourished. Since the death of them it hath
somewhat decayed." Lastly, we may mention three
famous clothiers who lived in the North Country early in
the sixteenth century—Cuthbert of Kendal, Hodgkins of
Halifax, and Martin Brian of Manchester—each of whom
kept " a great number of servants at work, spinners, carders,
weavers, fullers, dyers, and shearmen, etc., to the great
admiration of all that came into their houses to behold
them."

The movement towards a factory system, already fore- Opposition
shadowed in the career of Thomas Blanket, was disliked factory
by the Government, which was uneasy at the opportunity system.
it seemed to afford for unruly spirits to collect together in
one centre and stir up rioting and disorder. The famous
Weavers Act of Philip and Mary (1555) recited that " the
weavers of this realm have complained that the rich and
wealthy clothiers do in many ways oppress them; some by
setting up and keeping in their houses diverse looms, and
keeping and maintaining them by journeymen and persons
unskilful, to the decay of a great number of artificers which

were brought up in the science of weaving, their families
and households; some by ingrossing [accumulation] of looms
into their hands and possession, and letting them out at
such unreasonable rents as the poor artificers are not able
to maintain themselves; some also by giving much less
wages and hire for the weaving and workmanship of cloth
than in times past." It therefore forbade clothiers who
dwelt outside the older towns to keep more than one loom,
or woollen weavers more than two looms. This Act did
not affect urban centres and its operation was restricted
to country districts,[1] although in the eastern counties
attempts were made to limit the number of looms even in
towns. These efforts to check the development of a
capitalist class were unsuccessful, but the factory system
failed to maintain itself in the face of strong social anti-
pathy, the opposition of the Government, and the absence
of any vital economic necessity for the concentration of
workmen under a factory roof. The " factories " occasionally set up prior to the introduction of machinery were
mostly in the nature of charitable enterprises undertaken
from philanthropic motives. Arthur Young, for example,
mentions a factory at Boynton in 1768: " Sir George Strick-
land was so obliging as to show me his woollen manufactory; a noble undertaking which deserves the greatest
praise. In this country the poor have no other employment
than what results from a most imperfect agriculture; consequently three-fourths of the women and children were
without employment. It was this induced Sir George to
found a building large enough to contain on one side a
row of looms of different sorts, and on the other a large
space for women and children to spin. The undertaking
was once carried so far as to employ a hundred and fifty
hands, who made very sufficient earnings for their maintenance; but the decay of the woollen exportation reduced
them so much that now those employed are, I believe, under
a dozen." In the eighteenth century some of the clothiers
in the West Country and in Yorkshire employed men in
their own weaving sheds and thus created a miniature

---

[1] The Act did not apply to the northern counties.

factory. The advantages of the system were threefold. It enabled the employer to supervise in person the processes of manufacture; it prevented delay in the return of the work, which was wont to occur when a weaver wove in his own home for different masters; and it rendered more difficult any embezzlement of the raw material. On the other hand, the expense of building large weaving sheds, coupled with the strenuous opposition of the weavers, checked the growth of a factory system until the introduction of machinery made it an economic necessity. The cloth-finishers, however, generally worked in their employer's shop instead of their own homes, and they therefore stood outside the domestic system of industry.[1]

The clothiers were often in a large way of business. Even in the fourteenth century there were great employers of labour, and men like John Winchcombe and William Stumpe were prominent in the Tudor epoch. In the seventeenth century a Member of Parliament told the House of Commons (1614) that he and his partner maintained above three thousand workmen; and in the eighteenth century Daniel Defoe relates that he was told at Bradford in Wiltshire " that it was no extraordinary thing to have clothiers in that country worth from ten thousand to forty thousand pounds a man, and many of the great families, who now pass for gentry in those counties, have been originally raised from and built by this truly noble manufacture." The number of persons employed by a clothier naturally varied considerably. Some clothiers employed 150 or even 200 weavers, but not all the weavers on an employer's books worked for him alone.[2] In addition to the weavers the clothier had in his employment a large number of burlers, carders, spinners, cloth-finishers, and others; thus a wealthy clothier might employ altogether as many as 800 persons and even more. It is evident, then, that the capitalist employer was already the outstanding figure in the woollen industry long before the Industrial Revolution. None the less the West Country

The clothier as a large employer of labour.

---

[1] See below, p. 67.   [2] See below, p. 57.

clothier often enjoyed considerable leisure. Those whose business was conducted on a small scale were not required to make great exertions, as they were spared the duty of supervising the actual manual processes which were not carried on under their own roofs, and they disposed of their goods through the medium of factors at Blackwell Hall. Many clothiers therefore combined some other occupation with their calling—for example, they entered the malting or tanning trades or bought small farms and reclaimed the waste.

How the clothier obtained his material.   The clothier obtained his supply of raw material in one of three ways:[1] The " rich " clothier purchased his wool in the fleece direct from the wool-grower. The " meaner " clothier had neither the leisure to travel in the wool country nor the means to make large purchases of wool at shearing-time. He therefore bought the material from the wool-merchant, or wool-stapler as he was called, who acted as middleman between the grower and the clothier. The " poor " clothier could not afford to buy wool in its raw state, and instead bought yarn in the markets: " which yarn is weekly brought into the markets by a great number of poor people that will not spin to the clothier for small wages, but have stock enough to set themselves on work." It follows, then, that the wool-dealers served a very useful purpose. They acted as intermediaries between the clothier and the grazier, who usually lived in different counties a great distance apart. The carded wool grown in Norfolk, for example, was consumed in Yorkshire; the long staple grown in Lincolnshire was worked up in Norwich. Moreover, the wool-breeder could not afford to await the clothier's convenience, selling the wool in small quantities and allowing long credit, and the " wool-chapman " was able to take his stock off his hands. Nevertheless, hatred of the middleman was deep-rooted, and laws in restraint of wool-dealing were passed in the fourteenth, fifteenth, and sixteenth centuries on the ground that it enhanced prices.

[1] In the eighteenth century the West Country clothiers became increasingly dependent on Spanish wool. See below, p. 215.

For the disposal of his goods the clothier, unless he were a merchant exporter, relied upon agents, or factors as they were called, at Blackwell Hall. These factors fulfilled the same function in the final stages of the woollen industry which the wool-staplers served in the early stages. They were middlemen who thrust themselves between the manufacturers and their customers, the drapers or wholesale dealers. The factors were bitterly denounced as parasites on the industry. Intended originally to assist the West Country clothiers and Yorkshire merchants in selling their cloth in London—for clothiers could not afford the time to journey to London and remain there while the cloth was being sold—they raised themselves to be " the chief masters of the clothing trade." The root of the mischief lay in the fact that the clothiers were forced to give long credit to the drapers, the standard rule being six months, and even nine, twelve, and fifteen. As a result of handling large funds the factors grew rich. They started almost from nothing—" no more being required to set up a factor than an ink-box and two quires of paper "—and accumulated fortunes of " five and ten thousand pounds, and some of them forty and fifty thousand pounds a man." While the clothiers, it was said, " lived poorly and got little or nothing, the merchants lived splendidly and laid up money." It is not surprising, therefore, to find the economic literature of the seventeenth and eighteenth centuries filled with denunciations of the factors. One pamphlet[1] is written in the form of a play intended to show the contemptuous manner in which the factors, once the agents and servants of the clothiers, now treated their former masters. In one of the scenes the factors and clothiers dine together in a tavern. The factors sit apart at the head of the room, and after the dinner they propose that everyone should pay an equal share of the reckoning. The clothiers willingly agree, but make the discovery that the factors have been ordering for themselves the best wines and viands, while the inferior wines and meats were reserved for their own table; and the scene ends in great disorder.

[1] See Bibliographical Note.

The clothier not only suffered from long periods of credit he was also liable to be defrauded by absconding traders. A letter sent by the Privy Council to the Lord Deputy of Ireland records the commercial lapses of "one Brooke," a London merchant. "Whereas there is one Brooke, a young man of the City of London, that hath oft taken up cloths of divers clothiers of Kent and Suffolk amounting to the value of £1,500, and to defraud them of their money is, as we are informed, gone over into Ireland, whereby those poor men that have given him credit for this great sum are like to be undone, being a most lewd and dishonest practice. This shall be therefore to pray your Lordship to cause the said Brooke to be apprehended in what part soever he shall be found within that realm and safely sent up hither, that he may yield that satisfaction to those honest clothiers that have given him this credit which he ought to do, this his lewd kind of dealing being so odious as he deserveth in no sort to be protected."

The Tiverton incident.
We have shown the part played by the West Country clothier in the organisation of the woollen industry. We can best conclude our account with the story of the extraordinary commotion excited at Tiverton in 1765 by the death of one of the principal clothiers of the town: for it illustrates in a marked degree the clothier's importance. The Tiverton clothier had carried on an extensive woollen trade, and his workmen were apprehensive that the business "would be removed elsewhere unless some other merchant of fortune and capacity could be influenced to settle in Tiverton. They therefore applied to the Mayor and Corporation to elect" as a burgess, or member of the Corporation, a merchant of Exeter, "who had offered to reside in the town and conduct a considerable woollen trade in it." The greater part of the Corporation pledged itself to vote for him, but the Mayor refused to take the necessary steps, as he had promised. The weavers and wool-combers, greatly incensed, collected together in a large body, followed the Mayor through the streets when he entered the town, surrounded the house which he entered, and demanded a promise that he would give his vote for

their candidate. " After some time several of them, chiefly women, broke into the house through the windows, and into the room where the Mayor was, and greatly insulted him, pulling off his wig, striking him and twisting his nose, and threatening to kill him if he did not immediately sign a paper they then produced to him, by which he was to undertake to vote for Mr. Baring (the Exeter candidate) and to call a hall within eight days, in order to elect him to fill up one of the vacancies in the Corporation." The Mayor yielded to the threats and signed the undertaking. Other members of the Corporation were treated in similar manner and compelled to sign the document. The Mayor considered that he was in no way bound by a promise extorted from him under pain of death, and summoning military assistance he left the town. Before the arrival of the soldiers, the workmen again assembled their forces to the number of 300 and more, and after refreshing themselves with several " hogsheads " of cyder, they made a search for the Mayor in order to compel him to hold the election, and when they found that he had absconded they swore to kill him. They proceeded to a neighbouring village where the Mayor had his residence, smashed the windows, broke open the doors, wreaked vengeance upon his household effects, and explored the contents of his wine-cellar. They did as much damage as they could, destroying the tenters or cloth-racks, demolishing the weir across the River Exe by which water was conveyed to the Mayor's fulling mills, and attacking the houses of his tenants. The unions of the weavers and combers also posted up notices all over the town threatening a strike against any member of the Corporation who did not vote for their candidate. A fortnight later the election was held, but the Mayor had taken the precaution to secure a majority in favour of his own nominee—rumour said that money and liquor were freely expended—and Baring was not chosen. The people were greatly enraged at this disappointment of their hopes, and made an attack upon the Town Hall, breaking the windows and pelting the Mayor and his party with stones as they came out of the building and passed through the streets. The next day two of the rioters were arrested and conveyed to the county gaol at Exeter. On their way a determined effort was made to rescue them from the soldiers and constables. The Mayor, who accompanied the guard, was roughly handled, but the prisoners remained in safe custody. The route to Exeter lay through Silverton, and a number of people ran on ahead to give the inhabitants warning and stir them up against the approaching party. The rest of the story may be told in the words of Dunsford, the old historian of Tiverton: " When the constables arrived [at Silverton] they were beaten, wounded, and forced to remain in the street in great danger of their lives during the night. None of the inhabitants would take any of the constables into their houses, nor could they get entertainment from any public-house. In the meantime the soldiers who had halted at the head of the town, receiving intelligence of this obstruction, and that their attempting to pass that way might be productive of bloodshed, conveyed their prisoners circuitously through the neighbouring fields under cover of the night, and lodged them in the county gaol at Exeter early in the morning. At the following Assizes, about a month after, they were tried and sentenced to pay a fine of 13s. 4d. each and be imprisoned six months."

The West Country weavers. We have now to describe the condition of the various classes of domestic workers engaged in the woollen industry. The most important was the class of weavers. In the West Country the weavers did not work on their own, as they did in Yorkshire; they worked for hire on material supplied by the capitalist. They contracted with the clothier to weave the yarn which he delivered to them into cloth of a certain size; they carried it to their homes and did the work under their own roofs; when the cloth was woven they took it back to their employer and received the price of their work. This is essentially the wage system, since the manual workers had no property in the goods they manufactured. But although the weavers did not own the material they generally owned their looms. The price of a loom varied: some cost two, three, or four guineas, others even more, but a weaver might construct a loom with his own hands. The famous Weavers Act of 1555 limited weavers who lived outside the old urban centres of industry to two looms, but the restriction was not generally observed. Some weavers kept as many as five or six looms under their roofs; this was chiefly the case where the weavers had large families. The weavers as a rule did not confine themselves to one master; they took work from three, four, even five employers at once. The system had many advantages from the point of view of the weavers; if trade were dull with one clothier they might find work with another; they could also pick and choose what kind of work they pleased, and it heightened their feeling of independence to have more than one string to their bow. On the other hand, the system was inconvenient to the employer; not only was the work sometimes delayed several weeks, but when trade was brisk the clothier had no staff of workmen upon whose services he could exclusively rely.

Weaving was not confined to men. Women played an important part in the weaving branch of the woollen industry, just as they did in other branches. It was their recognised province: *Women in the weaving industry.*

> " By day the web and loom,
> And homely household talk shall be her doom."[1]

The employment of women was attacked, as we have seen,[2] in the fifteenth and sixteenth centuries, and in the case of one manufacturing centre, Cullompton in Devonshire, women were not allowed to learn weaving down to 1825; but as a rule women labour was not suppressed, and some women earned by weaving as much as men. At Trowbridge and Bradford in Wiltshire, in the eighteenth century, two weavers out of every five were women. Weaving was also carried on by women and girls in the North of England; it was usual, in any case, for the wife of a weaver to assist her husband in working the broad loom.

The weavers' earnings varied at different periods and in different parts of the country. In the year of the Armada

---

[1] Dryden.   [2] Above, p. 35.

(1588) a Yorkshire weaver was earning less than fivepence a day, and a century later his wages had scarcely increased, in spite of the great rise in prices due to the influx of American silver. According to evidence given in a trial of 1676, " weavers of cloth can hardly earn fivepence a day . . . and find themselves meat, though they be strong and able to work." The wages of weavers were probably no higher in the West Country or in East Anglia. At any rate the famous ballad of *The Clothier's Delight*[1] charged the clothiers with paying their weavers only sixpence a day:

" We will make [them] to work hard for sixpence a day,
  Though a shilling they deserve if they had their just
  pay."

Towards the end of the eighteenth century the earnings of weavers were round about ten shillings a week; roughly speaking they were a shilling or eighteenpence a day. At Leeds, for example, weavers engaged in making broad cloths earned 10s. 6d. a week the year round, if they were fully employed, otherwise they only made 8s.[2] At Norwich, they were said not to exceed, on an average, 5s. or 7s. a week; but when trade was brisk weavers might earn £1 1s. a week for fine work, and 12s. for coarse work. In the West they earned between 7s. 6d. (Somersetshire) and 12s. (Gloucestershire). The weaver was actually paid, not a weekly wage, but piece rates from which various deductions had to be made for expenses. On the whole we may say that a weaver received the gross sum of 40s. to 44s., or the net sum of 31s. to 35s. (after deducting expenses such as glue, candles, wear and tear of the loom, and so forth), for work which occupied him between two and three weeks; but as he was not regularly employed his average weekly earnings would be reduced accordingly. These, then, roughly were the " nominal " wages of the weavers. What were their " real " wages, or, in other words, what was the purchasing power of money ? At Leeds, in 1770, ten to eleven ounces of oatbread (the favourite food) could be bought for 1d.; eighteen to nineteen ounces of butter for 8d.;

---

[1] See below, p. 104.   [2] This was in 1771.

cheese was 4d. per pound; mutton, beef, and pork 4d. per pound; veal 2½d. per pound; milk ½d. per pint in summer, and 1d. or 1½d. in winter; house rent was 40s. a year, and firing 20s.

Weavers were not in employment all the year round; there were always times in the year when many were out of work. In periods of trade depression some employers might continue to give out work to weavers and prepare their cloth in anticipation of a revival of trade, but others did not get their cloth ready until the orders came. In the West Country it was not unknown for a weaver to be unemployed seventeen weeks together, and an unemployed artisan usually fared ill. In harvest time he might find work in the fields and earn two meals and a shilling a day at hay-making. Still the harvest comes but once a year, and as the textile workers in the West of England owned very little land, they were often employed, when out of work, in labour on the roads or forced to break stones and wheel heavy loads. Even where opportunities for rural employment existed the weaver would not find it a satis-factory substitute for weaving. Not only was rural work poorly remunerated, but the weaver, living a sedentary life, was not adapted physically for outdoor employment, and hard work roughened his hands, making him less fit for weaving—a fact overlooked by those who lay stress upon the opportunities for rural employment enjoyed by textile artisans prior to the Industrial Revolution. *Unem-ployment.*

How did a master-weaver start life ? In the days of the old gild system he was usually required to serve a period of apprenticeship, but in the eighteenth century, even before the Industrial Revolution, we find the institution of appren-ticeship in a state of dissolution. In the first place, although seven years still remained the recognised term for inden-tured apprentices, shorter or longer periods were common. In 1714 an apprentice bound himself to a weaver for four and a quarter years, and even shorter terms were not unknown; at the other end of the scale we hear of parish apprentices—pauper children apprenticed by the parish—who served fifteen or sixteen years; for parish officers, " to *Appren-ticeship under the Domestic System.*

save expense," were said to ruin the children " by putting them out, as early as they can, to any sorry masters that will take them, without any concern for their education or welfare." Whether a term of seven years was really necessary in the woollen industry became a burning question. In the case of weaving one view was that a lad " should be took to the loom for about an hour or two in the day, that he may get a knowledge of it gradually"; he needed constant supervision, for if he wove an entire piece straight off by himself he would spoil the work. Another view was that a boy of common capacity would learn weaving, including dressing the warp[1] and fixing it in the loom, in six months. "Respecting persons living in a manufacturing country," said a Gloucestershire clothier, " you do not speak of an instance of a savage from the woods or a porter taken out of London streets, but you speak of persons taken out of the country who know something of the trade. There is hardly a child who does not know something of the trade; he knows the nature of yarn, he puts his hand to one thing or another, and there is hardly a boy who does not put his hand to every part that he can."

Its changed character. In the eighteenth century the law of apprenticeship had become obsolete, and few attempts were made to enforce it in courts of law. The majority of clothiers probably never heard of the Elizabethan Statute of Apprentices, and did not know that they could be punished for employing a workman who had not served a legal apprenticeship. But although the eighteenth-century weaver did not trouble himself about the technicalities of the law of apprenticeship, there was a well-understood difference between a " legal " and an " illegal " workman. A legal workman was a man who served round about seven years at a trade before he set up for himself. He need not be regularly " indentured," provided he was taught by someone who knew his business. Not only the legal but also the social character of apprenticeship underwent a change. Instead of the apprentice residing with his master as in the olden

---

[1] See below, pp. 139, 186, *n*. 2.

days, it became an increasing practice, except in the case of
parish apprentices, to pay the boy wages in lieu of board
and lodging. In 1714 an apprentice bound himself to a
Gloucestershire weaver for four and a quarter years; the
contract stipulated that " he should find himself in food,
drink, lodging, and apparel, and might go home every
Saturday to Monday; his wages were to be, out of every
shilling made by his master, 2½d. in the first year, 3d. the
second and third years, 4d. the fourth year." This form
of apprenticeship was sometimes known as " colting," and
closely resembled the journeyman system.

When the period of training was completed the apprentice The
became a journeyman.[1] The number of journeymen journeyman
employed by a weaver depended upon his number of looms. under the
Before Kay invented the fly shuttle[2] two persons were Domestic System.
required to work the broad loom, the master-weaver and a
journeyman, but often the weaver's wife or daughter, or
an apprentice, supplied the place of a journeyman. In
former times the journeyman weaver was engaged for fixed
periods. The Statute of Apprentices (1563), for example,
made compulsory an engagement for twelve months, but
in the eighteenth century the journeyman was usually
engaged for the manufacture of one piece of cloth. The
method of payment was one-third of the price received by
the master from the clothier for weaving the cloth. In
addition to his piece-rate earnings the journeyman received
" small beer, lodging, and firing " where he had no home
of his own. This was called his " privilege," and was
valued at a shilling a week. Altogether, in the West
Country a journeyman in constant employment earned,
exclusive of his " privilege," about a shilling a day, and for
this he worked fourteen or fifteen hours daily. When he
had acquired by his industry a loom of his own he was then
able to set up as a master-weaver.

The position of a West-Country weaver in the eighteenth
century invites comparison with that of a modern factory
operative. The point of resemblance is that both are wage-

---

[1] For the term "journeyman," see above, p. 30.
[2] See below, p. 142.

Compari-
son of the
West
Country
weaver
and the
modern
artisan.

earners, neither of whom owns the raw material on which
he works. The differences are striking. The domestic
worker owned the instruments of production—that is, his
loom; he worked under his own roof, was free from exacting
supervision, and his time was his own to labour as he
pleased; also, he usually served more than one employer,
and so enjoyed greater economic independence as well as
increased security. The factory operative, on the other
hand, although he does not own the instruments of production, and works in a factory—under constant supervision—
for a single employer, has shorter hours, and is assured, as
a rule, of more continuous employment; he is also better
organised; and factory legislation now aims at providing
proper conditions under which his work may be carried on.

Spinning.

The spinning of yarn was generally the work of women
and children. It was peculiarly a female occupation, as
we see from the word " spinster " now applied to an unmarried woman. The Book of Proverbs praises the virtuous
woman as one who " seeketh wool and flax and worketh
willingly with her hands, . . . she layeth her hands to the
spindle, and her hands hold the distaff." An Old English
rhyme represents the division of labour among our primæval
parents in the well-known couplet:

" When Adam delv'd and Eve span
Who was then a gentleman ?"[1]

Pliny relates that at the nuptials of a Roman maiden a
distaff dressed with wool and a spindle trimmed with thread
were carried in the procession, presumably to put her in
mind of a housewife's duties; and Langland's exhortation
in *Piers the Plowman* shows that spinning was regarded in
mediæval England as the natural employment of women:

" Wives and widows . wool and flax spinneth;
Maketh cloth, I counsel you, and kenneth so your
daughters."

Children were taught to spin from their earliest years.
When Queen Elizabeth visited Norwich the worsted

[1] *Cf.* Goneril in *King Lear :* " I must change arms at home and
give the distaff into my husband's hands."

weavers gave a pageant in her honour; in the pageant were shown eight " small women children " spinning worsted yarn, while " a pretty boy," representing the city, recited verses:

" From combed wool we draw this slender thread,
  From thence the looms have dealing with the same,
And thence again in order do proceed
  These several works which skilful art doth frame:
And all to drive Dame Need into her cave,
Our heads and hands together labour'd have."

The work was often carried on in the open air. On sunny days women and children would betake themselves with their spinning wheels to some chosen spot and there pursue their labours; even as late as the nineteenth century girls were to be found in the Highlands of Scotland herding on the hillside busily spinning with their distaffs. Spinning occupied all the leisure moments of those engaged in it; the hours were therefore very long, though the work was light. One of the traditions of North Germany contains a warning against spinning on Saturday evening. " They have a story that there were two old women, good friends, and the most indefatigable spinners in the village. Their work did not cease even on Saturday evenings. At length one of them died; but on the following Saturday she appeared to the other, busy at her usual employment, and showed her burning hand, saying:

" ' See what I in Hell have won
Because on Saturday I spun.' "

In this country one day in the Calendar of Saints was named St. Distaff's Day. It was the morrow after Twelfth Day—that is, January 7—and it closed the season of Christmas festivities:

" Partly work and partly play
You must on St. Distaff's Day,
From the plough soon free your team;
Then come home and fother them:
If the maids a-spinning go,
Burn the flax and fire the tow,
Bring in pails of water then,
Let the maids bewash the men.

St. Distaff's Day.

> Give St. Distaff all the right:
> Then bid Christmas sport good-night.
> And next morning everyone
> To his own vocation."[1]

Employment of spinners. Sometimes the spinners worked on their own; they bought the raw material, spun it into yarn, and then carried it to the market for sale. As a rule they worked for hire on their employers' material, their employers being either clothiers, master wool-combers, or "market spinners" (*i.e.*, yarn-makers). The spinners were scattered over the whole countryside, and "spinning houses" or "packhouses" were therefore established in the villages for the distribution of the wool. The village shop often served as the pack-house, and the wool was conveyed to it by carriers or "packmen"; hither the spinners repaired for their material and returned it after it was spun into yarn. Spinning was thus essentially a "cottage" industry, and manufacturers were able to draw for their supply of labour upon a very extensive area. The worsted industry of the Norfolk towns, for example, was fed with yarn not only by the eastern counties—Suffolk, Cambridge, Bedford, and Hertford—but also by Yorkshire and even Westmorland.

Defects of hand-spinning. Hand-spinning had one serious defect. The spinner often lacked the requisite technical skill; the yarn was therefore neither uniform in quality, nor firm enough to stand the strain of the loom, and the cloth, as a result, was uneven in texture. The Suffolk clothiers drew attention to this evil as early as 1575. "The custom of our country is to carry our wool out to carding and spinning and put it to divers and sundry spinners who have in their houses divers and sundry children and servants that do card and spin the same wool, and some of them card upon new cards, and some upon old cards, and some spin hard and some soft, by reason whereof our cloth falleth out in some places broad and some narrow, contrary to our mind and greatly to our disprofit." There were sometimes as many as ten hands engaged on one chain,[2] and as it was spun very irregularly the thread was always breaking: a considerable

---

[1] Herrick.   [2] For the term "chain," see below, p. 136.

portion of the weaver's time, in fact, was spent in repairing broken threads. To remedy this it was proposed to establish spinning schools where children could be taught the art of spinning by experienced teachers. This idea was advocated by Yarranton, among others, in a book on *England's Improvement* (1677). "In all towns" in Germany, he wrote, " there are schools for little girls from six years old and upwards to teach them to spin, and so to bring their tender fingers by degrees to spin very fine. In all towns there are schools according to the bigness or multitude of the poor children. I will here show you the way, method, rule, and order how they are governed. First, there is a large room, and in the middle thereof a little box like a pulpit. Secondly, there are benches built round about the room as they are in our playhouses; upon the benches sit about two hundred children spinning, and in the box in the middle of the room sits the grand mistress with a long white wand in her hand. If she observes any of them idle, she reaches them a tap; but if that will not do, she rings a bell which by a little cord is fixed to the box, and out comes a woman. She then points to the offender, and she is taken away into another room and chastised. And all this is done without one word speaking. And I believe this way of ordering the young women in Germany is one great cause that the German women have so little of the twit-twat. And I am sure that it would be well were it so in England. And it is clear that the less there is of speaking the more there may be of working." In England spinning schools were sometimes established as part of the organisation of poor relief, and here poor children were taught by " spinning dames."

The spinners were very poorly paid for their toil. In the seventeenth and eighteenth centuries England's greatest industry rested on the basis of sweated labour. Evidence was given in a State trial, held in the reign of Charles I., showing that " the poor that spin, though they work very hard, cannot gain 4d. a day towards their living . . . the majority earn 2d. or 3d.," and at the close of the eighteenth century it was calculated that a spinner walked thirty-

Remuneration of spinners.

three miles, stepping back and forward to the wheel, in order to earn 2s. 8d. According to Arthur Young women at Leeds earned 2s. 6d. or 3s. a week; girls, thirteen or fourteen years old, 1s. 8d.; boys of eight or nine, 2½d. a day; a boy of six, 1d. a day. In most cases, no doubt, the earnings of a spinner were intended to serve not as her only source of income, but as an addition to the family budget. "The pay is not much," said a Lancashire woman, "but it helps to boil the pot." A woman, as Fitzherbert wrote in the sixteenth century, "cannot get her living honestly with spinning on the distaff, but it stoppeth a gap." None the less many poor women and children had to depend upon their scanty earnings for their daily subsistence, and even the small amount earned by a spinner, after working twelve hours a day, was liable to be reduced under various pretexts, such as "the dulness of trade," or "the custom of the trade." Another device of capitalist exploitation was to use false weights in weighing out the material to spinners. This was a legacy of mediæval times which is alluded to in *Piers the Plowman* :

" My wife was a weaver, woollen cloth she made,
　She spake to her spinsters to spin it soft,
　But the pound weight that she paid by weighed a quarter
　　more
　Than my own balance did when I weighed fair."

The fact that the spinners were unorganised made them powerless to resist industrial oppression.

The wool-combers. Two other classes of artisans engaged in the woollen industry merit attention: the wool-combers and the cloth-finishers. The wool-combers were in a better position than the weavers. Their numbers were limited, and their work was more highly remunerated. They were not tied to one particular locality, but were accustomed to travel about the country from place to place in search of employment. One reason for this roving life was that many of them were single men; and when work was scarce in their native town, they were not compelled to accept low wages to save themselves from starvation. During their wanderings they were kept by the institution to which they belonged; for the Combers' Union preferred to support its members in idleness rather than submit to a reduction of wages. When a wool-comber set out on his journeys he received from his club a certificate which testified that he was a member of the union, had behaved himself well, and was an honest man. This certificate entitled him to relief from every wool-combers' society affiliated to his branch, and enabled him to " travel the kingdom round, be caressed at each club, and not spend a farthing of his own or strike one stroke of work."[1] But anyone convicted of fraud forfeited his claim to the certificate and the privileges which it conferred.

The cloth-finishers were sometimes known as " cloth- workers," " cloth-dressers," " shearmen," and " croppers." The distinctive feature of this class was that their work was not carried on at home, as in the case of carders, spinners, and weavers, but was done in a workshop. This means that their industry—in the eighteenth century— was not a " cottage industry "; they worked together in large bodies, three men and one boy being engaged on a piece of cloth. The cloth-finishers were employed in different ways. Sometimes a number of clothiers had their cloths dressed at the same shop, where a master-dresser, as he was called, worked for them on commission and kept as many as forty or fifty men and boys. At other times the clothier employed cloth-finishers under his own roof. The story of Jack of Newbury represents the establishment of the great clothier as housing shearmen, rowers, fullers, and dyers, and in Yorkshire the merchant, who bought the cloth in an unfinished state from the clothier, often assumed direct responsibility for the final processes of the manufacture. This attempt of the clothiers and merchants to seize into their hands all the branches of the cloth manufacture was strenuously resisted by the master-shearmen and dyers.

The old domestic system of industry is often painted in very vivid colours. It is attractive, no doubt, to contem-

The cloth-finishers.

---

[1] Cf. *The Song of the Rambling Wool Combers*, who lived " regardless of your pity."

Defects of
the Do-
mestic
System in
theWestof
England: plate the artisan working in his own home, in the midst of his family, a free agent, not subject to the discipline of the factory bell, but at liberty to work or to play as the inclination seized him. The realities of industrial life did not, however, always correspond to the ideal picture sometimes presented of it. The domestic system, as it existed in the West of England, had several serious defects.

To begin with, the hours of labour were very long. " A shepherd," remarks Adam Smith, " has much leisure, a husbandman some, a manufacturer[1] none at all." We are told by a seventeenth-century writer that " a poor weaver sits at his loom from four in the morning till eight, nine, ten at night, but to get seven, eight, or ten shillings a week for a livelihood." In the middle of the eighteenth century fourteen hours, including meals, constituted a normal working day, while some weavers worked as much as fifteen or sixteen hours a day. A Wiltshire weaver told a Parliamentary Committee, which was investigating the conditions of the woollen industry in 1803, that " in winter we work as much by the candle as by daylight. I have worked from five to seven at night in winter, and from four to nine in summer "—that is, fourteen hours a day in winter, seventeen in summer. He was asked:

" How long would you be able to do that ?"—" As long as God Almighty gives me strength."

" But He will not give you strength more than your frame was originally intended for."—" I have done it for years."

" Do others do that ?"—" I hardly know anybody but what does; the greatest part of the inhabitants do that." This incessant toil left little or no leisure for education or recreation. Nor was it possible for the State to regulate the hours of employment; this only became possible under the factory system. To this day excessive hours have survived in those industries which are carried on in the homes of the workers: the man who works at home is never done. Moreover, the weavers often lived a long way from the clothier's house. Some weavers had six miles and even

---

[1] For the use of the term "manufacturer," see above, p. 41.

more to go, and six to come back, in fetching and carrying home their work. This wasted a great deal of the weaver's time, especially since he served more than one employer.

In the eyes of the employer the most serious defect of (ii.) Embezzlement the domestic system was the embezzlement of the raw of the material. material. At all periods complaints were general that carders and spinners and weavers appropriated the wool given out to them. Detection was difficult, and the numerous laws against embezzlement[1] failed to check the practice. In Scotland spinners or weavers who defrauded their employers were ordered " to be kept in prison till the market day, and there to stand in time of the market two hours with a paper mentioning their fault in great letters." A popular Scottish rhyme depicts the evil end of weavers who had been hanged for stealing yarn:

> " As I gaed up the Canongate,
>   And through the Nether-bow,
>   Four and twenty weavers
>   Were singing in a tow.

> " The tow gae a crack,
>   The weavers gae a girn:
>   Fie, let me down again,
>   I'll never steal a pirn.

> " I'll ne'er steal a pirn,
>   I'll ne'er steal a pow:
>   Oh fie, let me down again,
>   I'll steal nae mair frae you."[2]

A universal feature of the domestic system throughout (iii.) Employment the country was the employment of children. Nowadays ofchildren. child labour is looked upon, and rightly, as a great evil; in this respect public sentiment has changed, for in former times child labour was considered a good thing. Daniel

---

[1] As late as 1777 the so-called Worsted Act empowered the worsted manufacturers of the North (Yorkshire, Lancashire, and Cheshire) to appoint a Committee with inspectors for the detection and prosecution of embezzlement. In later years similar powers were given to Suffolk (1784), Leicestershire, Lincolnshire, and neighbouring counties (1785), and Norfolk and Norwich (1790).

[2] Gaed =went; tow =halter; gae =gave; girn =cry of pain; pirn =a quill on which yarn was wound; pow =(?) crab; nae mair = no more.

Defoe records with pride that in his day (1724) there was not a child in Taunton or the neighbourhood above five years old, " but if it was not neglected by its parents and untaught, could earn its own bread." Under the domestic system children were put to work as soon as they were able to render any kind of service, and it was remarked upon when children of six were " idle." In Westmorland children were employed in the manufacture of stockings as early as the age of four. The eldest son of Crompton, the inventor of the mule,[1] thus relates the experiences of his childhood:

" Soon after I was able to walk I was employed in the cotton manufacture. My mother used to bat the cotton-wool on a wire riddle. It was then put into a deep brown mug with a strong ley of soap suds. My mother then tucked up my petticoats about my waist, and put me in the tub to tread upon the cotton at the bottom. When a second riddleful was batted I was lifted out and it was placed in the mug, and I again trodded it down. This process was continued until the mug became so full that I could no longer safely stand in it, when a chair was placed beside it, and I held on by the back. When the mug was full quite, the soap suds were poured off, and each separate *dollop* (lump) of wool well squeezed to free it from moisture. They were then placed on the bread-rack under the beams of the kitchen-loft to dry. My mother and my grandmother carded the cotton-wool by hand, taking one of the *dollops* at a time on the simple hand-cards. When carded they were put aside in separate parcels ready for spinning."

The younger folk assisted their elders in various ways. They fetched the bobbins; they wound or " quilled " the spun yarn, they helped the weaver to prepare the loom for weaving, they learnt the preparatory processes like willey-ing, carding, scribbling, and slubbing;[2] and as they grew older they were able to spin and to weave—it was said to be very common for boys and girls to acquire the art of weaving by the time they were twelve years old. In some cases a child went to school in the daytime and worked in the morning and evening. The earnings of children were usually small. Those who were four to eight years old

---

[1] See below, p. 158.   [2] See below, pp. 130, 184.

earned a penny a day at quilling, from eight to twelve they earned twopence to fourpence a day at spinning, and from thirteen to fourteen years old eightpence a day at weaving; but the rates of wages varied considerably in different parts of the country.

As a rule children worked under the eyes of their parents, and in so far as the parents avoided exhausting toil the evils of child labour would be mitigated. But in earlier times children were not always treated humanely by their parents. An old man, who was brought up under the domestic system, declared that the days of his childhood were " really the days of infant slavery." " The creatures," he said, " were set to work as soon as they could crawl, and their parents were the hardest of taskmasters." On the whole, it would appear that the children of hand-loom weavers were employed at an earlier age, for longer hours, and for less wages, than the majority of children employed in factories. In any case the use of child labour was not due to the introduction of machinery, and it was only the creation of the factory system which made it possible in the nineteenth century to abolish it.

When we turn from the West to the North of England we are confronted with a very different kind of industrial society. The domestic manufacturers of Yorkshire, as the clothiers there were called, resembled neither the master-clothiers nor the master-weavers of the West Country; they differed from the latter because they owned not only their looms but also the material upon which they worked; they differed from the former because they were primarily manual craftsmen, rather than industrial or trading capitalists. They possessed, indeed, only " a very trifling capital," and depended upon the weekly sales of their goods for replenishing their store.[1] Every week they made a piece of cloth and brought it to market, " being compelled to sell the same at the week-end, and with the money received for the same to provide both stuff wherewith to make another the week following, and also victuals to sustain themselves and

The Domestic System in the North of England.

---

[1] This applies more particularly to the seventeenth century.

their families till another be made and sold." None the less they were not wage-earners. They bought the wool from the dealers, and in their own houses, assisted by their wives, children, and journeymen, they worked it up through all the different stages, and finally sold the manufactured cloth in the open market.[1] The number of looms owned by a domestic manufacturer varied according to circumstances; at the end of the eighteenth century most clothiers had two, and some three or even more. The Yorkshire clothier, unlike the West Country clothier, was himself a workman and wove in the loom. He was usually assisted by his wife and children, sometimes also by apprentices and journeymen. On an average a clothier probably employed at least ten persons.[2]

The family life of the West Riding clothier is portrayed in a colloquial poem " descriptive of the Manners of the Clothiers," written about 1730.[3] At the evening meal the master of the house gives instructions to his wife, apprentices, and journeymen, regarding the work of the morrow:

> " Lads, work hard I pray,
> Cloth mun be pearked[4] next market day,
> And Tom mun go to-morn to t'spinners,
> And Will mun seek about for t'swingers,
> And Jack, to-morn by time be rising
> And go to t'sizing mill for sizing.[5]
> And get your web and warping done
> That ye may get it into t'loom.

---

[1] The " domestic system " of Yorkshire is sometimes regarded as akin to the " gild system," except that there was no gild organisation among the Yorkshire manufacturers. The view here taken is that it was a primitive form of the " domestic system," as it existed in the West Country, since the Yorkshire clothier controlled all the processes connected with cloth-making, other than the finishing processes: whereas under the " gild system " (as here defined) there was no centralised control of the industry, and the workers in each branch retained their independence. See above, p. 27.

[2] In addition to the small manufacturers Yorkshire contained a class of large clothiers whose position was analogous to that of the West Country clothiers, and also (in the eighteenth century) a class of worsted makers who conducted their business on a large scale. But the typical figure of the Yorkshire industrial system was the small clothier engaged in woollen fabrics.

[3] For this poem see Bibliographical Note.

[4] Pearked =perched (i.e., tested for faults).   [5] See p. 186, n. 2.

Jo, go give my horse some corn,
For I design for t'Wolds to-morn.[1]
So mind and clean my boots and shoon,
For I'll be up i' t'morn right soon.
Mary—there's wool—tak thee and dye it."

His wife objects that she has her house-work to do: " To
bake and swing and blend, and milk, and bairns to school
to send," as well as " washing up morn, noon, and neet."
But the husband retorts:

" All things mun aside be laid,
When we want help about our trade."

The young folk are then left to themselves, and they sit
round the fire telling tales and " merry jokes,"

" Till ten gives warning by the clock,
Then up they start—to bed they run."

At five o'clock the next morning they commence again the
day's round.

In some parts of the North—for example South Lan- Weaving
cashire—weaving was carried on merely as a by-occupa- occupation: it was a means of supplementing the farmer's income. tion.
According to one account: " The farming was generally of
that kind which was soonest and most easily performed,
and it was done by the husband and other males of the
family, whilst the wife and daughters and maidservants, if
there were any of the latter, attended to the churning,
cheese-making, and household work, and when that was
finished, they busied themselves in carding, slubbing, and
spinning of wool or cotton, as well as in forming it into
warps for the loom. The husband and sons would next,
at times when farm labour did not call them abroad, size
(i.e., dress) the warp, dry it, and beam it in the loom, and
either they or the females, whichever happened to be least
otherwise employed, would weave the warp down. A
farmer would generally have three or four looms in his
house, and thus, what with the farming, easily and leisurely
though it was performed, what with the house-work, and
what with the carding, spinning, and weaving, there was

[1] The purpose of his journey is to buy wool.

ample employment for the family. If the rent was raised from the farm, so much the better; if not, the deficiency was made up from the manufacturing profits, and as the weaver was also the vendor, he had a pretty fair command of his own remuneration."

Weaving as the principal occupation. In other cases farming, and not weaving, was the subsidiary occupation. The following is a description of the parish of Mellor, near Manchester, in 1770. " In the year 1770 the land in our township was occupied by between fifty and sixty farmers; rents to the best of my recollection did not exceed 10s. per statute acre, and out of these fifty or sixty farmers there were only six or seven who raised their rents directly from the produce of their farms; all the rest got their rent partly in some branch of trade, such as spinning and weaving woollen, linen, or cotton. The cottagers were employed entirely in this manner except for a few weeks in the harvest. The great sheet-anchor of all cottages and small farms was the labour attached to the hand-wheel; and when it is considered that it required six to eight hands to prepare and spin yarn of (woollen, linen, or cotton) sufficient for the consumption of one weaver—this shows clearly the inexhaustible source there was for labour for every person from the age of seven to eighty years (who retained their sight and could move their hands) to earn their bread—say one to three shillings per week—without going to the parish." In Yorkshire itself the domestic manufacturers had really very little land, and they used it mainly to support a cow or a horse; in any case they were not as a rule arable farmers.

The Yorkshire apprentices. The institution of apprenticeship survived longer, in its old form, in the North of England than in the West. The Yorkshire manufacturers needed a thorough training in the various branches of the woollen industry, for though a man was employed as a rule on one operation, whenever it was necessary he could turn his hand to other operations. The nature of the instruction given to an apprentice is shown in the evidence of a West Riding master-clothier, who was asked to enumerate the various branches of the trade which he had learnt:

" I learnt to be a spinner before I went apprentice; when I went apprentice I was a strong boy, and I was put to weaving first."

" Did you also learn to buy your own wool ?"

" Yes; I had the prospect of being a master when I came out of my time, and therefore my master took care I should learn that." He was also taught to dye and full cloth.

" And you instruct your apprentices in the same line ?"

" Yes; we think it a scandal when an apprentice is loose if he is not fit for his business; *we take pride in their being fit for their business, and we teach them all they will take.*" Thus the old ideal of sound craftsmanship, embodied in the mediæval craft gilds, still persisted among Yorkshire masters.

In some cases the indenture itself made stipulations as to the nature of the instruction. In an agreement dated 1792 the master—a worsted clothier of Bingley—undertook to teach the apprentice the " art and mistery of a worsted stuff-maker in all its branches . . . and also shall and will take his apprentice, in the last year of his apprenticeship, to the market or into the country, and instruct him in the buying of wool, the apprentice finding his own horse and paying his own travelling expenses. And also shall and will allow unto his said apprentice one fortnight in each and every year during the said term (five years), to go to school to improve himself in learning."

As a system of social training the institution of appren- *Changes in the institution of apprenticeship.* ticeship also continued in the eighteenth century. We are told how " an eminent manufacturer in that age used to be in his warehouse before six in the morning, accompanied by his children and apprentices. At seven they all came in to breakfast, which consisted of one large dish of water-pottage made of oatmeal, water, and a little salt, boiled thick and poured into a dish. At the side was a pan or basin of milk, and the master and apprentices, each with a wooden spoon in his hand, without loss of time, dipped into the same dish, and thence into the milk pan; and as soon as it was finished they all returned to their work."

Yet even in the North of England the institution of apprenticeship in its old form was fast decaying. The masters disliked receiving apprentices in their own houses, and it was found to be cheaper to have children coming in the morning and going home again at night. On his part also the apprentice was often disinclined to complete his term of service, sometimes owing to ill-treatment, but mainly because as he grew older he wished to earn money by working for wages. It became very common for apprentices to run away, and the aid of the town crier was often invoked to bring the fugitive to justice. The following is an extract from the Crier's Register at Clare in Suffolk:

1704, 7th July. "Cryd in Clare Markett, one John Woods, Apprentice to John Snell, in Clare, who ran away from his master; the boy aboute 15 years of age, with a lank browne thick head of hair, and a round plump fulle vissage; he hath had the small pox; he had a light cullered coate and wescoate, and britches of sinniment culler and gray wollen stockens and a black hatt."

We also have a description of an "idle and disorderly" apprentice who had followed the road to ruin and found himself in gaol:

"Thomas Baldwin, aged 21 years, born in this city [Norwich] and brought up a worsted weaver, committed about six months since as an idle and disorderly apprentice, frequently running away from his master and wandering to London and other places; he is about 5 feet 2 inches high, brown hair, usually wears a striped worsted cap, of a clear complexion, and well-made lad; had on when apprehended an old blue and white chequered Scotch handkerchief about his neck, a green ragged waistcoat laced with cord and leather breeches."

But not all run-away apprentices ended their career in prison or on the gallows. A prominent Yorkshire manufacturer (Hirst), born in the last quarter of the eighteenth century, started life under very inauspicious circumstances, yet fought his way to the front. "I was born on the 14th January, 1777, in the parish of Huddersfield. My parents were very poor, but honest; and when I was seven years of age I was put to earn my own bread by spinning worsted on a hand-wheel. . . . I was apprenticed to Mr.

John Caton of Marsh, near Huddersfield, cloth-finisher, when about 15; but his conduct was so cruel that I was determined to leave his employ. Having stated my resolution to another boy who was similarly situated, we arranged to take our departure together. We decided on going to the Low Country, to get work in the harvest fields, and we reached Bawtrey the first night. After so long a walk, we were both so fatigued on the following morning that we were scarcely able to get out of bed. We then began to consider what we had done, and how we must proceed; for we found that the harvest would not commence for some weeks. We could not agree on the road we were to take and we parted company in consequence. I got work at a farm-house. . . . As the youth with whom I had left home did not like his situation he returned to Huddersfield and made it known where I was. We had then been about twelve months from home; and although the father of my companion was a professed fortune-teller, they had never been able to discover where we had gone to. My brother came over to see me and to take me back home; but my master was not willing to part with me until my engagement was expired."

It was unusual for an apprentice to set up as a master immediately he was " out of his time "; as a rule he became a journeyman. Sometimes the journeyman was hired by the year, in which case he worked the customary hours and received as wages eight to ten pounds a year in addition to his board; but payment by piece-work was the more general practice. A striking feature of industrial conditions in Yorkshire was the good feeling existing between the small clothiers and their workmen. In times of trade depression the domestic manufacturers rarely dismissed their hands. " Our men and masters," said a clothier, " are in general so joined together in sentiment and, if I may be admitted to use the term, love to each other, that they do not wish to be separated if they can help it. We always consider the masters and journeymen as one, and our interests are reciprocal." The Yorkshire clothier prided himself upon the fact that it was " almost a thing unknown

The Yorkshire journeyman.

to discharge a workman for want of employment. Winter
or summer, bad trade or good, we go on straight forwards,"
whether the stock was sold or left on their hands. " I have
been with domestic manufacturers when they were short
of work," said a journeyman, " and they used to see about
a job for me, and if one couldn't be got I was continued."
What happened, on the other hand, when a clothier had
extra orders ? " We ask another master, perhaps, whether
he will spare us such a man to weave for us." The reply
breathes the same spirit of communism which had inspired
the ordinances of the London Shearmen three centuries
before.[1]

Merits of the Yorkshire Domestic System.   The outstanding merit of the Yorkshire domestic system,
apart from the friendly relations between masters and men,
was the opportunity afforded to every workman of rising
in the world. In the North of England it was not difficult
for any wage-earner in the woollen industry to become a
master. Every journeyman who was careful and persevering worked with the idea of saving up money " by
good economy," and then setting up on his own as soon as
he could. " When I only got ten shillings a week," said
a successful clothier who began with one loom and ended
with twenty-one, " I saved one out of it." The domestic
manufacturer needed little capital; his wooden loom was
made with his own hands or cheaply purchased; his
other utensils were cheaply bought. The raw material
was easily obtained on credit by any young man of
good character, starting life on his own. A contemporary
tells us that he knew " many instances where persons were
not worth one shilling, but from the representation of their
neighbours that they were honest and industrious they
have got credit for any quantity of wool they could work;
and I could state an instance, among many others, of three
brothers of the name of Gudson, who lived in a hovel, and
had only two looms between them, borrowed or hired, and
they could not get a larger building. I was informed
respecting them that they were very honest and sober,
and could get credit for wool, but could not erect a building

[1] Above, p. 34.

or hire one larger. On this representation being made to me I built each of them a separate house; each immediately took separate journeymen, and all their children were set to work; they have flourished from that time and are in as comfortable a situation as any man would wish to be. I have known twenty other instances, and I am persuaded a sober, industrious man may get credit to any amount; indeed I believe credit is too easily given."

In addition to the clothiers, journeymen, and apprentices, The merchants. the industrial society of the North also contained a class of merchants to whom the domestic manufacturers sold their cloth in an unfinished state. In the Middle Ages cloth was always sold in a public place on fixed days of the week, and it was an offence against the law to buy or sell cloth privately. When commodities were sold secretly the owner of the market went without his tolls, and the public sale of cloth also facilitated the work of inspectors (aulnagers) whose duty it was to see that the manufacturers had observed the statutory regulations as to size and quality.[1] In London the famous centre of the cloth trade was Blackwell Hall, and in other towns a separate place was set aside for the sale of cloth; for example, in the North the Thursday market of York, in the East the Worsted Seld of Norwich, in the West the Touker Street Market of Bristol, and many others. In general the system of public markets survived only in Yorkshire, where the cloth markets constituted one of the most striking features of the old domestic system. The most important was Leeds, and we have a vivid account of it in Defoe's *Tour of Great Britain*.

" The market itself is worth describing, though no description can come up to the thing itself. The street[2] is a large, broad, fair, and well-built street, beginning at the bridge and ascending gently to the north. Early in the morning there are tressels placed in two rows in the street. Then there are boards laid across those tressels, so that the boards lie like long counters on either side from one end of the street to the other. The clothiers come early in the morning with cloth, and few clothiers bring more than one

The cloth market at Leeds.

---

[1] See below, p. 113. [2] Briggate.

piece, the market being so frequent. At six or seven o'clock in the morning the market bell rings," and in a few minutes, without hurry or noise, " all the boards are covered with cloth, and behind every piece of cloth the clothier standing to sell it. As soon as the bell has done ringing the merchants and factors and buyers of all sorts come down. When they see any cloths that suit their occasion they reach over to the clothier and whisper, and in the fewest words imaginable the price is stated; one asks, the other bids; and 'tis agree or not agree, in a moment. The merchants and buyers generally walk down and up twice on each side of the rows, and in little more than an hour all the business is done. Thus you see ten or twenty thousand pounds value in cloth, and sometimes much more, bought and sold in little more than an hour."

The Cloth Halls.   In the eighteenth century several cloth halls were erected in Yorkshire towns to take the place of the open market; at Halifax in 1700, at Wakefield in 1710, at Leeds in 1711.[1] As industry developed, larger halls became necessary; for example, a second White Cloth Hall was opened at Leeds in 1755 and a third in 1775. At the opening of the second hall at Halifax in 1779 verses were composed in honour of the wool-combers' patron, and though crude in quality, they possess a certain historical interest:

> " When Adam and his Consort Eve
> Lived in a garden fair,
> They dressed themselves in green fig-leaves
> For want of better wear:

> " But we, their sons, are wiser grown
> Than leaves of fig to pull;
> We clothe ourselves from head to foot
> With ever honour'd wool.

> " O let us not forget the good,
> The worthy Bishop Blaize,
> Who came from Jersey here to us
> As ancient history says.

[1] This was the White Cloth Hall. Coloured cloths were still sold in the open market in Briggate until the erection of the Coloured Cloth Hall in 1756. A cloth hall was opened at Huddersfield in 1766 and at Bradford in 1773.

" He taught us how to comb our wool
The source of all our wealth,
Then let us still remember him,
While we have life and health."

Leeds contained at first two halls, one (built in 1711) for white cloth, the other (built in 1756) for coloured cloth; and the two together ultimately contained room for about four thousand cloth-stalls. A great many clothiers did not possess stands in the halls, but were allowed to expose their cloth for sale on payment of sixpence for each cloth. None but those who had been apprenticed, or " legally brought up," were allowed to purchase stands in the official halls; and those who were not lawful clothiers used to assemble in Potter's Field, whence originated a third hall bearing the significant title of Tom Paine Hall. The official halls viewed with great jealousy their upstart rival; and, in order to prevent merchants frequenting it, they changed the hour of the market, holding it at the same time as the Tom Paine Hall. Eventually the White Cloth Hall was constrained to admit all clothiers to its privileges, whether they had served an apprenticeship or not. The same procedure was observed in the halls as in the open market: the manufacturers taking up a position behind the stands, the merchants passing along and making purchases, the bell ringing at the end of an hour. One recent development, however, must be noticed. Great quantities of cloth were sold which had never been " pitched " (exposed to sale) in the market. It was an increasing practice for domestic manufacturers to carry a single piece of cloth to the hall as a sample, and the merchant gave orders for others to be made according to the pattern shown. When the cloths were ready they were brought to the merchant's house without ever coming into the halls. Sometimes merchants themselves gave out patterns, but the manufacturer who made goods to order was considered equally a master-clothier with the one who worked on his own lines and exposed his cloth for sale in the halls.

How did the merchants dispose of their goods? To Classes of merchants: answer this question we must observe that there were three

kinds of merchants: (1) some supplied shops; (2) others
supplied the factors at Blackwell Hall; (3) others were
exporters.

(i.) The
travelling
merchants.   The travelling merchants, who supplied the shops, are
described by Defoe. He tells how they used to " go all
over England with droves of pack-horses and to all the fairs
and market towns over the whole island. Here they supply
not the common people by retail, which would denominate
them pedlars indeed, but they supply the shops by wholesale or whole pieces; and not only so, but give large credit
too, so that they are really travelling merchants, and as
such they sell a very great quantity of goods; 'tis ordinary
for one of these men to carry a thousand pounds value of
cloth with them at a time." Aikin, the topographer of
Lancashire, adds that the pack-horses " brought back
sheep's wool which was bought on the journey and sold
to the makers of worsted yarn at Manchester, or to the
clothiers of Rochdale, Saddleworth, and the West Riding
of Yorkshire. On the improvement of turnpike roads
waggons were set up, and the pack-horses discontinued;
and the chapmen only rode out for orders, carrying with
them the patterns in their bags."

Their ar-
duous life.   To picture the arduous existence of a travelling merchant,
we must turn to the account which Thomas Walker gives
in his *Original* of a Lancashire merchant who lived a generation before the Industrial Revolution. " He sent the
manufactures of the place into Nottinghamshire, Lincolnshire, Cambridgeshire, and the intervening counties; and
principally took in exchange feathers from Lincolnshire
and malt from Cambridgeshire and Nottinghamshire. All
his commodities were conveyed on pack-horses, and he
was from home the greater part of every year, performing
his journeys leisurely on horseback. His balances were
received in guineas and were carried with him in his saddle
bags. He was exposed to the vicissitudes of the weather,
and to great labour and fatigue, and to constant danger.
In Lincolnshire he travelled chiefly along bridle-ways,
through fields where frequent gibbets warned him of his
peril and where flocks of wild-fowl continually darkened the

air. Business carried on in this manner required a combination of personal attention, courage and physical strength not to be hoped for in a deputy; and a merchant then led a much more severe and irksome life than a bagman afterwards, and still more than a commercial traveller of the present day."

Travelling in the eighteenth century was extremely slow according to modern standards. " The increased speed with which everything connected with the trade is transacted," wrote Edward Baines, the historian of the cotton industry, in 1870, " is startling to men who remember the old times and ways. Time was, as men yet active in business well remember, when the Manchester merchant coming to Bradford took three days for the outward and return journey. Starting from the cotton metropolis on Wednesday morning with a post-chaise and pair of horses, one ridden by a postilion, he got as far as Halifax, where he stayed the night. Next day, by way of the lofty table-land of Catherine Slack and Queensbury . . . he reached Bradford, completed his business, dined, and returned to Halifax. On Friday, after his early breakfast, he saw his Halifax dyers or other business connections for an hour, and then away by Todmorden and Blackstone Edge to Manchester again. The travellers by the Bradford and Manchester market express train would think chaos come again were they to return, if only for a month, to the habits of their immediate predecessors." The dangers of travelling were multiplied many fold by the execrable state of the roads. Arthur Young's denunciation of the road between Preston and Wigan deserves to be quoted in this connection. " I know not, in the whole range of language, terms sufficiently expressive to describe this infernal road. To look over a map, and perceive that it is a principal one not only to some towns, but even whole counties, one would naturally conclude it to be at least decent; but let me most seriously caution all travellers who may accidentally purpose to travel this terrible country, to avoid it as they would the devil; for a thousand to one but they break their necks or their limbs by overthrows or breakings down.

Travelling in the eighteenth century.

They will meet here with ruts, which I actually measured four feet deep, and floating with mud only from a wet summer; what, therefore, must it be after winter? The only mending it receives is the tumbling in some loose stones, which serve no other purpose but jolting a carriage in the most intolerable manner. These are not merely opinions but facts, for I actually passed three carts broken down in these eighteen miles of execrable memory." The road to Warrington is described as " most infamously bad." " Any person would imagine the people of the county had made it with a view to immediate destruction; for the breadth is only sufficient for one carriage; consequently it is cut at once into ruts." Elsewhere he writes: " It is impossible to describe these infernal roads in terms adequate to their deserts. . . . Let me persuade all travellers to avoid this terrible country, which must either dislocate their bones with broken pavements or bury them in muddy sand."

(ii.) Merchants who supplied Blackwell Hall.

Of the London factors we have already spoken,[1] and it is only necessary to add that one class of Yorkshire merchants, like the West Country clothiers, made it its business to supply Blackwell Hall with cloth which the factors sold on their behalf to the drapers.

(iii.) Merchant exporters.

The third class of merchants comprised the merchant exporters. In the sixteenth and seventeenth centuries the best method of pushing the oversea trade had been a thorny subject of controversy. Nowadays an English merchant is free to trade with the whole world; in earlier times he was required to be a member of a company which was assigned a territorial sphere within which it had a complete monopoly of trade. The ideal of mediæval commerce, which lasted beyond the Middle Ages, was " a well-ordered and ruled trade," in which production was limited, prices were high and stable, and commodities were well wrought. Thus the Merchant Adventurers, who traded in cloth to Northern Europe, prided themselves on the fact that they did " keep up the price of our commodities abroad by avoiding an over-glut, whereas when trade is free, many sellers will make wares cheap and of less estimation." The

[1] Above, p. 53.

system of chartered companies had certain definite advantages: it prevented excessive competition among traders, which flooded the market with goods and lowered prices to the benefit of foreign buyers; it also enabled the Government to control trade and advance the interests of the State as they were then understood. Its great drawback was that it retarded the expansion of trade, it curtailed competition and checked enterprise. A merchant adventurer, for example, was limited in the extent of his trade for a period of fifteen years. He was not allowed to export more than four hundred cloths during the first three years of membership, then the number rose annually by fifty, so that in his fifteenth year he was able to export a thousand cloths. The enemies of the chartered companies were the " interlopers " who were outside their fellowship, but " intermeddled " with their trade. They appealed to the traditional liberty of Englishmen and defied the trading companies' monopoly. The centre of the interlopers was the West of England, for the West Country clothiers in particular resented the claim of London merchants to control the export of their cloth. At the Revolution (1688) the interlopers triumphed, and trade was thrown open to all merchants. An Act for encouraging the woollen manufactures allowed all persons to export cloth to any part of the world, a saving clause reserving the monopoly of four companies only—the Levant, Eastland, Russian, and African.

Merchant-exporters had commercial agents in all parts of the world; and we get interesting glimpses of the duties they were expected to perform in a series of instructions drawn up about the year 1582 for the guidance of an English factor in Turkey. The writer assumes as an axiom that " of the many things that tend to the common benefit of the State no one thing is greater than clothing," and proceeds: " This realm yieldeth the most fine wool, the most soft, the most durable in cloth," and " there is no commodity of this realm that may set so many poor subjects on work, as this doth, that doth bring in so much treasure, and so much enrich the merchant, and so much employ the navy of this realm, as this commodity of our wool doth.

Commercial agents.

7

Ample and full vent [sale] of this noble and rich commodity is it that the commonwealth of this realm doth require." After this exordium, the factor is told how he may best serve his country. " Forasmuch as it is reported that the woollen cloths dyed in Turkey be most excellently dyed, you shall send home unto this realm certain pieces of shred to be brought to the Dyers' Hall, there to be showed, partly to remove out of their heads the too great opinion they have conceived of their own cunning, and partly to move them for shame to endeavour to learn more knowledge. To amend the dyeing of England learn to know all the materials and substances that the Turks use in dyeing, be they herbs, plants, berries, or mineral matter. If you shall find that they make any cloth of any kind not made in this realm, that is there of great use, then bring of the same into this realm some ' mowsters ' [samples], that our people may fall into the trade and prepare the same for Turkey. For the more kinds of cloth we can devise to make, the more ample vent of our commodity we shall have, and the more sale of the labour of our poor subjects that else for lack of labour become idle and burdensome to the commonweal. And in England we are in our clothing trade to frame ourselves according to the desires of foreign nations, be it that they desire thick or thin, broad or narrow, long or short, white or black. Thus," concludes the writer, " may you help to drive idleness, the mother of most mischief, out of the realm, and win you perpetual fame, and the prayer of the poor, which is more worth than all the gold of Peru and of all the West Indies."

The Grand Tour. In the eighteenth century it was a recognised part of an English merchant's training in life to travel abroad as a young man, and make himself personally acquainted with the conditions of foreign countries. " There are very few commercial houses," said a merchant at the end of the century, " but what send their sons abroad to inspect the state of the manufactures as well as to form connections, and so promote the sale and extension of our manufactures." In addition, merchant-exporters had correspondents in all the chief continental cities.

CHAPTER III

STATE CONTROL OF THE WOOLLEN AND WORSTED INDUSTRIES

THE woollen industry from its infancy was the subject of State regulation. As the staple manufacture of the country its prosperity was always considered a matter of the greatest national importance. The clothiers succeeded, in the words of Adam Smith, "in convincing the wisdom of the nation that the safety of the commonwealth depends upon the prosperity of their particular manufacture." The Government lavished upon it the most unremitting care and attention, and created for its protection an elaborate code of industrial and commercial legislation. We shall examine first the commercial regulations, and it will be shown how every interest in the country was rendered subservient to the assumed needs of the clothing industry; how agriculture and commerce were shackled, Ireland and the Colonies hampered in their development, in order that the woollen manufacturer might have an adequate supply of raw material and the undisputed possession of markets at home and abroad.

We have seen above how English wool—"the goddess of merchants" as the "moral Gower" called it[1]—was regarded in the Middle Ages as the basis of English wealth. It was the staple article of export, one of the main sources of the royal revenue—in the year 1421 the amount raised by the Government on wool was 74 per cent. of the entire customs revenue—and an invaluable instrument in our diplomatic relations with foreign countries. The author of

State protection of the woollen industry.

Prohibition of the export of wool.

---

[1] He apostrophises it as "the beautiful, the white, the delightful one. The love of you stings and binds so that the hearts of those who make merchandise of you are not able to disengage themselves from you."

a pamphle written in the fifteenth century, entitled *England's Commercial Policy*, voiced the common opinion that no country was able to dispense with English wool, and he argued that this gave us the means by which " we might rule and govern all Christian Kings." Edward III., in particular, had known how to use the industrial resources of the country as a bait to draw the great manufacturing towns of Flanders from their allegiance to the French King, and the mere threat to withhold the wool-supply sufficed to humble the proud commons of Bruges, Ypres, and Ghent. Occasionally an embargo was placed by English rulers on the export of wool, but the prohibition was usually short-lived, and even while nominally in force was easily evaded by the purchase of licences, granted for revenue purposes, allowing wool to be carried out of the country. The manufacturers who wanted an abundant supply of raw material at low prices fought hard against the policy of free trade. Throughout the Tudor period they had been steadily advancing in wealth and power, and under the Stuarts they were strong enough to overcome the opposition of the landed interest and force their wishes upon the country. The seventeenth century witnessed the thoroughgoing adoption of an industrial protective policy, which is known in history as the Mercantile System. A complete change was made in the commercial policy of the realm, and the transport of wool beyond the sea was forbidden, not as a temporary expedient, but as a permanent feature of England's new trade policy. James I. issued proclamations for the " keeping of our subjects from idleness by restraining of the wool of this realm from exportation "; these were repeated by Charles I. and Cromwell, and embodied in an Act of Parliament at the Restoration. Thus the industrial revolution of the fifteenth century, which had been due to the growth of the woollen industry, was now followed in its turn by a commercial revolution in the seventeenth century.

The wool smugglers.   In spite of all its efforts to check the export of wool, the Government was unable to repress an illicit trade which sprang up immediately in defiance of the law. We are told that forty thousand packs of wool were conveyed to Calais alone from the coasts of Kent and Sussex; and whether the estimate is trustworthy or not, wool was certainly exported clandestinely to the Continent in large quantities. The people of Faversham, among other places, are said to have grown " monstrous rich " by " that wicked trade," and the smugglers brought back with them cargoes of French and Dutch liquors. An account of the smugglers is contained in various pamphlets written by William Carter, their indefatigable adversary. " The methods or ways of these evils are—first, in Romney Marsh in Kent, where the greatest part of rough wool is exported from England, put aboard French shallops by night, ten or twenty men well armed to guard it; some other parts there are, as in Sussex, Hampshire, and Essex, where the same methods may be used but not so conveniently. The same for combed wool from Canterbury; they will carry it ten or fifteen miles at night towards the sea—with the like guard as before." As a measure of precaution, while the wool was afloat, it was " pressed into barrels with screws, and then the barrels were washed over with brine-water." This was done that they might pass for beef, or herrings, in order to deceive the cruisers who might possibly examine the cargo. " These barrels are not put on board in ports where they are liable to be examined, but are conveyed into creeks from whence they are shipped off." Wool in its raw state (fleece wool) was worth in Ireland fourpence per pound, and combed wool tenpence; in France the first was sold for half a crown a pound, the second for five-and-six-pence or six shillings: " so that the temptation is really almost too great to be withstood, especially by such who only measure their consciences by their gain." The wool smugglers were called " owlers," and their desperate character was shown in the hardihood with which they attacked the coastguardsmen, who were often " obliged as it were to stand still and see the wool carried off before their faces, not daring to meddle." The severity of the punishments did nothing to " discourage the active spirits, and they readily risked their necks for twelvepence a day."

An exciting incident, in which William Carter was con-

cerned, occurred at Romney Marsh in 1688. "Having procured the necessary warrants, he repaired to Romney Marsh,
where he seized eight or ten men who were carrying the wool
on horses' backs to be shipped, and desired the Mayor of
Romney to commit them. The Mayor, wishing no doubt
to live a peaceful life among his neighbours, admitted them
to bail. Carter and his assistants retired to Lydd, but
that town was made too hot to hold them—they were
attacked at night; adopting the advice of the Mayor's son,"
whom they afterwards suspected to be in league with the
smugglers, "the next day, December 13, came towards
Rye. They were pursued by some fifty armed horsemen
till they got to Camber Point; so fast were they followed
that they could not get their horses over Guildford Ferry;
but, luckily, some ships' boats gave them assistance so that
the riders got safe into the town, which had been ' put
into much fear.' " " Had not the boats belonging to
several vessels gave their attendance and took us in,"
deposed one of the witnesses, " we might have been destroyed." On another occasion William Carter arrested a
smuggler at Folkestone, " but the women of the town
came out of their houses and gathered up stones upon the
beach which they flung about my ears so violently that,
having no help, I was forced to quit my prisoner, hardly
escaping myself."

Attempts
to repress
the smug-
gling of
wool.

The evils of smuggling, " that wicked trade," as Defoe
termed it, attracted considerable attention. James II.
found it necessary to issue a proclamation in 1688, de-
nouncing " persons evilly-disposed " who had assumed
" by open force and violence with armed companies of
men the liberty to convey and transport wool into parts
beyond the seas; and also to rescue the same out of the hands
and possession of our officers of the Custom, and in riotous
and tumultuous manner have beaten and wounded our
officers and those acting in their aid." After the Revolution the clothiers took up the matter (1701), and addressed
a complaint to Parliament that, " notwithstanding this
kingdom is at great charges in maintaining vessels and men
to prevent the exportation of wool, yet within these two

years many thousands of packs of wool have been exported into France and other foreign parts." The Government, unable to devise any remedy, transferred the responsibility to Parliament, and the Speech from the Throne recommended the Legislature to " find time to consider of some better and more effectual method to prevent the exportation of wool, and to improve that manufacture which is of great consequence to the whole kingdom." Many schemes were proposed for preventing the export of wool. The favourite expedient was to establish official registers to " keep sight of all wool from its being shorn till it is completely manufactured." This proposal was made in 1717, but the Commissioners of Trade reported that the scheme would be very expensive, if not—through the multiplicity of accounts—wholly impracticable. The idea was revived a few years later, and the House of Commons passed a resolution declaring that " a public register of the wool grown in Great Britain and Ireland is the most effectual method for preventing the exportation thereof to foreign parts." No practical effect, however, seems to have been given to this resolution.

It is a striking testimony to the importance of the woollen industry that the Act forbidding the export of wool remained on the Statute Book more than a hundred and fifty years. One result of the embargo on wool was to create that rivalry of interests between agriculture and industry which, in one form or another, has ever since been a feature of our economic system. The manufacturer demanded cheap raw material and cheap food, and he came into conflict with the farmer over the first in the eighteenth century, and over the second in the nineteenth century. Hence the woollen manufacturers found it necessary to exercise the utmost vigilance in warding off attacks upon a privilege which had been wrested from the rulers of the State in the teeth of bitter opposition on the part of the landed interest. The graziers raised a violent agitation against their confinement to the home market. An interminable argument was carried on in an unceasing stream of pamphlets and broadsheets. The manufacturers urged that foreign competition, and in

Conflict between manufacturers and graziers.

particular French competition, could be extinguished by
refusing to supply other countries with raw material. " Our
fathers bravely pulled down the exorbitant power of France
at the expense of their blood and their treasure, but never
thought of the way to give her a more deadly wound than
she could receive by the loss of ten battles and twice as
many towns." The export of wool, protested the manufacturers, would be an unparalleled disaster; it would
" change the current of their wealth, destroy their industry
and enterprise, deprive the poor of their employment, add
to the poor rates, and diminish the rental of the land."
" Ere the next generation," cried a panic-stricken " Cheshire
Weaver," after recounting the fatal consequences attending
the smuggling of wool, " England will be no more." The
advocates of free trade endeavoured, on their part, to show
the folly of a system in which wool, the " coveted vineyard,"
was " watched with as much care and jealousy as the Golden
Apples of the Hesperides." The embargo on wool was
pronounced unnecessary since foreign countries could carry
on their textile manufactures without English or Irish
wool; it encouraged illicit trading, and it was injurious to
the landed interest upon which fell the main burden of
taxation. The only wool admitted to be peculiar to England
was combing wool:

> " If any wool peculiar to our isle
> Is giv'n by nature, 'tis the comber's lock,
> The soft, the snow-white, and the long-grown flake."[1]

In spite of their arguments the efforts of the wool-growers
to secure a limited exportation of wool proved unsuccessful;
and in 1788 the penalties on the export of sheep or wool
were made even more stringent than before. The severity
of the penalties imposed at one period or another called
forth Adam Smith's bitter reflection that the laws, " which
the clamour of our merchants and manufacturers has
extorted from the Legislature for the support of their own
absurd and oppressive monopolies," may be said, " like the
laws of Draco, to be all written in blood." The protection

[1] Dyer, *The Fleece.*

given to the woollen industry does not appear to have had good results. It tended rather to produce stagnation. Sheltered from foreign competition, " petted and favoured," in Huskisson's phrase, by the Legislature, English manufacturers made no real attempt to improve the state of the industry, to introduce new fabrics and new designs, or to show adequate enterprise in the opening up of new markets. The statistics of the foreign trade in the eighteenth century, contrasted with those of the nineteenth century, when the exports of woollen manufacture grew in spite of the overpowering competition of the cotton industry, seem to show the defects of a policy which gave the English manufacturer the undisputed control of the home market, and removed all occasion for initiative and enterprise.

The embargo on wool was combined in the eighteenth century with an embargo on the emigration of skilled artisans. In earlier times England reaped great benefit from the settlement of aliens, and she was now anxious to prevent other countries using English technical skill to build up their own industries. In the troubled reign of Charles I. weavers and wool-combers crossed over to Holland, where every encouragement was given to textile workers, and in 1649 a writer drew attention to " the great number of cloth-workers, weavers, dyers, cottoners, and pressers repairing from England " to the Continent. An Act of 1718 imposed heavy penalties on those who induced English workmen to leave the country in order to teach the arts of cloth-making in foreign lands. " Divers ill-disposed persons, as well foreigners as subjects of this kingdom by confederacy with foreigners, have of late drawn away and transported and have also made divers attempts to entice, draw away, and transport several artificers and manufacturers of and in wool . . . out of his majesty's dominions into foreign countries, by entering into contracts with them to give greater wages and advantages than they have or can reasonably expect within this kingdom, and by making them large promises." The offender on the first occasion was to be punished with a fine not exceeding £100, and three months' imprisonment; and on the second occasion with a fine imposed at the discretion of the Court, and twelve months in prison. The Act did not prevent the emigration of English textile workers, and one case is recorded of a Yorkshire man who settled in Altona in 1732, " and now (1738) there is at that place above a hundred looms, and those that are gone over lately are to set up the making of stuffs and stockings and narrow goods, and have carried their engines and other utensils along with them."

Compul-
sory use of
English
cloth.   To prevent the export of material and the emigration of artisans was only one part of our commercial policy; the other part was to prevent the importation of goods, manufactured abroad, which competed with native commodities. It was a recognised maxim of trade that " the importation of such goods as hinder the consumption of our own, or check the progress of any of our manufactures, is a visible disadvantage." The use of native cloth was therefore enjoined on all as a patriotic duty. As far back as the thirteenth century Englishmen were urged not to " seek over-precious garments," but to content themselves with home-spun garments, and at various periods in the Middle Ages it was forbidden to import foreign cloth. A strong agitation in favour of the compulsory wearing of English cloth sprang up in the seventeenth century. Just as Queen Elizabeth established a compulsory Lent certain days in the week in order to foster the fishing trade, so her successor endeavoured to compel his subjects to wear native instead of foreign textiles. A Bill " for the better vending of the cloth of this kingdom " was introduced into Parliament in 1621, but met with some opposition. " It is hard," said a member, " to make a law whereby we shall not know our wives from our chambermaids." Others, however, approved the Bill, and suggested the addition of a clause " that none under the degree of a baron should mourn in anything but cloth." After the Restoration the agitation was renewed. In 1665 a Statute was passed enacting that the dead must be buried in woollen cloth, " forcing the dead," as Arthur Young said, " to consume what the living were inadequate to purchase."

> " Since the Living would not bear it,
> They should, when dead, be forc'd to wear it."

A few years later (1668) the House of Commons presented
an address to the King, praying him to encourage the
wearing of English manufactures " by his own example
and his Queen's." Recognising that practice is better than
precept, they also wisely resolved " that the House begin
themselves to show a good example herein to the nation."
A subsequent resolution (1677) enjoined " all persons what-
soever to wear no garment, stockings, or other sort of
apparel, but what is made of sheep's wool only from the
Feast of All Saints to the Feast of the Annunciation of Our
Lady inclusive." These efforts to promote the compulsory use of English cloth were renewed after the Revolution. In 1697 the Commons ordered the insertion of a
clause " that all magistrates, judges, students of the
Universities, and all professors of the common and civil
law do wear gowns made of the woollen manufacture."
In short, as a pamphleteer wrote at the beginning of the
eighteenth century, " both the Living and the Dead must
be wrapt in woollen, indeed no other law is wanted but
only one, that our perukes should be made of wool."

The woollen manufacturers considered the home market
as their natural preserve. They sought therefore to exclude
not only foreign cloth, but all foreign textiles which competed with the native woollen manufacture.[1] The East
India Company, for example, imported textile fabrics from
the East as a substitute for woollen and worsted goods.

> " When first the Indian Trade began,
> And ships beyond the Tropicks ran,
> In quest of various Drugs and Spices,
> And sundry other strange devices,
> Saltpetre, Drugs, Spice, and like Trading,
> Composed the bulk of all their Lading:
> Bengals and Silks of Indians making,
> Our merchants then refus'd to take in,
> Knowing it wou'd their country ruin."

[1] Complaint was made against the wearing of silk in the reign of
James I. See below, p. 109.

But when men's " chiefest Aim " became " private Gain,"
Indian silks were imported, and—

> " Our Ladies all were set a gadding.
> After these Toys they ran a madding.
> And like gay Peacocks proudly strut it
> When in our Streets along they foot it."

Great alarm was therefore felt lest Indian silks and muslins
should become " the general wear." " I question not,"
said one writer, " but we shall have cotton cloth and knaves
to make it a fashion and fools enough to wear it." " The
general fancy of the people," declared another writer,
" runs upon East India goods to that degree that the
chints and painted calicoes which before were only made
use of for carpets, quilts, etc., and to clothe children and
ordinary people, became now the dress of our ladies; and
such is the power of a mode, that we saw some of our
persons of quality dressed in Indian carpets which a few
years before them chambermaids would have thought too
ordinary for them: the chints were advanced from being
upon their floors to their backs; from the footcloth to the
petticoat; and even the Queen herself at this time was
pleased to appear in China and Japan, I mean China silks
and calico. Nor was this all, but it crept into our houses
and bedchambers; curtains, cushions, chairs, and at the
last the beds themselves were nothing but calicoes and
Indian stuffs, and in short everything that used to be
made of wool or silk, relating either to the dress of the
women or the furniture of our houses, was supplied by the
Indian trade." It was said that Englishmen could not
compete with Eastern labour, since " the people in India
are such slaves as to work for less than a penny a day,
whereas ours here will not work under a shilling." Some
of the West Country clothiers pointed out that we had
begun to export to India very great quantities of woollen
goods in exchange for their silks, and the effect of prohibiting Indian textiles would be to diminish our woollen
exports. In spite of their arguments the Government
yielded to the outcry (1700), and forbade the use of Indian

silks in England on the ground that " it is most evident that the continuance of the trade to the East Indies in the same manner and proportions as it hath been for two years last past must inevitably be to the great detriment of this kingdom by exhausting the treasure thereof, and melting down the coin, and taking away the labour of the people, whereby very many of the manufacturers of this nation are become excessively burdensome and chargeable to their respective parishes." The prohibition of Indian silks had an unexpected result, for it encouraged the English cotton manufacturers to seize their opportunity to capture the market from which their Indian rivals had been expelled. " As if this nation was never to want a set of men to undo her," complained the indignant weavers, " no sooner were the East India chints and printed calicoes prohibited from abroad, but some of Britain's unnatural children, whom we call Drapers, set all their arts to work to evade the law of prohibition, to employ people to mimick the more ingenious Indians, and to legitimate the grievance by making it a manufacture." The weavers raised a great clamour and attacked in the open streets those who wore cotton dresses, the " calico-madams," or " calico Picts," as they were called, even tearing the clothes off their backs. Parliament was forced to pass another Act (1720) prohibiting the use of printed painted calicoes, since " the wearing and using " of calicoes " does manifestly tend to the great detriment of the woollen and silk manufactures of this kingdom." In this way the infant cotton industry was sacrificed to the woollen industry, in order that nothing might impair the prosperity of the leading manufacture of the realm.

While the controversy over the East India trade was at its height, another quarrel sprang up in connection with Ireland. The Irish farmers had been forbidden in 1667 to export cattle to England in order that the English farmer should have no competitor in the home market; they therefore turned their attention to grazing. As a result, wool became plentiful and meat cheap, and the abundance of raw material coupled with the cheapness of living attracted

Competition of the Irish woollen industry.

English artisans from the West of England. " These erected a manufactory (great in respect to Ireland) at Dublin, which hath been carried on ever since and increases daily. There came also over, much about the same time, sixty families from Holland, setting up another at Limerick, which by occasion of the succeeding wars decayed. But, after these, more of the English clothiers came and fixed about Cork and Kinsale, where they continue and are grown not inconsiderable. Some French have since resorted to Waterford to make druggets[1] there, and other commodities of their fashion. And about a year or two ago some merchants of London raised another manufacture at Clonmel, managing it by their agents. There is more cry than wool in this matter: For I dare and do assure you that, modestly speaking, the whole quantity of what we work up in Ireland amounts not to the half of what any one clothing county in England does." The English woollen manufacturers, alarmed at this new development, raised a great outcry and predicted the most fatal consequences to their trade. Ireland was able to compete successfully with England owing to the conditions under which the Irish industry was carried on. In England, according to one writer, a wool-comber earned nine to ten shillings a week, the wool was prepared with oil costing 7½d. to 8d. a pound and more, and " the woman that spins it would think sixpence a day small wages." In Ireland, on the other hand, " the spinner would be content to earn threepence a day, and herself goes through the whole process from the sheep's back until the worsted is ready for the loom, preparing it with the worst butter at twopence or threepence a pound mixed with a mucilaginous[2] juice got from fern roots." The spinning could be done by girls of six or seven years old, and the weaving was also done very cheaply, as " the women of every peasant manufacture clothing and blankets for the family."

The protestations of the manufacturers that English

---

[1] A kind of stuff, all of wool, or wool and silk mixed, or wool and linen mixed.

[2] Mucilage is a substance obtained from plants.

trade was being undermined bore fruit in the Act of 1698, Laws against the Irish and Colonial woollen manufactures.
which forbade the export of Irish wool or woollen manu-
factures except to England and Wales. Thus " the Irish
woollen fabrics," in the words of Arthur Young, " were
destroyed by one of the most infamous Statutes that ever
disgraced a Legislature." A generation later the Act against
the Irish woollen manufactures was said to have " laid the
foundations of all the misfortunes of both kingdoms. It
drove abroad all our [*i.e.*, Irish] woollen manufacturers,
who set up in different countries," and—so ran the current
opinion—it " taught our neighbours to steal from us a
manufacture we entirely engrossed before." Another
writer pointed out that the English persecution in trade
had the same effect as the French persecution in religion,
in causing an exodus of Ireland's most industrious sons.
He showed the fallacy of the argument on which the sup-
pression of the Irish woollen industry had been based.
Suppose it were true that Ireland could work cheaper than
Yorkshire or Lancashire: " would it hurt the British Empire
more than it hurts her that Yorkshire or Lancashire should
work cheaper than Devonshire or Cornwall ? Can any
man of open understanding consider Ireland but in the
light of four or five great counties added to England advantageously for water carriage cut by a large navigable
river ?" The English plantations in America were treated
in the same way as Ireland, for one clause of the Act of
1698 ordered that " no wool, woollen yarn, cloth, serge,
bays, kersies, says, friezes, druggets, cloth-serges, shalloons,
or any other drapery, stuff, or woollen manufactures what-
soever " should be exported from the colonies, or even
transported from one colony to another. The English
woollen trade with the American Colonies was considerable,
amounting to one-half of the total export trade with the
plantations.

In their efforts to secure the undisputed control of the Export of undyed cloth.
home market manufacturers and merchants were in com-
plete harmony; in their attitude towards the export trade
a serious cleavage of interests manifested itself. The
merchant exporters demanded a free hand in foreign trade,

but their claim to ship cloth abroad in a raw state, undyed and unfinished, brought them into collision with the clothiers. The struggle between the trading and industrial capitalists extended over many centuries. The trading capitalists defended themselves on the ground that the export of white and undressed cloth promoted national prosperity, since foreign traders were unwilling to buy cloth which was dyed and finished. They contended that English cloth-workers had the buying and selling of the wool, as well as the carding, spinning, weaving, fulling, and the first sale of the cloth; while foreigners had only the dressing and shearing of certain cloths, " whereby the inhabitants there be a little relieved and a few number of them[1] for a time set to work." If, then, " the realm of England should all covet and they to have no relief nor comfort of the same," there was a danger lest other countries might concert ways and means to exclude our cloth altogether. The industrial capitalists, on the other hand, urged that if the cloth were finished at home it would " set many thousands of people more on work for dressing and dyeing, and likewise employ more ships and mariners for bringing in dyeing stuffs." The export of white cloth was several times prohibited by Statute, but in spite of Acts of Parliament nearly 96 per cent. of the cloth exported from England under the Tudors went from these shores undyed. In 1541 Chapuys, the envoy of the imperial court, wrote to the Regent of the Netherlands that " some days ago the cloth-makers and cloth merchants here came before the Council against the shearmen to get the Statute repealed which forbids the exportation of cloths of more than £3 value unless dressed, alleging that the shearmen dressed them so ill that the people of the Low Countries would no longer buy English cloth; at least there was not a piece of dressed cloth from here that did not sell there for two ducats less than if it were not dressed, and besides the loss of these two ducats they lost other two in getting them ready. The majority of the Councillors seem to be in favour of the

---

[1] It was estimated that 50,000 persons in the Low Countries were employed in dyeing and finishing English fabrics.

repeal of the Statute, but" the envoy feared "the King will not consent just because it will benefit the people of those countries; and therefore English merchants would be glad of a proclamation in Flanders against the importation of English woollen cloth, to see whether the King would not then grant their request." Later he reported that the King would not revoke the Statute against the export of undressed cloth since he derived a great profit from *licences for exportation.*

Under Elizabeth and James I. attempts were made to foster a native dyeing industry. The Government recognised that the best way to discourage the export of raw cloth was to improve the native arts of cloth-finishing. " We have often and in divers manners expressed ourselves," declared James I., " what an earnest desire we have that, as the reducing of wools into clothing was the act of our noble progenitor, King Edward the Third, so the reducing of the trade of white cloths, which is but an imperfect thing towards the wealth and good of this our kingdom, into the trade of cloths dyed and dressed might be the work of our time." The export of rough white cloth was therefore prohibited (1614), and a patent for dyeing was granted to Alderman Cockayne. The scheme of the Government met with great opposition. When the Merchant Adventurers were summoned before the Privy Council and " there pressed whether they would dye and dress all the cloth " at home, they " concluded it to be impossible." The project was also attacked in the House of Commons. " If to be done with a pen or an argument at Council Table," said a member sarcastically, " Mr. Alderman Cockayne will do it." As for the proposal to bring in five thousand foreign craftsmen to dye and dress cloth, " we have too great a clothing commonwealth already." The experiment was not attended with success. " The Dutch prohibited the importation of dyed and dressed cloths from England, and Cockayne and his company not only dyed and dressed the cloths worse and dearer—which are ever the consequences of monopolies—than they were in Holland, but these being restrained to a company they could not dress or dye the cloths made in England. Whereupon the making of cloths

Cockayne's patent.

8

stood at a stand, and infinite numbers of poor people who were employed in making cloths lay idle and were reduced to a starving condition." The clothiers complained that their cloth lay on their hands; the cloth-finishers protested that they were in a worse plight than before, " and indeed it is found that there hath not been a cloth dyed or dressed since Christmas more than usual "; the export trade was greatly reduced; the customs revenues fell off; " and many other inconveniences " followed " both at home and abroad." The scheme was perforce abandoned (1617)—in spite of Bacon's counsel to " blow a horn to let the Flemings know your majesty will not give over the chase "—and the King sadly confessed that " time discovereth many inabilities which cannot first be seen." " We intend," he therefore added, " not to insist any longer upon specious and fair shows which produce not the fruit our actions do aim at . . . perceiving that the former grounds proposed to us by the undertakers of that work consisted more in hopes than in effects." The question came again to the front after the Revolution, when, in order to remove any doubts as to the exact legal position, the export of white cloth was expressly permitted by law in 1707.[1]

Commercial treaties.

Although divided on the question of the export of white cloth, manufacturers and merchants alike recognised the importance of pushing the woollen trade overseas, and in this their efforts were warmly seconded by the Government. Henry VII., in particular, concluded numerous commercial treaties intended to provide an outlet for the woollen manufacture. The most memorable was the Magnus Intercursus (1496), which ensured a free market for the sale of English cloth in the Netherlands. Indeed, one reason why the Tudors encouraged voyages of discovery was to find new markets for our woollen fabrics. In 1541, according to the report of Chapuys, the Privy Council deliberated about " sending out two ships to discover a passage between

[1] The Merchant Adventurers had been authorised by Elizabeth to export a certain quantity of unfinished cloth, and a patent was also granted by Charles II. to the trustees of the Countess of Portland. Upon the expiry of the patent the export of white cloth was held up; hence the Act of 1707.

Iceland and Greenland, where it was thought the great cold would cause a good sale for woollen cloth, and with this view" the King "retained here for some time an experienced pilot from Seville; with whom, however, he could not agree as to terms, and the undertaking has been abandoned." Another notable treaty was the famous Methuen Treaty concluded with Portugal in 1703. A writer stated in 1693 that the Portuguese were taking off our hands 180,000 pieces a year, and he contended that this quantity would be largely increased if we dealt with them for wine. In order to develop a native cloth manufacture the Portuguese began to exclude English goods, but in the Methuen Treaty they removed the prohibition on condition that the wines of Portugal were admitted into England at two-thirds of the duty levied on French wines. The Methuen Treaty was viewed with so much favour in England that it was the means of preventing a commercial treaty with France until 1786. The negotiators of the Treaty of Utrecht (1713), for example, were unable to bring about a reduction of tariffs owing to the fear that our trade with Portugal would suffer by the admission of French wines upon the same terms as the Portuguese. " The preserving our looms and the rents of Great Britain," contended *The British Merchant*, " was of greater consequence to the nation than gratifying our palates with French wine," and public opinion supported this view.

The commercial policy of the State in its relation to the woollen industry was thus essentially a protective policy; it was designed to give the English clothiers the undisputed possession of the home and foreign markets, and it was, on the whole, consistently maintained down to the nineteenth century. The industrial policy of the State, on the other hand, falls into two well-defined periods, the dividing-line between them being drawn roughly at the Revolution of 1688. In the first period the State imposed restrictions upon industrial capitalism in the interests of the working classes; in the second period the capitalist manufacturer was allowed comparatively a free hand. The control of

The industrial policy of the State.

industry in the earlier period embraced four main points:
(1) wages; (2) unemployment; (3) technical training; and
(4) standardisation. We shall deal first with the wage
problem.

(i.) The wage problem.

The grievance of low wages was as old as the capitalist
system itself. As early as the fifteenth century a popular
pamphlet on *England's Commercial Policy*, one of the earliest
expressions of industrial discontent known to us, summed
up in a telling phrase the economic position of the textile
workers under a capitalist régime:

" The poor have the labour, the rich the winning."

In the next century (1539) the Suffolk and Essex weavers
attributed their destitute state to a conspiracy of " the
rich men," the clothiers, " to hold and pay one price for
weaving of cloths," and a price which was not enough to
support their families even by working day and night, holy
days and work days. In 1621 a member of Parliament
complained in the House of Commons that clothiers " give
not the poor competent wages—threepence a day and no
more to divers." A famous ballad, which is said to have
been chaunted about the streets in the time of Charles II.,
recited in rude rhymes the grievances of the workers in
cloth against their employers. It is entitled *The Clothier's
Delight, Or the Rich Men's Joy, and The Poor Men's Sorrow,
Where is exprest the craftiness and subtility of many clothiers
by beating down their workmen's wages.* The opening verses
run as follows:

" Of all sorts of callings that in England be,
　There is none that liveth so gallant as we;
　Our trading maintains us as brave as a Knight,
　We live at our pleasure and take our delight;
　We heapeth up riches and treasure great store,
　Which we get by griping and grinding the poor.
　　And this is a way for to fill up our purse,
　　Although we do get it with many a curse.

" Throughout the whole kingdom, in country and town,
　There is no danger of our trade going down,
　So long as the Comber can work with his comb,
　And also the Weaver work with his lomb;

The Tucker and Spinner that spins all the year,
We will make them to earn their wages full dear.
   And this is a way for to fill up our purse,
   Although we do get it with many a curse.

" In former ages we us'd to give
So that our work-folks like farmers did live;
But the times are altered, we will make them know
All we can for to bring them all under our bow;
We will make to work hard for sixpence a day,
Though a shilling they deserve if they had their just pay.
   And this is a way for to fill up our purse,
   Although we do get it with many a curse."

What was the attitude of the State towards the wage problem ? In the fourteenth and fifteenth centuries the regulation of wages was one of the functions of the gild system.[1] In the sixteenth, seventeenth, and eighteenth centuries this function was assumed by the State.[2] As early as the reign of Edward III. the wages of agricultural labourers were fixed by Parliament, and in the next reign Justices of the Peace were authorised to assess the wages of various classes of artificers provided they did not exceed a stated maximum. In 1563 Parliament enacted the important Statute of Apprentices expressly in order, as the preamble recites, to " yield unto the hired person both in the time of scarcity and in the time of plenty a convenient proportion of wages." This famous measure ordered the Justices of the Peace in every county and city, at the annual Easter Sessions, to " rate and appoint " the wages of labourers and artificers. There was some room for doubt whether the Statute applied to textile workers, and in 1597 the Justices were empowered " to rate wages of any labourers, weavers, spinsters, and workmen or work-women whatsoever." The Act of 1597 was confirmed in the next reign (1604) with two significant additions: (1) A Justice who was also a clothier was not allowed to be a " rater of wages for any artisan that dependeth upon the making of cloth "; and (2) penalties were imposed upon

State regulation of wages.

----

[1] See above, p. 32.
[2] In the sixteenth century the wages of textile workers were sometimes fixed by the municipality—*e.g.*, at Coventry.

any employer who paid less than the authorised wages.[1] These two clauses serve to show that the Government was actuated by a real desire to safeguard the economic interests of the textile workers. In any case, the system of assessment of wages was evidently popular among the weavers and spinners, who pressed for its enforcement. In 1623, for example, they presented a petition to the Justices of Wiltshire in these terms: " May it please you to be informed of the distressed estate of most of the weavers, spinners, and others that work on the making of woollen cloths, that are not able by their diligent labours to get their livings by reason that the clothiers at their will have made their works extreme hard, and abated wages what they please. And some of them make such their workfolk to do their household businesses, to trudge in their errands, spool their chains, twist their list, do every command, without giving them bread, drink, or money for many days' labour." They asked the Justices " to appoint certain grave and discreet persons to view the straitness of works, to assess rates for wages according to the desert of their works, now especially in this great dearth of corn, that the poor artificers of these works of woollen cloth may not perish for want of food whiles they are painful in their callings." In 1631 the weavers of Sudbury complained to the Privy Council that the " poor spinsters, weavers, and combers of wool are much abridged of their former and usual wages " by the clothiers, " who are now grown rich by the labours of the said poor people." A Commission was appointed to enquire into the matter: " and in case any particular person shall be found, either out of the hardness of his heart towards the poor or out of private end or humour, refractory to such courses as the said Commissioners shall think reasonable and just," he was to be brought before the Council. The employers declared that they were willing to pay reasonable wages if the rate were

[1] The Act of 1604 was thus a Minimum Wage Act, but in some parts of the country the Justices continued to fix maximum rates which the clothiers were forbidden to exceed. In these cases the wages actually paid fell much below the maximum authorised by the Justices.

made binding on all alike. This response served incidentally to justify the action of the State in regulating wages, for it showed how the pressure of competition forced good employers to follow in the wake of bad employers. The Justices doubtless lacked the necessary technical qualifications for framing complicated piece-lists, and these were often drafted by a joint committee of clothiers and weavers, and submitted to the Justices for ratification. A noteworthy instance of State intervention, " for the general good of the whole Commonwealth," was the issue of a proclamation in 1636 stating that, in view of the increase in the " reel-staff "—" a fifth or sixth part longer than had been accustomed "—the wages of spinners were to be increased " after the rate of twopence in the shilling more than heretofore they have had paid unto them," and " all labourers and other artificers employed about the trade of clothing and yarn-making should have the like increase of wages."

Connected with low wages was another evil which per- Truck sisted for many centuries—namely the payment of truck wages. Combers, spinners, and weavers were often obliged by their employers to take the greatest part of their wages in provisions or goods, which were rated at extravagant prices, sometimes double their real worth. Some clothiers even forced their weavers to become their tenants and to pay high rents for their houses whether they occupied them or not; and others made them buy their bread and other necessities at particular shops. Another device was to defer the payment of wages until they amounted to a considerable sum and then compel the work-people to take promissory notes payable at a future date: this not only drove the workmen into debt, but they also had to forfeit part of their earnings in order to get the notes discounted. The workers kept up a ceaseless stream of protests against these evil practices, and for centuries the Legislature passed laws against them. In the reign of Edward IV. (1464) Parliament, following the lead already given by municipal enterprise half a century before, affirmed that labourers in the cloth industry had been driven to take a great part of their wages in pins, girdles, " and other unprofitable wares " at less than their value, and ordered clothiers to pay their workfolk " lawful money for all their lawful wages." This injunction was revived at intervals in the following centuries, but legislative action was not very effective in checking a system which inflicted great hardships upon the workers and was the burden of repeated complaints to Parliament. In 1637 some weavers complained that their employer not only reduced their wages, but also made them accept payment in truck. The Privy Council committed the offender to prison, and did not release him until he had paid his workmen double the amount they had lost, together with the plaintiffs' costs. One reason for the failure of the laws against truck was the want of a summary method of punishing those who disobeyed the law; when the magistrates imposed penalties on the clothiers they removed the trials to Westminster, and the expense of carrying on prosecutions in such circumstances was beyond the resources of the poor.

(ii.) Unemployment.

The intervention of the State was also demanded on behalf of unemployed artisans. The Tudors and Early Stuarts insisted that an employer should not turn his men adrift in times of depression. In 1586 the Privy Council addressed the Justices of Somersetshire in the following terms: " Whereas their lordships are informed that the poorer sort of the people inhabiting about the city of Bath and other towns on the easterly parts of the county of Somerset, wont to live by spinning, carding, and working of wool, are not set on work, whereby in this time of dearth of corn and victual they lack their common and necessary food, a matter not only full of pity, but of dangerous consequence to the State if speedy order be not taken therein; her majesty, therefore, tendering the one and careful of the other, hath given commandment that they forthwith . . . consider of the present inconvenience and how it may be redressed, and for that purpose especially they are hereby authorised to call before them the clothiers and other men of trade in the several places within the county where the people do complain of lack of work, and in her majesty's

name to require and command such of them as have stocks
and are of ability to employ the same as they have heretofore done, so as by them the poor may be set on work;
and if any of them upon any frivolous excuse$ shall refuse
to obey her majesty's commandment herein, they shall
certify their names and what their excuses be, that consideration may be had of them accordingly." In some
cases the Justices were able to report that the employers
were fully alive to their responsibilities. " The clothiers
here do yet continue to keep their poor in work, as in former
times they have done, although it hath been to their great
losses; and so they are contented to do as long as they may
occupy their trade without undoing of themselves." In
another case, " one Will Bennett, a very ancient and good
clothier, doth offer to live by brown bread and water,
rather than his great number of poor people should want
work, if he had means to keep them in work."

One of the most memorable depressions in the annals of The trade
the woollen industry began in 1620. The Government depression of 1620-4.
appointed a Commission to investigate the causes, and
" after many days spent in this weighty service " the Commission presented a report in which they enumerated
several " grounds and motives " for the decay of trade.
They found "the chiefest cause" to be " the making of
cloth in foreign parts in more abundance than in former
times, being thereunto chiefly enabled by the wools and
other materials transported from the kingdoms of England,
Scotland, and Ireland." They also included " the false
and deceitful making of cloth," the heavy duties imposed
on exported cloth, the monopoly of the Merchant Adventurers, the war in Germany, " the scarcity of coin at home,
and the baseness of foreign coins compared unto ours,"
and, finally, " the too little use of wearing cloth at home
and the too much of silks and foreign stuffs." Whatever
the cause of the depression, the effects were serious and
widespread. The export of cloth was reduced by nearly
two-thirds, and the clothiers unanimously protested that
" these times do more than threaten to throw us and every
one of us, yea, many thousands of poor and others that

depend upon us, into the bottomless pit of remediless destruction." In one Wiltshire town forty-four looms stood idle for half a year, " by which means eight hundred persons are now miserably distressed for want of employment." " We much fear," the Justices of Gloucestershire wrote to the Privy Council, " that the peace hereof will be very shortly endangered, notwithstanding all the vigilance we use or can use to the contrary," since workmen " do wander, beg, and steal, and are in case to starve as their faces (to our great griefs) do manifest." The depression was general throughout the kingdom and the Council actively bestirred itself. It summoned representatives of the clothiers to the capital, and issued a circular letter to the Justices of the clothing counties enjoining them to call the clothiers together and require them to keep their workfolk in employment. The clothiers were not to be allowed to dismiss their artisans at pleasure, for " those who have gained in profitable times must now be content to lose for the public good till the decay of trade be remedied." The incidents we have cited do not stand alone, and it was in fact a recognised practice for work-people out of employment to solicit the intervention of Judges of the High Courts or the local magistrates.

Pressure on merchants.

Pressure was also brought to bear upon merchants in order to compel them to take unsold cloth off the clothier's hands. In 1528 the trade in Flanders was interrupted by the outbreak of war. The clothiers were urged to keep their workfolk in employment, but they declared that they could not hold out more than two or three weeks unless the merchants continued to buy as usual. Wolsey summoned the merchants before him and thus addressed them: " Sirs, the King is informed that you use not yourselves like merchants, but like graziers[1] and artificers; for when the clothiers do daily bring cloths to your market for your ease, to their great cost, and there be ready to sell them, you of your wilfulness will not buy them, as you have been accustomed to do. What manner of men be you ? I tell

---

[1] At this period the graziers were in ill repute owing to the enclosures. See above, p. 19.

you, that the King straitly commandeth you to buy their
cloths, as beforetime you have been accustomed to do,
upon pain of his high displeasure."

In the Middle Ages the responsibility for the technical (iii.) Technical train-
training of weavers and shearmen rested with the gilds. ing.
As we have seen,[1] the custom of seven years' apprenticeship
was general throughout the country. In the case of the
shearmen of Norwich an apprenticeship of seven years'
duration was enforced by Statute as early as 1495, and in
the case of the weavers of broad woollen cloths in 1552;
a few years later (1563) it was made compulsory on all
artisans. There were also legal restrictions as to the
number of apprentices whom a master might take. Thus
the Act of 1497 forbade worsted weavers to employ more
than two apprentices at a time, and the Statute of Apprentices (1563) compelled every master in the cloth-making
industry who had three apprentices to employ a journeyman. These laws, while intended to protect the journeymen from the competition of cheap labour, and to ensure
that the cloth was not spoilt by the inferior workmanship
of half-trained assistants, set limits to the growth of industrial capitalism, which was also kept in check by restrictions
on the number of looms permitted to each weaver.[2]

State control of the woollen industry was not confined (iv.) Stan-
dardisa-
to questions of wages, unemployment, or technical training; tion.
it embraced also the actual processes of the cloth manufacture. Nowadays a manufacturer is free to make cloth
as he pleases—long or short, fine or coarse. In earlier times
the Government sought to standardise industry—that is,
to maintain a uniform standard of quality and measurements. The famous Assize[3] of Cloth under Richard I.
(1197) fixed statutory measures and assigned four or six
men in each borough to enforce its regulations. The principle of legal measurements was also embodied in Magna
Carta, which enjoined that there should be " one width of
cloth, whether dyed, russet or halberget—to wit, two ells
within the lists."[4] But the Government did not adhere to

---

[1] Above, p. 30.   [2] Above, p. 50.   [3] *I.e.*, law.
[4] The English ell=45 inches; list=border or edge of a cloth.

a consistent policy. Sometimes, as a concession to the immigrant weavers or foreign merchants, cloths were allowed to be made of any length: " A man may make the cloths as long and as short as a man will." At other times the Assize was revived, and elaborate regulations as to the measurements of cloth were then laid down.

The question of quality also engaged the attention of the Government. It was forbidden to mingle different kinds of wool in the same cloth—for example, to use lamb's wool or flocks with ordinary sorts of wool.[1] " Clothiers," complained Parliament in 1552, " study rather to make many than to make good cloths," and " instead of substantial making of cloth do practise sleight and slender making, some by mingling of yarns of diverse spinnings in one cloth, some by mingling fell wool and lambs' wool, or either of them, with fleece wool, some by putting too little stuff, some by taking them out of the mill before they be full thicked, some by overstretching them upon the tenter and then stopping with flocks such breaks as shall be made by means thereof, finally by using so many subtle sleights[2] and untruths as when the cloths so made be put in the water to try them, they rise out of the same neither in length nor breadth as they ought to do." Parliament did not succeed in destroying the evils which it lamented, and an Elizabethan writer, Leake, echoed the opinion of the mediæval chronicler[3] when he wrote: " I am fully of opinion that generally for all cloths the laws were never yet observed in any place within the realm." In the seventeenth century John May, an aulnager's deputy, enumerated in detail the deceits practised in the woollen industry in his day: the mixing of different qualities of wool which made the cloth uneven, and the frauds perpetrated in weaving, fulling, and dyeing—for example, using a coarser yarn for the middle than the ends of the cloth, " which is so far as commonly the merchant or buyer looks into them," and straining or

---

[1] An Act of 1467 made an exception in favour of the Devonshire industry. The cheap fabrics (friezes, Kendal cloths, etc.) were generally exempted from State control. Flocks=the refuse of wool.
[2] *I.e.*, tricks.　　　　　　　　　[3] Above, p. 15, *n*. 1.

stretching cloth unduly: " If a gentleman make a livery
for his man, in the first shower of rain it may fit his page
for bigness !"[1] To guard against defects in the manufacture of cloth, and to enforce obedience to the Assizes,
a special office, the aulnage, was instituted. This office
already existed in the last quarter of the thirteenth century,
for in 1279 two men were appointed " to view all cloths
exposed for sale "; six years later they were replaced by
a " Keeper of the Assize." The functions of the aulnager
were to test the measurements and quality of every piece
of cloth, affixing his seal when the cloth was sound or
confiscating it when defective, and so ensuring uniformity
of " length, breadth, weight, and goodness "; he also collected the subsidy and fees, which varied according to the
size and nature of the cloth.[2]

Perhaps the most remarkable exercise of State control
is seen in a Statute of Henry VII. (1489), fixing the retail
prices of cloth: " Forasmuch as drapers, tailors, and other
in the City of London and other places within this realm,
that use to sell woollen cloth at retail by the yard, sell a
yard of cloth at excessive price, having unreasonable lucre,
to the great hurt and impoverishment of the King's liege
people, buyers of the same, against equity and good con-
science," the maximum retail price of cloth grained was
fixed at 16s. a broad yard, and " out of the grain " at 11s.
a yard.[3]

The Civil War profoundly affected the economic life of Changed
the country. It destroyed the power of the absolute attitude
monarchy, and this reacted upon industrial conditions. State after
The system of State control established in the sixteenth War.
century depended for its successful working upon the extent
to which the monarchy, acting through the agency of the

---

[1] The practice of stretching cloth unduly was prohibited by
numerous Statutes. In 1597 it was even forbidden to use tenter-
frames, but the Justices apparently refused to put the Act into
operation.

[2] A whole cloth of assize paid a subsidy of 4d. and the aulnager's
fee of ½d. A kersey paid only 1d. as subsidy.

[3] Henry himself bought scarlet cloth as low as 6s. 8d. the yard.
The Act was repealed in 1624.

Privy Council, maintained its hold over the local authorities. Under the Tudors and Early Stuarts the Council actively intervened on behalf of distressed artisans. But after the Great Rebellion its authority was fatally impaired; its control almost completely relaxed, and the industrial legislation of the sixteenth century was allowed to fall into disuse. The Revolution of 1688 completed the process of disintegration, and Parliament came directly under the influence of the capitalist classes, who now demanded their liberation from the shackles of State control. The instantaneous success of Adam Smith's *Wealth of Nations*, published nearly a century after the Revolution, was largely due to the fact that he gave articulate expression to ideas towards which the leaders of industry had long been feeling their way. We shall indicate briefly in the following paragraphs the new attitude of the State towards industrial problems.

(i.) The wage problem.

Two examples of the assessment of wages in the woollen industry after the Revolution will show the altered condition of affairs. In 1728, after the system had passed out of living memory, the Justices of Gloucestershire revived it at the Quarter Sessions, and fixed the wages of textile workers. The assessment was not observed by the clothiers, who no longer dreaded as in Tudor and Stuart days a summons before the Privy Council. Nearly thirty years later, in 1756, the weavers of Gloucestershire secured from Parliament a re-enactment of the assessment clauses of the Elizabethan Statute, but the clothiers, who had been taken by surprise, fought strenuously against the Act. They drew up a document which their workmen were asked to sign, in which the latter acknowledged themselves well satisfied with their wages and agreed to remain at work upon the same terms at which they were then employed. Shortly afterwards the Justices held their Michaelmas Quarter Sessions, and both sides presented petitions to the Court. The weavers complained that the clothiers had ignored the rates fixed by the Justices at the beginning of the reign (1728); their sufferings had since increased owing to the great reduction in their wages, " insomuch that the

weavers cannot get above fourpence for sixteen hours'
labour upon many sorts of work." The clothiers responded
with a counter-petition in which they protested against the
compulsory assessment of wages. Their argument was
threefold. They asserted that the system was not workable
on the ground that it was impossible to settle beforehand
an equitable rate for weaving. Many factors needed to be
considered: the number and size of the threads, the weight
of the chain,[1] the fineness of the weft, the breadth of the
cloth, the differences in technical skill. They postulated
also the doctrine of Industrial Freedom. " We think it
repugnant," they declared, " to the liberties of a free people
and the interest of trade that any law should supersede a
private contract honourably made between a master and
his workman." And, finally, they contended that the Act
was subversive of authority: " The weavers by this Act
will be rendered more our masters than we are now theirs."

The clothiers seem to have marshalled their case so State
effectively that the Justices were won over to their stand- of wages
point and refused to issue any order. This profoundly doned.
dismayed the weavers, who, having secured an Act of Parliament in their favour, had confidently expected the Justices
to act upon it. Infuriated at their disappointment, the
weavers created a great disturbance and declared a strike;
for six weeks work was suspended, and the whole county
was in a state of uproar. To calm the disorders the men's
leaders proposed a meeting with the employers. At this
meeting, which was held at Stroud, the weavers put forward
the piece-lists drawn up in 1728; the clothiers advanced an
alternative scheme whereby the weavers were to appoint a
committee of eleven or thirteen clothiers who should meet
every quarter and assess wages. This proposal was re-
jected, and a mob thereupon burst into the room in which
the negotiations were taking place, dragged back the
clothiers as they endeavoured to escape from the windows,
and forced them to concede all their demands. At the
next session the Justices, in order to pacify the county,
confirmed the rates prescribed in 1728 and the men returned

[1] *I.e.*, the warp. See below, p. 136.

to their work. The triumph of the weavers was short-lived, for very few employers observed the assessment, but continued to pay their workmen upon the old footing. The clothiers soon began to agitate for a repeal of the Act. They carried their case to Parliament, where they represented the " ill consequences which have arisen from the Act whereby the Justices of the Peace have power to make rates for the payment of wages to weavers employed in the woollen manufacture." They repeated the arguments which had served them so effectively in their legal duel with the weavers, and their solicitations prevailed. Parliament, turning a deaf ear to the prayer of the weavers not to subject them " to the arbitrary will and power of the clothiers," annulled the measure which it had passed in the previous session. For nearly two centuries the right of the State to fix wages had been recognised as a cardinal principle of industrial regulation; and though in practice the right had fallen into disuse, its survival on the Statute Book had vested in the authorities a reserve of power to which they could always turn in the last resort for the protection of the working classes. The repeal of the Act of 1756 signified that the system of wage assessment was now definitely discarded in the premier industry of the country. The principles of *laissez-faire* received legislative sanction in the woollen manufacture half a century before they were adopted as the authoritative basis of State action.

(ii.) Unemployment. As regards unemployment the Government, after the Revolution, no longer required the clothiers to keep their men employed in times of trade depression, but distress was now relieved through the machinery of the Poor Law.

(iii.) Technical training. Industrial capitalism claimed the right not only to make its own contract with labour—as regards wages and length of employment—independent of any external interference, but also to draw freely upon an unlimited supply of labour. The survival of apprenticeship after the Revolution was a matter of local custom rather than State compulsion.[1] Parliament openly abandoned the legal enforcement of the

---

[1] The authorities at Leeds tried to maintain the system of apprenticeship down to the middle of the eighteenth century.

system at the beginning of the eighteenth century.[1] In 1700 the wool-combers of London and Peterborough presented petitions setting forth that "great numbers of persons of all other trades have intruded into the petitioners' trade, so that they cannot get a livelihood," and that many of these intruders take fourteen or more apprentices to work them for a year or two, after which they become journeymen, "to the ruin of such as have legally served apprentices to the said trade." The petitions of the woolcombers were accompanied by others from the worsted and woollen weavers of Somersetshire and Devonshire, in which they complained of the intrusion of "many unskilful persons who for a little money have just learned to weave," the result being to "sink the wages usually given" and to make them chargeable to the parish, "when their masters turn them out of employment." Parliament declined to take any steps in response to these petitions, and pronounced the maxim which was to mould its economic policy throughout the century: "*Trade ought to be free and not restrained.*"

The breakdown of the industrial code established for (iv.) Standardisation. the protection of the woollen industry was shown, finally, in the decay of the aulnage. Even in the sixteenth century the Government had found it difficult to standardise industry. One of Thomas Cromwell's agents was warned by the cloth-makers that, if they were compelled to make cloth according to the Assize, it would cause them to forbear cloth-making, for it was impossible to keep the size of the cloth limited as the Act required, nor could the weavers afford to provide the necessary "lomes and slees." In reply he "bade them take heed and beware, for if by obstinacy or wilfulness they left their cloth-making any murmur or sedition among the people for lack of work would be laid to their charge. To this they said obediently they would do what they could." Nevertheless it was found expedient to suspend the operation of the Act. In

[1] An Act of 1724 contained a clause that clothiers who "make or cause to be made any broad cloth in the West Riding" should serve an apprenticeship of seven years, but the clause was omitted in 1734 in an Act to "explain and amend" the previous Statute.

the next century[1] complaints were frequent that the system of search had broken down, and after the Restoration (1662) a corporation was erected in the West Riding[2] expressly on the ground that " divers abuses and deceits have of late years been had and used in the manufacture of broad woollen cloth "; it was composed of clothiers under the rule of a governing body, whose duty it was to appoint inspectors to examine cloths and seal them. The policy of standardising industry was severely condemned by Sir Josiah Child, who expressed the views of the woollen manufacturers when he pleaded for freedom in industry. " All our laws," he wrote, " that oblige our people to the making of strong, substantial, and, as we call it, loyal cloth, of a certain length, breadth, and weight, if they were duly put into execution would, in my opinion, do more hurt than good, because the humours and fashions of the world change, and at some times, in some places (as now in most), slight, cheap, light cloth will sell more plentifully and better than that which is heavier, stronger, and truer wrought; and if we intend to have the trade of the world we must imitate the Dutch, who make the worst as well as the best of all manufactures, that we may be in a capacity of serving all markets and all humours. I conclude all our laws limiting the number of looms, numbers or kind of servants, or times of working, to be certainly prejudicial to the clothing trade of the kingdom in general." He recommended that clothiers should be left at liberty " to make what cloth and stuffs they please, how they will, where and when they will, of any length or sizes."

Relaxa-
tion of
control.

The Revolution was followed, in this as in other directions, by a complete relaxation of industrial restraints. " As the worthy makers of those good laws are now asleep," it was complained in 1691, " so are their laws too, and every man may make his cloth at his own choice." The aulnage survived only as an instrument of extortion—

---

[1] At the end of the sixteenth century the aulnager's function of measuring cloth was largely taken over by cloth searchers appointed first by the Justices of the Peace and afterwards (in the West Riding) by the Corporation of Clothiers.

[2] See below, p. 119, *n.* 2.

" very burdensome to the subject and a great hindrance
to the woollen trade "—and its officials did not trouble
themselves about the size and quality of the cloth, but
were content merely to enforce payment of the duty. The
manufacturers themselves affixed the seals on their cloths
without submitting them for inspection. The original
design of the institution was entirely lost sight of, the
makers having " an uncontrolled liberty to make bad cloth
of what material they will "; and in 1724 it expired.[1] A
few years later (1738) Parliament openly discarded the
system of standard measurements in Yorkshire in the case
of narrow woollen cloths, and in 1765 in the case of broad
woollen cloths.[2] At the opening of the nineteenth century
a clothier told a Parliamentary Committee that " at this
time we make goods to suit every customer and every
clime." The attempt to standardise the cloth trade was
thus necessarily abandoned. It was manifestly impossible
to manufacture cloths according to statutory measurements
in view of the variety of fabrics now exported abroad to
meet the tastes of foreign buyers; nor was it considered
necessary to prevent the straining and stretching of cloth
since the manufacturer was the one most interested in
maintaining the credit of his cloth, and therefore the most
concerned not to stretch or strain it injuriously; while,
lastly, the use of various ingredients forbidden by law
was now required owing to improvements in the art of
dyeing. The argument in short was that, however necessary statutory control of the woollen manufacture might
have been in earlier times to give credit to the industry
by preventing abuses, competition could now be trusted
to secure this end. " The interest of the seller," now ran

[1] In 1699 Parliament enacted that the aulnage should come to an
end upon the expiration of the sixty years' grant made to the Duke
of Richmond and Lenox in 1664.
[2] The Corporation of Clothiers in the West Riding, which had been
vested with the power of appointing local searchers, expired in 1685.
In 1708 the influence of the leading men in Yorkshire secured the
passage of an Act fixing the measurements of Yorkshire broad cloth,
and this was followed in 1724 by the institution of inspectors who
were to be appointed, as formerly, by the Justices. The system of
inspection lasted into the nineteenth century, even after statutory
measurements were abandoned.

the maxim of trade, " is sufficient security to the buyer for fair dealing."[1]

Rise of Trade Unionism. The changed attitude of the State towards the wage problem and the technical training of workmen was one of the factors in the rise of Trade Unionism. Capital and Labour were no longer controlled by an external authority, but were left free to determine, according to their respective strength, wages and the general conditions of employment. The textile workers found that they must depend upon their own efforts for the maintenance of " the standard of life," and the Revolution of 1688, which brought to a final close the era of benevolent autocracy, was soon followed by an outburst of trade union activity.

Eighteenth century combinations. The combinations formed among textile artisans in the eighteenth century were the forerunners of the great trade unions of the nineteenth century. The ostensible purpose of these associations was to serve as benefit clubs for the relief of the sick. In Gloucestershire, for example, the members of a club paid twopence a week and received six shillings a week in times of sickness. But benefit clubs easily develop into trade societies, for when men who are engaged in the same occupation meet together at regular intervals they inevitably begin to discuss trade grievances. Our knowledge of the early trade union movement is derived mainly from the accounts given by the employers, which are naturally one-sided. One account stated that at Tiverton the wool-combers and weavers " have combined and formed themselves into clubs and unlawful assemblies, and have taken on themselves an arbitrary power to ascertain their wages in their respective businesses

---

[1] In the eighteenth century a curious legend was industriously circulated concerning an elaborate fraud perpetrated on the Russian Government. In 1724 " an able merchant did declare to the House of Commons the abuses [in English cloth] he himself had experienced and that he had been concerned in clothing the army of Russia with the Yorkshire cloth, but that the cloth was so ill-managed, that by one shower of rain upon a day of review, the clothing of the whole army shrunk to such a degree that it brought discredit upon the cloth and lost the trade absolute." The story was repeated at intervals in the eighteenth and nineteenth centuries, connected with various historical personages, and lost nothing in the re-telling (see Bibliographical Note).

and trades; by means whereof many tumultuous and riotous meetings and outrages have been by them frequently had and committed not only on their masters, but also on their fellow-labourers who refused to join with them in such their practices; by breaking into houses, spoiling of wool, and cutting and destroying the pieces in the looms and the utensils of trade; whereby several poor persons have been reduced to penury and want; and such offenders have not only insulted the chief magistrates, but also abused and threatened the constables and other peace officers who are thereby deterred from executing justice on them." The unruly character of the weavers is shown in the description of a riot at Crediton in Devonshire, where they were headed by a captain who threatened dire consequences to the masters if they did not raise their wages. On this occasion the weavers carried about with them a chain of serge which they had cut off from a loom, and declared that they would treat in similar fashion the cloth of other masters who refused to comply with their demands. When the constables seized some of the ring-leaders, the mob surrounded the Court House, pelted the Justices with stones, and eventually drove them to flight, after which they rescued the prisoners. There was seemingly little respect for authority. At Taunton, where a number of rioters had been apprehended, a thousand men collected together, forced their way into the Court, beat the constables, assaulted the Justice, and rescued several of the prisoners. When the Town Clerk read the proclamation for dispersing the mob, " they pulled off his hat and wig, and put dirt upon his head." As a result of the representations made by the employers, Parliament passed an Act in 1726, which recited that " great numbers of weavers and others concerned in the woollen manufactures in several towns and parishes in this kingdom have lately formed themselves into unlawful clubs and societies, and have presumed, contrary to law, to enter into combinations and to make by-laws, or orders, by which they pretend to regulate the trade and the prices of their goods, and to advance their wages unreasonably, and many other things

to the like purpose. And the said persons so unlawfully
assembling and associating themselves have committed
great violences and outrages upon many of his majesty's
good subjects." The Act henceforth forbade, under penalty
of imprisonment, all combinations of weavers and wool-
combers formed with the object of regulating industry and
improving the conditions of labour.   This Act was intended
by its authors to stifle at its birth the trade union movement, but one thing in fairness should be remembered.
It was not a purely one-sided measure, for it also contained
regulations for the better payment of wages.   While the
State refused to recognise the right of working men to
combine together for the protection and advancement of
their economic interests, it still accepted, in principle at
least, the duty of safeguarding the economic welfare of the
industrial masses.   The real criticism against the Act of
1726 is that it did not affect equally both sections of the
industrial community.   The employers remained free to
exercise a right which was refused to working men, and the
clothiers, as Adam Smith expressly tells us, entered into
combinations, " always conducted with the utmost silence
and secrecy," in order to maintain their common interests.

The West
Country
weavers.

After an interval of a dozen years (1738) the wild passions
of the West Country weavers, which the lapse of time had
done nothing to soften, flared up once again under the
spur of a fresh grievance.   A great riot broke out at Tiverton owing to the misdeeds of one Grimes, a publican.   The
latter was accustomed to purchase cloth which the merchants
had returned to the makers as defective, and to sell it
again to the same merchants at reduced prices.   The
merchants encouraged the practice because it increased
their profits, but the artisans of Tiverton were infuriated
at the dishonest trickery by which their earnings were
sensibly curtailed.   One fine morning they collected together
in a large body, and, joined by the workmen from the
neighbouring villages, marched on the Red Lion Inn, situated on Pound Hill, broke into the house, and finding great
quantities of serges there threw them into the street, hang-
ing some upon the signpost and tearing others to pieces.

The publican himself was discovered in the oven of a bake-house at the bottom of Pound Hill; he was promptly "horsed" on a staff which was borne horizontally on the shoulders of the crowd, carried through the streets, and at length deposited on the mayor's doorstep. A few years later the weavers and wool-combers of Tiverton attacked the inn of another publican who was charged with similar mal-practices. On this occasion they set the house on fire, but extinguished it again on discovering his little child in a cradle. The Wiltshire weavers were equally noted for their turbulent character and the rude violence with which they proclaimed the wrongs under which they smarted. In 1738 they assembled together in a riotous manner from the villages round Bradford and Trowbridge, and made an attack upon the house of a clothier who had reduced the price of weaving. They smashed open the doors, consumed or spoiled the provisions in the cellar, drank all the wine they could, set the casks running, and ended up by destroying great quantities of raw material and utensils. In addition to this exploit they extorted a promise from all the clothiers in Melksham that they would pay fifteen pence a yard for weaving, but their further course was arrested by the appearance of the military upon the scene. For the destruction of property three of the rioters after-wards suffered execution. Another great tumult occurred at Bradford (Wiltshire) in 1752. Thirty weavers had been committed to prison; the next day above a thousand weavers assembled, armed with bludgeons and firearms, beat the guard, broke open the prison, and rescued their companions.

The wool-combers were also organised in unions, and their relations with the employers were far from friendly. A worsted manufacturer of Nottinghamshire declared in 1794 that "the manufacturers are entirely at the mercy of their combers and must pay them whatever wages they demand, particularly when trade is in a flourishing state, insomuch that if a manufacturer displeases one wool-comber all the others either quit his service entirely or until he appeases the offended member, and no other wool-

Unions among the wool-combers.

comber will work for him so long as he continues under the
displeasure of any of the members of their society." A
strike of journeymen wool-combers took place at Norwich
in 1752. "The journeymen retired from the city to a
heath about three miles off, called Rackheath, where they
erected booths for themselves, and about 300 of them
being supported by purse clubs lived without any irregu-
larities." They demanded the dismissal of one Trye, whom
they declared to be an informer. The masters, after holding
out for five weeks, acquiesced in the demand. The union
at Tiverton was formed as early as 1700, and an episode
in its history throws vivid light upon the determined character of its members. The merchants of Tiverton had
begun to import large quantities of combed wool from
Ireland, where the price of spinning was only half the price
in England. Irish worsted yarn was in consequence much
cheaper than English yarn, and the manufacturers used it
to make white serges. The wool-combers saw themselves
menaced with the extinction of their industry, for the more
combed wool brought into this country, the less would be
the demand for their labour. Alarmed at this prospect,
they determined (1720) to take the law into their own
hands. Collecting their forces together, they attacked the
houses of those merchants who had brought over the most
yarn and spoilt all the worsted they could find. Large
quantities were hung on signposts as trophies of their
victory, and they also rifled the houses of several makers
who had begun the manufacture. "Several of the merchants fortified their houses. The magistrates assembled
a great number of constables and attacked the combers
upon the Oat Hill." A terrible battle ensued. "The
combers seized a horse's load of wood coming into the
town, tore it all up into bats, and fought for a long while
with the constables, but at last were overpowered and
many of them taken prisoners. These were rescued for a
time, but afterwards with the assistance of the military
were again taken, sent to the county gaol, and tried for
their lives, but escaped other punishment." The manufacture of serges with Irish wool was, however, soon dis-

continued as they were found unequal to those made with wool which had been combed and spun in this country.

The organisation of the cloth-finishers first emerges into prominence at the very end of the eighteenth century, and an interesting account of the Yorkshire union,[1] the "Croppers' Society"—corresponding to the Cloth-Dressers' Society in the West of England—is given in the *Report on the State of the Woollen Manufacture* (1806): Unions among the cloth-finishers.

"It appears that there has existed for some time an institution or society among the woollen manufacturers consisting chiefly of cloth-workers. In each of the principal manufacturing towns there appears to be a society composed of deputies chosen from the several shops of workmen, from each of which town-societies one or more deputies are chosen to form what is called the Central Committee, which meets as occasion requires at some place suitable to the local convenience of all parties. The powers of the Central Committee appear to pervade the whole institution; and any determination or measure it may adopt may be communicated with ease throughout the whole body of manufacturers. Every workman on his becoming a member of the society receives a certain card, or ticket, on which is an emblematical engraving, the same—the Committee are assured—both in the North and the West of England, that by producing his ticket he may at once show he belongs to the society. The same rules and regulations appear to be in force throughout the whole district; and there is the utmost reason to believe that no cloth-worker would be suffered to carry on his trade, otherwise than in solitude, who should refuse to submit to the obligations and rules of the society. A stated weekly contribution, greater or less according to existing circumstances, is required from every member, and of course the sum raised in this way may be, and in fact has been, very considerable. . . . It appears that from the fund liberal weekly allowances have been made to whole shops of workmen who have turned out, as it is called—*i.e.*, who have illegally

---

[1] In Yorkshire there was unrest among the cloth-finishers, worsted weavers, and wool-combers throughout the eighteenth century.

combined to quit the service of some particular master who has become obnoxious to them, and thereby to force him into a compliance with their terms. It likewise appears that the society, which by embracing only the workmen in the woollen manufacture throughout so large a district must both from its numbers and its pecuniary resources have become a very powerful body, had formed a sort of confederacy, cemented as it appears by mutual contributions and payments, with various other classes of artificers nowise connected with the woollen trade; and that these connections and the effects of them were not confined to the clothing district, but that they extended to various parts of England, and, your Committee have reason to believe, into Scotland also."

Objects of the Union. The objects of this combination among the cloth-workers were fourfold: (1) to raise wages; (2) to prescribe the age at which apprentices should be taken; (3) to regulate the number of apprentices in accordance with the number of journeymen; and (4) to resist the introduction of machinery. While the Industrial Revolution was at its height a great trial of strength between Capital and Labour was provoked at Leeds over the question of apprenticeship. The employers were accustomed to take apprentices " of any age and for any time; that was left entirely to the discretion of the parent and the master—sometimes for four years, and sometimes for seven years; in short all lengths of time, as it suited the parties." In 1803 a prominent manufacturer at Leeds, Mr. Gott, took two apprentices over fifteen years of age. This violated the rules of the shearmen, which forbade apprentices to be taken over the age of fifteen—a boy over fifteen would not have completed his apprenticeship at the age of twenty-one, and would then be doing a man's work without receiving a man's pay— and the manufacturer was called upon to dismiss the apprentices. He declined to do so, on the ground that they were indentured for seven years. In consequence all his shearmen laid down their tools after they had finished the work upon which they were engaged and quitted his service. Unable to fill their places, he applied to the merchants of Leeds, over forty of whom agreed to come to his assistance and dress his cloth for him. He accordingly sent some pieces of cloth to twenty or thirty merchants in Leeds, but the men refused to handle the goods which came from his shop; not one of the merchants was able to get a single piece of cloth dressed, and they were warned by their foremen that if they persisted in the attempt, their men would also quit their service. A deadlock ensued, and the upshot was that the matter was referred to arbitration; the magistrates of Leeds were called in, and the employers agreed not to take any apprentices over fifteen years old nor for less than seven years. This was a victory for the shearmen, who had maintained their traditional practices in the face of the efforts of the capitalists to break loose from restrictions which obstructed the free development of their business.

CHAPTER IV

PROCESSES AND INVENTIONS

The
stages of
cloth-
making. In order to understand the inventions which revolutionised the woollen industry, we must first gain some notion of the main technical processes involved in the preparation and manufacture of cloth. The different stages of cloth-making are described in a poem printed in 1641:[1]

" As first, the Parter, that doth neatly cull
The finer from the coarser sort of wool.
The Dyer then in order next doth stand,
With sweating brow and a laborious hand.
With oil they then asperge it, which being done,
The careful hand of Mixers round it run,
The Stock-carder his arms doth hard employ
(Remembering Friday is our Market Day).
Then Knee-carder doth (without control)
Quickly convert it to a lesser roll.
Which done, the Spinster doth in hand it take,
And of two hundred rolls one thread doth make. . . .
The Weaver next doth warp and weave the chain,
Whilst Puss his cat stands mewing for a skein,
But he, laborious with his hands and heels,
Forgets his cat, and cries: Come boy with quills.
Being fill'd the Brayer doth it mundify
From oil and dirt that in the same doth lie,
The Burler then (yea, thousands in this place)
The thick-set weed, with nimble hand doth chase. . . .
The Fuller then close by his stock doth stand,
And will not once shake Morpheus by the hand.
The Rower next his arms lifts up on high,
And near him sings the Shearman merrily.
The Drawer, last, that many faults doth hide
(Whom merchant nor the weaver can abide)
Yet he is one in most cloths stops more holes
Than there be stairs to the top of Paul's."

[1] R. Watts, *The Young Man's Looking Glass.*

The first process was the sorting of wool. " The perfect The sorting of wool. and principal ground of cloth-making," declared a Statute of 1554, " is the true sorting of wools." The long wool had to be divided from the short wool; and the different qualities —there were often as many as ten grades of wool in a single fleece—carefully sorted.

" In the same fleece diversity of wool
Grows intermingled, and excites the care
Of curious skill to sort the sev'ral kinds. . . .
Nimbly with habitual speed,
They sever lock from lock, and long and short,
And soft and rigid, pile in sev'ral heaps."[1]

The wool, after being sorted, was scoured in order to dis- The cleaning of wool solve the grease. This was done in a stream: the short wool was put in baskets, and the water was " drained through the baskets, leaving the wool behind, which was dried in lofts or in the sun. Long wool for combing was washed with two poles, having crooks at one end, which were twisted reverse ways, squeezing the water out like wringing a towel." The wool had to be cleansed from miscellaneous impurities; in the case of unwashed merino wool foreign matter made up more than one-half its weight. The farmer often branded the sheep with pitch and tar; this was detrimental to the wool, which also suffered from excessive marking. The manufacturer was therefore obliged to waste a considerable quantity of wool in clipping off the damaged parts. Another evil with which manufacturers had to contend was the fraudulent winding of wool. This was " a crime of ancient date." As early as 1532 it was enacted " that no person should wind within any fleece clay, lead, stones, tail, deceitful locks,[2] cotts, eals, comber, lambs' wool, or any other thing whereby the fleece might be more weighty, to the deceit and loss of the buyer." In some parcels of wool one-fifteenth of the weight was lost owing to marking and deceitful winding; and in the middle of the eighteenth century petitions were presented to Parliament from sixty centres of the woollen industry complaining of these practices. The cause of the growers

[1] Dyer, *The Fleece*.   [2] The coarse ends of the wool.

was taken up by John Smith, the author of *The Memoirs of Wool*, who defended them from the accusations of the manufacturers, " the inveterate antagonists to wool-growers for ages and centuries."

Willeying. When the wool was dry[1] it was beaten with rods to cleanse it from dust and to disentangle the locks; this was called willeying. It was then picked to free it from any refuse which had escaped the rods. After these operations the wool was in a condition to undergo the preliminary processes of manufacturing—namely, carding or combing.

Branches of the woollen industry The woollen industry was divided into two main branches: the clothing branch, or manufacture of short, carded wool; and the worsted branch, or manufacture of long, combed wool.[2] The term " cloth " was used where both warp and weft were spun from carded wool; and the term " stuff " (or tammy) denoted that warp and weft were made from combed wool. A third category, serge, was created by the mixture of carded and combed wool—the weft being carded yarn, and the warp combed yarn. These " three fundamental sorts," as they were called, were subdivided into a great number of others, " according to certain qualities added to them, and different ways of working." Combing wool, as we learn from a list given to Parliament in 1794, was used in the manufacture, among others, of sagathies, duroy, estamanes, shalloons, poplins, lastings, callimanco, bombazine, stuff-damask, camblets, crapes, russells, druggets, sanfords, and baize.

Carding. The long wool, as we have said, was combed, and the short wool carded. After the wool had been sorted and cleansed from impurities it was carded in order to disintegrate the locks of wool, and straighten out and interlace the fibres. Carding was done by means of hand-cards, which resembled hand-brushes in shape, the backs being made of stout card or wood, 12 inches long and 5 inches wide, and the fronts being fitted with short pieces of wire (instead of bristles) set in a leather cover. The wool was spread in small quantities upon one of the cards, and

---

[1] Or even before it was washed.
[2] Short wool can now be used in the worsted manufacture.

brushed and combed with the other until all the fibres were disentangled from the locks and crossed in every direction, after which it was stripped off the card in soft fleecy rolls termed " slivers." Originally the cards were held one in each hand, but afterwards one of the cards was made a fixture, and its size was also increased, so that a greater quantity of wool could be spread on it. A later improvement was to suspend the card from the ceiling, which relieved the operator from bearing its weight. The new type of cards bore the name of " stock cards."

The sliver, or fleecy rolls in which the wool was taken Roving. off the hand-cards, was converted into a thick, coarse thread called " roving," and the rovings were then spun into a fine twisted thread termed " yarn." The process of roving was analogous to the process of spinning, and the two operations involved the use of the same instrument. A description of spinning will therefore serve as a description of roving. We must first, however, say a word about the process which corresponded to carding in the worsted industry—namely, wool-combing.

Three implements were employed in wool-combing: a Combing. pair of combs, a post to which one of the combs was fixed, and a comb-pot or small stove for heating the teeth of the combs. The comb was a piece of wood shaped like the letter T. The perpendicular part served as the handle, while the head or horizontal part, which usually measured 3 inches in width, contained long, pointed teeth. These teeth were " finely tapered, made of well-tempered steel, and generally arranged in three rows about thirty in each, and placed nearly at right angles to every part of the wood." The wool was hung upon the teeth of the comb affixed to the post, " in such a manner as to project over the front of the head; when sufficiently filled and firmly fixed, another comb of the same kind was drawn through the wool so as to unravel and lay each hair of it smooth and even." The comb not only served to lay the fibres parallel with each other, but also to separate the long wool (the " top ") from the wool of shorter staple (the " noil ").

Unhealthy
nature of
the em-
ployment. The work of the wool-combers was both unpleasant and unhealthy. According to an account written in 1845, " the wool-combers assort the wool chiefly in an apartment of their own dwelling. The work is done over a fire of charcoal, which sends forth volumes of carbonic acid gas, and the workpeople are obliged to keep their windows open in all weathers to prevent or to mitigate the evil effects of the gas. They are roasted to perspiration on one side, and have often a current of cold air rushing upon them from the window. They look pale and cadaverous, and are short-lived, few reaching fifty years of age." The discontent which prevailed among them may be attributed, in part, to the " harassing and enfeebling nature of their employment; their ill-ventilated and unhealthy dwellings." It was, indeed, an argument in favour of machinery that the hand-comber, " confined to noisome abodes," was " enervated by the heat and effluvium of charcoal fires."

Spinning:
(i.) The
distaff and
spindle. The original method of spinning—the word means to draw out and twist the fibres of wool so as to form a continuous thread—was the distaff (or " rock ") and spindle. The distaff was a cleft staff, about a yard long, with a forked top on which a fleece of wool, called the " lint " or " tow," was loosely wound. It was held under the left arm, or sometimes carried in the girdle of the spinner in order to give freedom to the hands. The method of spinning was to draw a continuous lock of wool from the fleece through the fingers of the left hand, and twist it between the forefinger and thumb of the right with the aid of a pendent spindle. This spindle was a slender rod, constructed of reed or other light wood, and measuring 8 to 12 inches in length. An incision was made at the top for attaching the thread to the spindle, and as the spindle was perpetually revolving it served to draw out and produce a more finely twisted thread. The lower end of the spindle was inserted in a whorl—a ring, or weight, usually made of stone, but sometimes of metal or wood—with a hole bored through the centre to admit the spindle. The main use of the whorl was to act as a flywheel to the whirling spindle, keeping it steady by its weight and making it revolve

uniformly. It also served a subsidiary purpose in preventing " the thread from becoming unravelled by shuffling
down from the centre to the end." Another form of
spindle was " an elongated cone of wood, the lower end
being the thicker and acting as the weight "; this kind of
spindle needed no whorl to serve as a flywheel. As the
spinner gradually lengthened the thread with her fingers,
the spindle touched the ground and a " length " was said
to be spun. The thread was then wound upon the spindle,
another portion of the " tow " was attached to the top of
the spindle, and the spinner set to work upon a fresh
" length."

This mode of spinning, which was prevalent in ancient Antiquity
times, is thus described by Catullus: and late
survival of
" rock "
spinning.

> " The loaded distaff, in the left hand placed,
>   With spongy coils of snow-white wool was graced;
> From these the right hand lengthening fibres drew
> Which into thread, 'neath nimble fingers, grew."

The discovery of whorls in the Pictish towers (brochs)
affords evidence of the use of the distaff and spindle in
these islands in the remotest times, and they were still
known in the second half of the nineteenth century. Dyer,
whose poem, *The Fleece*, was published in 1757, wrote:

> " Many yet adhere
> To th' ancient distaff, at the bosom fix'd,
> Casting the whirling spindle as they walk."

More than a century later the spindle and whorl were in
use among the fishermen of the west coast of Scotland. One
advantage of the distaff was that the work could be done
on the hillside, and a generation ago a traveller in the
Highlands could still meet girls " herding on the hillside
and busily spinning with the distaff."

The rock and spindle were eventually superseded by the (ii.) The
spinning-wheel, which was erroneously supposed to have spinning
wheel.
been introduced into England by an Italian in 1505, but
was really known in this country at least as early as the
fourteenth century.[1] The purpose of the spinning or hand-

---

[1] It is mentioned in the *Records of Nottingham*.

wheel, as it was called, was to give motion to the spindle
by means of a revolving wheel. Instead of being suspended
by the thread, the spindle was " mounted in a frame and
turned by a belt passing over a large wheel." The process
is thus described by Guest: " In spinning with the hand-
wheel the roving was taken fast hold of betwixt the left
forefinger and thumb at 6 inches distance from the spindle.
The wheel, which by a band gave motion to the spindle,
was then turned with the right hand, and at the same time
the left hand—holding the roving fast as before mentioned—
was drawn back about half a yard. The roving was thus
drawn out into weft,[1] the necessary twist was then given
by a few turns of the wheel, and finally the weft was wound
upon the spindle." Adam Smith asserts that the exchange
of the rock and spindle for the spinning-wheel enabled a
spinner to perform more than double the quantity of work
with the same quantity of labour. At first the wheel was
turned by one hand, and the thread twisted and drawn out
by the other; subsequently the wheel was turned by a
treadle and crank which the spinner worked with her foot.
This left the spinner free to employ both her hands in
spinning the thread. " In my memory," stated the writer
of a treatise on *Silk, Wool, Worsted, Cotton, and Thread*
(1779), " wool was spun on the long wheel only, which
was tedious and irregular, the wheel being at least five feet
perpendicular with one spindle. This wheel was turned by
a peg with the right hand, and the wool spun from the left
by the hand being extended as the wheel was turned. The
next invention was a one-handed wheel, so-called from its
motion being continued with one hand, and the yarn spun
with the other, and twisted with a spindle and flyer. In
1750 a wheel was invented to spin with both hands, turned
with the feet."

Defects of
hand-spin-
ning. We have already pointed out the defects of hand-spun
yarn arising from the irregular quality of the thread.[2]
Individual spinners sometimes achieved remarkable per-
formances. Thus at the end of the eighteenth century the
Highland Society of Scotland was shown " a specimen of

---

[1] *I.e.*, thread.   [2] Above, p. 64.

the singularly fine woollen yarn, spun by Miss Ann Ives,
of Spalding in Lincolnshire, which, though strong, is drawn
to such a fineness that a pound weight of the yarn measures
no less than 168,000 yards in length, which is equal to
95 miles." But as many as ten hands might be employed on a single chain, and the yarn was therefore very
uneven in quality. Another serious defect was the in-
adequateness of the supply. In spite of the multitude of
spinners they were unable to furnish weavers with the
necessary quantity of yarn. It is estimated that one loom
gave work to half a dozen spinners or more, and the progress
of the textile industries was checked by a yarn famine.
In farming districts the spinning was largely done in the
winter, and here the weavers experienced great difficulty
in carrying on their work during the summer months. " I
have known our stock of yarn so low in the summer," stated
a worsted manufacturer, " that weavers have sometimes
had to wait a few days for warps." It has been said that
one-half the weavers' time was generally consumed in
waiting for work. They went from house to house in
search of yarn. " It was no uncommon thing for a weaver
to walk three or four miles in a morning, and call on five
or six spinners, before he could collect weft to serve him for
the remainder of the day; and when he wished to weave a
piece in a shorter time than usual a new ribbon or gown
was necessary to quicken the exertions of the spinner."
The difficulties arising from the shortage of yarn were
aggravated after the introduction of the fly shuttle[1] since
the productive power of the weaver was greatly increased,
and as a result also the demand for supplies of yarn. " The
spinners in those days," we are told by one who had known
the conditions which existed before the Industrial Revolution,
" were the masters of the weavers, and they often took a
most unfair advantage of their position. If two or three
buyers appeared together in a rural district, the intelligence
spread with telegraphic rapidity from house to house, and
the price of yarns immediately rose one-third or even
one-half." The large clothier was able to send his wool

[1] See below, p. 142.

away into country districts, but the weaver who was dependent upon the resources of his immediate neighbourhood was seriously handicapped. This scarcity of yarn was a serious obstacle to the progress of the woollen industry. An increase in the demand for cloth could not be met automatically by an increase in the output of weft and warp. The rapidity with which the machinery used in spinning cotton was applied to spinning worsted was the result of a long experience of the shortcomings of the old hand-yarn manufacture.

Weaving. Weaving has been defined as the art by which threads are crossed and interlaced. We may expand this definition by saying that a piece of cloth is made up of longitudinal threads laid parallel to each other and intersected by transverse threads. The longitudinal threads constitute the warp or chain, the transverse threads the weft or woof.[1] The process of weaving consists in inserting the threads of the weft between the alternate threads of the warp.

Tasks of the weaver. The first task of the weaver is to arrange the warp in order on the loom. This was termed " looming," and unless the warp was " put square " (fixed properly) on the loom, every thread at an equal tension, the texture of the cloth would be uneven. The loom was framed like an oblong box, four upright posts being joined together by two long and two short posts. At one end of the loom was the warp beam, at the other end the cloth beam. The warp threads were laid parallel to each other extending lengthwise across the loom from one beam to the other, and as the cloth was woven it was wound upon the cloth beam, and fresh warp was paid out by the warp beam. In the middle of the loom the warp passed through two sets of healds. These healds were small parallel cords, or wires, stretched vertically between two horizontal bars, each cord having a loop, or " eye," for the admission of a single thread of the warp. The even threads of the warp passed through the loops of one leaf[2] or set of healds, the odd threads

---

[1] The weft was also called " abb " and " shute."
[2] A " leaf " was the name given to a set of healds; it was also termed " gear."

through the loops of the other leaf. There were thus two series of warp threads, the odd and the even, the former controlled by the first set of healds and the latter by the second set. The healds were worked by two treadles, and when one treadle was depressed by the foot, it lifted the other treadle as well as the shaft of healds connected with it. This contrivance enabled the weaver to raise alternately one section of the threads of the warp for the passage of the weft. The warp threads were then inserted in the "batten," or "sley," a movable wooden frame designed on the principle of a comb, with a large number of dents through each of which several threads of the warp were passed to keep them in position.

When the warp was prepared in the manner we have *Operations involved* described, the weaver seated himself at the loom and with *in weaving.* his foot depressed the right treadle. This raised the left treadle, and, as explained above, made an opening or "shed" in the warp. Through the shed the weaver now swiftly threw the shuttle—a piece of wood tapering to a point at each end, and containing a cavity or chamber for the reception of the "bobbin" or "quill," a small reed pipe on which was wound a quantity of weft. As the shuttle shot across the warp from the right side of the loom to the left, the weft unrolled itself from the bobbin and escaped through a small hole or eye in the side of the shuttle. The weft thread was then beaten home and packed close by the batten against the stretch of cloth already produced by former throws ("picks," as they are called) of the shuttle. The left treadle was now in its turn depressed; this caused the right treadle to rise, and with it the alternate series of warp threads, forming another shed for the passage of the shuttle from the left side to the right.

> " And now he strains the warp
> Along the garden-walk, or highway side,
> Smoothing each thread; now fits it to the loom,
> And sits before the work: from hand to hand
> The thready shuttle glides along the lines,
> And ever and anon, to firm the work,
> Against the web is driv'n the noisy frame
> That o'er the level rushes, like a surge."

The art of weaving, apart from the laborious work of fixing the warp on the loom, thus involved three distinct operations: opening alternate sheds in the warp by means of the treadles; casting the shuttle through each shed when opened; and driving home the weft threads with the batten. The swiftness of the shuttle became proverbial:

> " My days are swifter than a weaver's shuttle and are spent without hope."

A single weaver was able to work a narrow loom; he threw the shuttle with his right hand and caught it on the other side with his left; but two weavers were needed for the broad loom, one at each end, to receive and return the shuttle thrown by his partner.

Nature of the employment. Hand-loom weaving, as Dr. Gaskell pointed out in 1836, " is not easy labour; the position in which the weaver sits is not the best for muscular exertion, as he has no firm support for his feet, which are alternately raised and depressed in working the treadles. He has thus to depend for a fulcrum chiefly on the muscles of his back, which are kept in constant and vigorous action, while one order of muscles is employed with little power of variation in moving the shuttle and beam. These processes, when carried on for many successive hours, are very wearying, and the exertion required becomes, after a while, laborious. The weaver who worked hard, therefore, actually toiled—a condition widely different from that of the steam-loom weaver." Another criticism of hand-loom weaving is that the most experienced weavers rarely wove cloth uniform in texture; they could not throw the shuttle nor drive home the batten, from beginning to end, with the even force and mechanical precision of a power loom, and a weaker or stronger blow at once affected the texture. Nor could a hand-loom weaver work at the speed of a steam-loom, which was able to make many more times the number of " picks " per minute. The power loom not only reproduced the human movements, but it accelerated their speed, and combined with them an endurance that was inexhaustible.

Burling. Weaving was not the final process in cloth-making, for, as Langland wrote:

" Cloth that cometh fro the weaving is naught comeley to
    wear,
Till it is fulled under foot, or in fulling-stocks,
Washen well with water, and with teasles scratched,
Tucked and tented, and under tailor's hand."

After the cloth was woven it was scoured, in order to get
rid of the oil used in scribbling and of the size with which
the warp was dressed—burled, that is, the knots and
extraneous particles in the cloth were picked out—and (in
the case of woollen cloth only)[1] it was fulled.

The essential difference between woollen and worsted Fulling.
fabrics was that the former were thickened and felted—
that is, the fibres instead of lying parallel with each other
were inextricably interlaced until the woven pattern of the
cloth often ceased to be visible. The process of felting
is known as fulling: the cloth, after it had been woven and
burled, was soaped and beaten in a damp state with heavy
wooden hammers, so as to make it warmer, opaque, and
more durable. The original process of fulling consisted in
trampling the cloth underfoot until it was sufficiently shrunk
—a piece of cloth often shrinks up to two-thirds of its
original length, and about half its original width; on this
account the fuller was sometimes called a " walker." The
first improvement in the art of fulling cloth was to substitute a sitting posture for an erect one, enabling the
operation to be performed with greater rapidity and ease.
Thomas Pennant, who visited the North of Scotland in
1774, and came across a survival of the ancient mode of
fulling cloth with hand and foot in the Isle of Skye, gives
the following entertaining description of it:

" On my return am entertained with a rehearsal, I may Pennant's
call it, of the Luaghad, or walking of cloth, a substitute description of fulling
for the fulling mill: twelve or fourteen women, divided into in 1774.
equal numbers, sit down on each side of a long board ribbed
lengthways, placing the cloth on it: first they begin to work
it backwards and forwards with their hands, singing at the
same time as at the Quern:[2] when they have tired their
hands, every female uses her feet for the same purpose, and

---

[1] Some worsteds are now lightly milled.   [2] I e., mill-grinding.

six or seven pairs of naked feet are in the most violent agitation, working one against the other: as by this time they grow very earnest in their labours, the fury of the song rises; at length it arrives to such a pitch that without breach of charity you would imagine a troop of female demoniacs to have been assembled.

"They sing in the same manner when they are cutting down the corn, when thirty or forty join in chorus. The subjects of the songs at the Luaghad, the Quern, and on this occasion, are sometimes love, sometimes panegyric, often a rehearsal of the deeds of ancient heroes, but all the tunes slow and melancholy."

Late survival of the old mode of fulling.

Over a century later another writer describes "a picturesque sight" in the Highland districts: "A dozen or more Highland lassies set round in two rows facing each other. The web of cloth is passed round in a damp state, each one pressing and pitching it with a dash to her next neighbour." The process is slow and tedious, but the time is beguiled with song, each one taking up the verse in turn, and all joining in the chorus. "Should a member of the male sex be found prowling nearby he is—if caught—unceremoniously thrust into the centre of the circle and tossed with the web till, bruised with the rough usage and blackened with the dye, he is glad to make his escape from the hands of the furies."

Fulling mills.

The use of fulling mills in place of "hand and foot" dates from very early times; they afford apparently the first example of the application of motive power to the textile industries. The fullery consisted of wooden hammers or shafts—hinged to an upright post and worked by water-power—and hollow vessels, known as "stocks" or fuller's pots, which were used to hold the cloth as it was pounded by the strokes of the hammers. Dyer's account of the fulling mills runs:

> "Next, from the slacken'd beam the woof unroll'd,
> Near some clear sliding river, Aire or Stroud,
> Is by the noisy fulling mill receiv'd;
> Where tumbling waters turn enormous wheels,
> And hammers, rising and descending, learn
> To imitate the industry of man."

The use of water mills for purposes of fulling cloth aroused Opposition to their use. great opposition. As early as 1298 London prohibited fulling at the mills instead of " by might and strength of man, and that is with hand and foot." The prohibition was removed in 1417 on the ground that water mills involved less cost and were equally serviceable, but it was revived again in 1437. This antagonism to machinery driven by power was doubtless one of the main reasons for the delay in its introduction into industry. In 1485, for example, the owner of a fulling mill in the Stroud Valley was attacked by a crowd of " malefactors, *vi et armis*— viz., with swords, sticks, bows and arrows, scythes, jakkes, armour, etc.—with intent to murder him, so that he was many times affrighted and disturbed." The opposition to the mill eventually died down, but another grievance was voiced at Pontefract in 1739. Complaint was made to the Justices that " it is, and for many years last past hath been, a common practice to mill narrow cloth upon Sundays, and that the cloth-makers are now arrived to such a scandalous and shocking degree of prophaning the Sabbath this way, that they even contrive to bring more cloths to be milled upon Sunday than any other day. Whereby both masters and servants are guilty of a public neglect of the holy duties of the day, and by certain consequence are insensibly drawn into the commission of all manner of sin and wickedness, to the great displeasure of Almighty God, the scandal of the kingdom, the evil example of their neighbours, and the breach of all laws, both divine and human."

After the cloth was fulled it was stretched on tenters Finishing processes. in the open air to dry, and then " dressed " or finished. The finishing process involved two operations: " rowing " —that is, drawing out the loose fibres from the cloth with teasles[1] so as to raise a " nap " on the surface; and " shearing "—that is, cropping the nap as closely as possible, so as to impart a smooth appearance to the surface. Blemishes in the cloth were then repaired by the " drawer," after

---

[1] Teasle = a plant with prickly leaves.

which the cloth was pressed between heated plates and packed for the market.

Dyeing. Dyeing was a process in itself. Sometimes the wool was dyed after it was washed, but before it was woven, wool-dyed cloth being termed "medley cloth." White and medley cloth were made out of the same material, but the wool of the medley cloth was dyed before weaving. Most of the cloths made in Wiltshire were said to be dyed in the wool; on the other hand, the cloths made in Gloucestershire were chiefly dyed in the piece—that is, after being woven.

According to Luccock, an authority on wool, the methods of dyeing were distinctly primitive in Yorkshire. He wrote: " But indeed what can we expect but faint, muddy, and uncertain colours, where wool is dyed, as is too much the custom in Yorkshire, without being scoured, in pans unwashed, and with materials mixed together upon a floor unswept, where a little before perhaps have been mixed ingredients calculated to produce a totally different tint ?"

The inventions. All the inventions whose history we have now to relate were first intended for the cotton industry and afterwards applied to the worsted and woollen industries. To this statement two exceptions must be made: the fly shuttle was first introduced into the woollen industry, and the combing machine was only used in the worsted industry.[1]

Kay's fly shuttle. John Kay, the inventor of the fly shuttle, was born in 1704 at Walmersley, near Bury in Lancashire. He was educated on the Continent, and when he grew to manhood was given charge of a woollen manufactory at Colchester owned by his father. In 1733 he patented the famous invention which enabled one weaver to do the work of two, and which ushered in an era of revolutionary changes in the organisation and distribution of the textile industries. The main feature of Kay's device was the new mode of casting the shuttle. The batten[2] was flanked on each side by a shuttle race-board along which the shuttle ran on

---

[1] Paul's carding machine should perhaps be added to the list of exceptions.
[2] See above, p. 137.

wheels. The boards were connected by means of a cord with a lever, or " picking peg," held in the weaver's right hand. A jerk of the " picking peg " gave the necessary impetus to the shuttle, which was driven to and fro across the warp mechanically without being thrown by the weaver's hands, one of which was thus left entirely free to work the batten and beat together the weft threads. The speed at which the shuttle could now be thrown gained for the new contrivance the name of " fly shuttle." Robert Kay, a son of John Kay, afterwards invented the drop box, which enabled the weaver to use a variety of shuttles, each containing a different coloured weft. The invention of the fly shuttle, or " spring loom," enabled a weaver to dispense with assistance in weaving broad cloth; it removed his dependence on a journeyman,[1] whose irregular habits, arising from idleness, drunkenness, or sickness, had often hindered his work. In this sense we may say that one weaver was now able to do the work of two. Still, hand-loom weaving is not merely a matter of throwing a shuttle; it also involves the laborious task of binding the warp threads on the loom and repairing broken threads. The workman had to do all this on the spring loom single-handed, and some weavers maintained that the work could not be done in the same time. The fly shuttle certainly increased the production of cloth, one weaver instead of two being now required to work a loom, and it enabled the workman to earn more money. It also effected an improve-ment in the weaver's health; he was able to sit upright instead of having to lean forward, and was therefore less subject to breast disorders. On the other hand, the work was apparently more strenuous, and the common or double-handed loom still had its use for older weavers.[2]

[1] Owing to the demand for weavers, due to the increase in the manufacture of yarn, the journeymen were soon employed on their own.

[2] When Kay's fly shuttle was introduced into the North of Ireland, the new process of weaving attracted large crowds, and one woman " was enthusiastic in her admiration of it. Clapping her hands, she exclaimed in Scoto-Hibernic phraseology: ' Weel, weel ! the warks o' God's wondtherful, but the contrivance o' man bates Him at last !' "

Kay's ill-fated career. It has been said that Kay's invention called forth " that opposition of the working classes to the abridgment of processes of labour which was so conspicuous a fact for nearly a century afterwards in British industry." But from the earliest times the textile workers had always displayed a resolute antagonism to " the abridgment of processes of labour." They fought strenuously against the use of fulling and gig[1] mills in the finishing processes of the cloth industry, and their opposition to Kay and the long series of inventors who succeeded him sprang from a traditional dislike of innovations, coupled with a deep-rooted fear that machinery would take from them their means of livelihood. In the case of inventions like the fly shuttle, the folly of resisting improvements was soon rendered manifest, for the hand-loom weavers were the first to benefit by changes which gave them a more perfect command over their instruments. Kay's ill-fated career is a melancholy illustration of the evil destiny which has pursued most of the English inventors; their lives have been usually one long tragedy, sometimes relieved by transitory gleams of success, but more often shrouded in obscurity and gloom. The weavers of Colchester resisted the introduction of the fly shuttle, and their opposition drove Kay to the North of England, where he settled in Leeds. Here he found himself in conflict with the West Riding clothiers, who adopted his invention but refused to pay for its use. In order to protect themselves in this mean and dishonest conduct they even established an association under the name of " The Shuttle Club," which bore the costs of the lawsuits brought by Kay in defence of his rights. The inventor secured verdicts in his favour, but the barren triumphs he achieved in the courts of law did not restore his ruined fortunes; his resources were exhausted in fighting the combination formed against him, and, harassed by the inveterate animosity of clothiers and workmen, he retired to Bury.

His exile. In spite of his unhappy experiences the ardour of the inventor did not forsake him, and he turned his attention

[1] See above, p. 141, and below, p. 188.

to improvements in spinning. This gave occasion for renewed disturbances. In 1753 a mob broke into his house, wrecked everything it could lay its hands upon, and would probably have killed the inventor but for the intervention of two friends, who carried him to a place of safety in a wool-sheet. Abandoning the country which had given so rude a welcome to his inventive talent, Kay went into exile abroad. He applied to the Government for some recognition of his services, but met with no response. One letter has survived in which he records in brief, touching terms the pathetic history of his career: " I have a great many more inventions than what I have given in; and the reason that I have not put them forward is the bad treatment that I had from woollen and cotton factories in different parts of England twenty years ago; and then I applied to Parliament, and they would not assist me in my affairs, which obliged me to go abroad to get money to pay my debts and support my family." His end is unknown beyond the fact that he is said to have died in obscurity and poverty in France, where " not a stone tells where he lies." This was the fate which befell the first great inventor in the textile industries, whose vital improvements in the weaving of cloth conferred inestimable benefits upon his countrymen.

Who first conceived the idea of automatic spinning ? The claims of four different men have been widely canvassed: Lewis Paul, John Wyatt, Richard Arkwright, and Thomas Highs. The problem has never been satisfactorily solved, though certain facts are beyond all reasonable dispute. In the first place the mode of spinning by rollers was undoubtedly known a generation before Arkwright, with whose name the invention is commonly associated, set up his first machine in the house of a Preston schoolmaster. The date of its invention is 1738, for in that year a patent was taken out in the name of Lewis Paul, and the specification explaining the nature and scope of the machine anticipates the vital principles of the water-frame. It states that the sliver " is put between a pair of rollers," and " being turned round by their motion, draws in the

The origin of automatic spinning.

raw mass of wool or cotton to be spun in proportion to the velocity of such rollers. A succession of other rollers, moving proportionately faster than the rest, draw the rope, thread, or sliver, into any degree of fineness that may be required." In addition " the bobbin, spole, or quill, upon which the thread is spun, is so contrived as to draw faster than the first rollers give and in such proportion as the sliver is proposed to be diminished." This description of the machine which bears Paul's name demonstrates that Richard Arkwright, whatever his other merits, was not the original inventor of the mode of spinning by rollers.

Lewis
Paul.

The career of Lewis Paul, the reputed inventor of the first English machine on which thread was ever spun without the aid of human fingers, is obscure. He was the son of a French refugee who settled in this country during an era of religious persecution in France. "We have no information as to his bringing up, but gather from his papers that Lewis led a gay life as a young man, fell into bad company, and to pay his debts mortgaged the valuable property in the parish of St. Bride's which his father had left him. He was evidently on the high road to ruin unless he reformed his habits, and that speedily. He had the courage to break off his connection with his former associates, though by that time his purse was nearly empty; and he proceeded to apply himself to business connected with invention." The only other personal detail worth relating is that he was the friend and correspondent of Dr. Johnson. In his enterprises Paul associated himself with a skilled mechanic, John Wyatt, and the latter has been credited with the real authorship of the invention. This was the expressed belief of Wyatt's descendants, and it was shared by one of the earliest and sanest investigators into the history of the textile inventions. " The merit of conceiving the principle of spinning by rollers," according to Baines, " is the glory of Wyatt." The opposite view awards " the merit and honour of being the sole inventor " to Paul alone, Wyatt having no part in the invention beyond advancing money to his principal and serving in his employment.

The letters and papers of Paul and Wyatt have come to light, and they appear to show that Paul was the inventor of roller spinning and Wyatt the mechanic who carried out his ideas. A memorandum, in the handwriting of John Wyatt, discovered among his papers, has established this point. " *Thoughts originally Mr. Paul's.*—1. The joining of the rolls. 2. Their passing through cylinders. 3. The calculation of the wheels, by which means the bobbin draws faster than those cylinders. This I presume was picked up somewhere before I knew him." Wyatt only claimed for himself various mechanical improvements which his experience as a trained mechanic would enable him to introduce into Paul's machine. Another piece of evidence is that Paul, who owed Wyatt over £800, undertook to give his assistant the plan which he himself was using for " erecting, making, and perfecting proper machines or engines and spindles for the spinning of wool or cotton." Wyatt also received the right to set up 300 spindles for the spinning of wool or cotton " according to the new invention of Lewis Paul," and the contract contains this significant passage: " The said Lewis Paul shall and will give unto the said John Wyatt . . . such further instructions for the erecting, making, and perfecting of the machines or engines and spindles as shall be requisite and needful for the effectual working and management of the same." This language would seem to admit only of one conclusion—that Paul, not Wyatt, was the inventor of the machine which was the subject of the contract.

A mill was erected at Birmingham (1738-1743), and another mill was afterwards started at Northampton with money furnished by Cave, the editor of *The Gentleman's Magazine*. Dyer, in his poem *The Fleece*, alludes to Paul's invention in the following terms: Dyer's description of Paul's machine.

> " We next are shown
> A circular machine of new design,
> In conic shape: it draws and spins a thread
> Without the tedious toil of needless hands.
> A wheel, invisible, beneath the floor,
> To ev'ry member of th' harmonious frame

Gives necessary motion.   One, intent,
O'erlooks the work: the carded wool, he says,
Is smoothly lapp'd around those cylinders,
Which, gently turning, yields it to yon cirque
Of upright spindles, which, with rapid whirl,
Spin out, in long extent, an even twine."

The enterprise was successful at neither place.   Paul was short of capital, and his letters to Wyatt reveal the straits to which he was often reduced in his desperate efforts to raise the necessary funds.   Even Wyatt himself saw for a time the inside of a debtors' prison.   Another reason for Paul's failure to reap the fruits of his inventive genius and to achieve the commercial success which afterwards attended Arkwright's own efforts in the same field was doubtless the imperfect nature of his machine.   Although the principle was identical in both cases, Paul's machine was inferior to his successor's in point of construction.   Harassed by financial cares, deficient perhaps in the priceless virtue of perseverance, at times even sceptical as to the value of the " old gimcracks," as Wyatt contemptuously termed the machines, they failed to show that singular devotion to details which was the true secret of Arkwright's success.

Fate of Paul's invention.   The subsequent fate of Paul's invention has given rise to much controversy.   The problem is whether the invention entirely lapsed, or whether it was revived in the next generation.   The claims of two inventors have been upheld, the one Richard Arkwright, the other Thomas Highs, a reed-maker of Leigh.   In the absence of authentic information we must content ourselves with stating the various alternatives, one of which must contain the solution of the problem.   It is possible that the knowledge of Paul's invention came to the ears of either Highs or Arkwright, and that one or the other constructed a machine on its principles; and it is possible, again, that one of them conceived the idea of roller spinning independently, rediscovering a secret which had been forgotten.   The most favourite theory is that Arkwright was indebted in some way or other to Highs; he may have stolen the idea fullfledged, or may have obtained some hints from Kay, a clockmaker, who was in Highs's confidence. The latter hypothesis has been stated after this fashion: " Arkwright was set to think of roller spinning by what he had heard of Highs's experiment, and did not scruple to borrow some hints from Kay. At the same time his rollers may have been altogether different from Highs's—workable while Highs's were unworkable—and Arkwright may fairly claim to be the virtual, though not the actual, inventor of roller spinning." But it is necessary to repeat that all these hypotheses are in the main pure conjecture, and are never likely to be satisfactorily determined. One thing alone is certain: the successful application of automatic spinning was the work of Arkwright.

Richard Arkwright, one of the greatest " captains of industry " in this country, and the most prominent figure in the history of the textile industries, was born at Preston in 1732. He was the youngest of thirteen children, and the impoverished circumstances of his parents threw him at an early age upon the world with none of the advantages of education to help him in the struggle for existence. He was apprenticed to a barber, and settled in Bolton, where he obtained some reputation for his skill as a wig-maker. He had no knowledge of mechanics, and no practical acquaintance with industrial processes, but he had a quick, alert mind, an insatiable curiosity, and a genius for assimilating and developing the ideas of others. His natural gifts more than compensated for any deficiency of technical training, and he showed marked determination in pursuing his opportunities to the utmost. Among the manufacturers in whose midst Arkwright lived the shortage of yarn must have been a constant topic of conversation, and the wealth which awaited the fortunate discoverer of a new process fired the imagination of the poverty-stricken wig-maker. He was drawn irresistibly to mechanical experiments, and chance threw him, about the year 1767, in the path of a clock-maker, Kay,[1] whom he employed to construct his apparatus. It is possible that Kay communicated to him the nature of Highs's machine—this point, as we have said,

Richard Ark- wright.

---

[1] Not to be confused with the inventor of the fly shuttle.

has never been satisfactorily cleared up—or perhaps Arkwright had heard rumours of the factory at Northampton and stumbled by accident upon the secret of Paul's invention. In any case, whether his knowledge was the fruit of his own ingenuity or the reward of a dishonourable ruse, Arkwright came into possession of the secret which was destined to revolutionise the textile industries and create the factory system.

Difficulties of the inventor.

Arkwright had now reached the first milestone along the road which was to lead him to fame and fortune; but to achieve his goal took him many years of unwearied application and devoted labour. He was almost penniless, and his poverty is shown by the story that on the occasion of a " great election " at Preston, " the wardrobe of the future knight was in so tattered a condition that a number of persons subscribed to put him into decent plight to appear at the poll-room." He enlisted the practical sympathy of a friend, Mr. John Smalley, a liquor merchant and house-painter, whose faith in Arkwright's machine led him to open his purse-strings and provide the necessary means. The machine was set up in the parlour of the house owned by the head-master of the Preston Free Grammar School, and in this atmosphere of learning the ex-barber pursued his mechanical investigations. Shortly afterwards came the news of the riots in the neighbourhood of Blackburn which had been provoked by Hargreaves's spinning jenny, and Arkwright and Smalley, fearing to draw upon themselves the attentions of the machine-wreckers, removed to Nottingham. Here they entered into partnership with two manufacturers, Mr. Samuel Need and Mr. Jedediah Strutt, and thus secured the valuable help of experienced business men whose abundant command of capital completely solved the pecuniary problem. In 1769 Arkwright took out a patent for his machine, and this event marked the second milestone in his career. Yet his difficulties were not at an end; indeed, throughout his lifetime Arkwright was engaged in one long struggle against adverse circumstances; there was for him no royal road to success, and whatever our opinion of his methods we cannot but admire

the undaunted resolution with which he pursued his goal in
the face of all the obstacles which harassed his course. Of
these obstacles the least formidable was the hostility of
the working classes, although in an outburst of popular
fury they destroyed his mill at Chorley in 1779. More
serious was the persistent hostility of his industrial rivals,
those in Lancashire even refusing to buy his yarn in spite
of its superior quality. "It was not," he afterwards
declared, "till upwards of five years had elapsed after his
first patent and more than £12,000 had been expended in
machinery and building that any profit accrued to himself
and his partners." His chief difficulties, however, arose
from the infringement of his patent rights. Every successful inventor has been the victim of unscrupulous attempts
to rob him of the fruits of his enterprise, and Arkwright
was no exception to the rule. He was driven to defend
himself in a court of law (1785), and obtained judgment in
his favour. The verdict caused a great sensation among
his fellow-manufacturers, who had installed his machinery
in their factories without taking the precaution of securing
Arkwright's permission, and they made a vigorous effort to
secure a reversal of the judgment. A few months later a
fresh trial was held. Highs and Kay came forward to
swear that Arkwright was not the inventor of the machines
which were patented in his name; the widow and son of
Hargreaves swore that the improvements in the carding
machine were the work of Hargreaves—we now know that
Arkwright was, as he claimed, the author of these improvements about which Hargreaves was informed by one of
Arkwright's workmen—but the decisive factor in the case
was Arkwright's own fatal admission that the specification
of his patent was obscure. Every patentee is required by
law to draw up a specification "particularly describing and
ascertaining the nature of his invention and in what manner
the same is to be performed," in order that anyone may
know how to use the patent when the copyright has expired.
The specification in which Arkwright described his machines
was admittedly obscure. He endeavoured to justify his
action on the ground that he desired to preserve his secret

from foreigners, but the general opinion was that he was more concerned to protect it from his fellow-countrymen, and judgment was given for the defendants. As a result the patent was cancelled, and the water-frame, together with the carding machine, became the common property of the manufacturing world. The story is told that after his defeat Arkwright overheard one of his opponents say: " Well, we've done the old shaver at last !" To this the ex-barber rejoined: " I'll find a razor in Scotland to shave you all with yet," and entered into negotiations with David Dale, afterwards the father-in-law of Robert Owen, for the erection of mills at New Lanark. The story may be untrue —the details at least are not perfectly accurate—but it is not impossible that Arkwright's fertile imagination had conceived the ambitious project of dethroning Lancashire from her dominant position in the cotton industry, and making Lanark, as he said, " the Manchester of Scotland."

His success. In spite of his failure to drive his fellow-manufacturers from the field which his enterprise had opened up, Arkwright achieved both fame and fortune. In 1786 he received a knighthood at the hands of George III., and the following year was made High Sheriff of Derbyshire. " Wealth flowed in upon him with a full stream," for he not only reaped a rich harvest by the sale of his machines before his patent rights were cancelled, but he entered into several partnerships which gave him a controlling interest in numerous concerns where his unrivalled skill in business, shrewd judgment, and remarkable faculty for organisation enjoyed abundant scope. In this direction, indeed, lies his real merit and his permanent contribution to the stock of economic ideas. He was not an inventor of the first rank, for he did not originate the process of spinning by rollers, the pivot of all his other achievements; but he knew how to turn the inventions of others to practical account; possessing the inventive faculty, he was able to develop and bring to perfection the germs of the great ideas contained in the rude, imperfect machines which he used as the basis for his own creations. Above all he was the founder of the factory system; not indeed that he erected the first

factory in England,[1] but he built up great business enterprises which formed the model for similar undertakings in
every part of the country.   In co-ordinating all the various
parts of his vast industrial structures; in organising and
disciplining large bodies of men, so that each man fitted
into his niche and the whole acted with the mechanical
precision of a trained army; in carrying on under the same
roof all the manifold processes involved in the preparation
and spinning of yarn; in combining division of labour with
effective supervision from a common centre, Arkwright
displayed the qualities of a master-mind and inaugurated
a new epoch.

The character of Richard Arkwright as a man is portrayed
in the following sketch based upon the evidence of contemporaries: " The most marked traits in the character of
Arkwright were his wonderful ardour, energy, and perseverance.   He commonly laboured in his multifarious
concerns from five o'clock in the morning till nine at night;
and when considerably more than fifty years of age—feeling
that the defects of his education placed him under great
difficulty and inconvenience in conducting his correspon-
dence and in the general management of his business—he
encroached upon his sleep in order to gain an hour each
day to learn English grammar, and another hour to improve
his writing and orthography !   He was impatient of whatever interfered with his favourite pursuits; and the fact is
too strikingly characteristic not to be mentioned, that he
separated from his wife not many years after their marriage
because she, convinced that he would starve his family by
scheming when he should have been shaving, broke some
of his experimental models of machinery.   Arkwright was a
severe economist of time; and that he might not waste
a moment he generally travelled with four horses and
at a very rapid speed.   His concerns in Derbyshire, Lancashire, and Scotland were so extensive and numerous as
to show at once his astonishing power of transacting business and his all-grasping spirit.   In many of these he had
partners, but he generally managed in such a way that,

Character of Arkwright.

[1] See above, p. 49.

whoever lost, he himself was a gainer. So unbounded was his confidence in the success of his machinery and in the national wealth to be produced by it that he would make light of discussions on taxation, and say that *he* would pay the national debt ! His speculative schemes were vast and daring; he contemplated entering into the most extensive mercantile transactions and buying up all the cotton in the world in order to make an enormous profit by the monopoly: and from the extravagance of some of these designs his judicious friends were of opinion that, if he had lived to put them in practice, he might have overset the whole fabric of his prosperity."[1]

Description of the water-frame. The leading feature of the water-frame was the use of rollers. The roving was inserted between a pair of rollers placed in a horizontal position, one above the other. These rollers revolved in contact, and as they revolved they compressed and drew the roving from the bobbins. Another pair of rollers, which revolved five times as fast, received the roving from the first pair, and their rapid revolutions reduced the thick roving into a fine thread. A twist was imparted to the thread by means of revolving spindles with which the roving was connected as it was drawn out of the second pair of rollers. The first machine erected by Arkwright at Nottingham was turned by horses. This proved an expensive method, and in order to utilise the resources of water-power Arkwright built a mill at Cromford in Derbyshire, which was worked by a water-wheel and was therefore called the " water-frame."[2]

Other inventions of Arkwright. The machine patented in 1769 was adapted only for the final process of spinning—namely, to convert the rovings into yarn; the first process, turning the sliver into rovings, was still done by hand. A few years later (1775) Arkwright patented other inventions which enabled all the preliminary operations connected with spinning to be done by machinery. He appears to have been the first to adapt the system of spinning rollers to the process of roving, and for this purpose he invented the roving frame built on the same principle

---

[1] He died in 1792.
[2] After the application of steam it became known as the "throstle."

as the water-frame. He was also the first apparently to
introduce the "drawing" process—a kind of preparatory
spinning intended to straighten the fibres and reduce the
thickness of the roving after it left the roving frame.

Arkwright's most important achievement, after the *The card-ing ma-chine.* water-frame, was a machine for carding by revolving
cylinders instead of hand-cards. The idea was originally
conceived both by Daniel Bourne and Lewis Paul. The
machine which the latter invented was "a horizontal
cylinder covered with parallel rows of cards and turned by
a handle. Under the cylinder was a concave frame, lined
internally with cards exactly fitting the lower half of the
cylinder, so that when the handle was turned the cards of
the cylinder and of the concave frame worked against each
other and carded the wool," the teeth of the cards on the
cylinder and on the concave frame being in close contact.
"This bears the closest resemblance to the modern carding
machine, except that the concave frame is now placed over
the cylinder and in Paul's machine it was under."

The carding machine of Paul had three defects: (1) there
was no "feeder," and the wool was therefore applied to
the cylinder by hand; (2) the machine had to stop while
the cardings were taken off by a movable comb; and (3) a
continuous carding was made by uniting short pieces with
the hand. The first defect, the absence of a feeder, was
removed as the result of an invention (1772) attributed to
John Lees, a Quaker of Manchester. This consisted of a
"perpetual revolving cloth" on which the cotton or wool
was spread, and which fed the cylinder with material. The
main improvement in the carding machine was the work
of Arkwright, who brought to maturity the earlier ideas.
He invented in 1775 the crank and comb—a "plate of
metal, finely toothed at the edge like a comb which, being
worked by a crank in a perpendicular direction, with slight
but frequent strokes on the teeth of the card, stripped off
the cotton in a continuous filmy fleece." A subsequent
improvement (1785) ensured a continuous carding by means
of a comb joined to the cylinder and worked by a crank.
The series of inventions associated with Arkwright's name

thus enabled all the preliminary processes of the cotton and woollen industries to be done by machinery instead of by hand. Henceforth wool could be carded, made into rovings, and spun into yarn, without the aid of human fingers.[1]

James Hargreaves.

The second of the great inventions in the spinning of cotton and wool was the work of James Hargreaves, a weaver of Standhill, near Blackburn. The story runs that he " received the original idea of his machine from seeing a one-thread wheel overturned upon the floor, when both wheel and spindle continued to revolve. The spindle was thus thrown from a horizontal into an upright position, and the thought seems to have struck him that if a number of spindles were placed upright and side by side, several threads might be spun at once." This lucky inspiration gave birth in 1767 to the spinning jenny.

The jenny.

The jenny was a frame, in one part of which was set a row of eight rovings, and in another part a row of eight spindles. The rovings were inserted between two flat pieces of wood, termed a " clove," which opened and shut something like a parallel ruler, and held the roving firm as in a clasp. A portion of each roving was then connected with a spindle, and the clove travelled along the horizontal bars of the frame away from the spindles, drawing out the threads and reducing them to the proper fineness. At the same time the spinner turned a wheel which made the spindles revolve and twist the thread. The clove then returned towards the spindles in order to " cop the weft "— that is, wind the spun yarn upon the spindles.

Its introduction into the woollen manufacture.

The jenny is said to have taken its name from the fact that it performed the work of a female. In the case of cotton the yarn was apparently spun only for weft, but in the woollen industry not only the weft, but also the warp was spun on the jenny. The introduction of the jenny into the woollen manufacture followed closely upon its invention, and it does not appear correct to say that " the great textile inventions did not extend to wool till much later," and that " many years elapsed before the contrivance

[1] The carding machine was in use in the woollen industry by the end of the eighteenth century.

of Hargreaves was applied to spinning wool." The number
of spindles used in the jenny did not remain stationary.
It was found possible for a spinner to take care of 60 or
70, and even as many as 120 spindles at one time, and
wages were trebled in consequence.

The water-frame and the jenny differed in various ways. The water-
In the first place the water-frame, although originally jenny con-
employed to reduce the rovings into yarn, and not to turn trasted.
the slivers into rovings, was subsequently adapted for this
purpose; the jenny was used apparently only for the final
process of spinning. In the second place, the thread spun
on the water-frame was harder, that is, more firmly twisted,
and was suitable for warps, whereas the thread spun on
the jenny was soft, and therefore suitable for weft. In
the third place, the jenny was an implement which the
artisan was able to work in his own cottage with his own
hands. The water-frame was a machine which required
more than human strength to give it motion. The difference
between the jenny and the water-frame thus became the
starting-point of a new economic order. The invention of
the former was compatible with the retention of the domestic
system of industry; the adoption of the latter brought in
its train the establishment of the factory system.

For some time Hargreaves endeavoured to keep the Har-
secret of his machine locked in the breasts of his household. history.
He knew its value, and feared to excite the suspicions of
his neighbours. He used the jenny, therefore, only to
provide weft for the cloth woven at his own loom. But
the noise of his invention was soon bruited abroad; and
an angry mob of spinners, deluded with the notion that
the spinning jenny would rob them of their bread, burst
into Hargreaves's house and wrecked the machine. The
inventor, like Kay in earlier days, was driven from his
native town (1768) and sought refuge in Nottingham; there
he entered into partnership with a joiner who was able to
scrape together enough money to start a small factory.
The business was carried on " with moderate success " until
his death in 1778. Hargreaves had taken out a patent for
the jenny in 1770, but an unfortunate circumstance pre-

vented him from enjoying the fruits of his invention. He
discovered that some of the Lancashire manufacturers were
using his machine without paying for it, and announced his
intention to appeal to the protection of the law. " The
manufacturers thereupon sent a representative to Nottingham with an offer of £3,000 in return for permission to set
up his machine. Hargreaves, however, demanded £7,000,
and at last stood out for £4,000. The negotiations being
broken off, the actions proceeded; but before they came
to trial Hargreaves's attorney was informed that his client,
before leaving Lancashire, had sold some jennies to obtain
clothing for his children (of whom he had six or seven);
and in consequence of this, which was true, the attorney
gave up the actions in despair of obtaining a verdict."
None the less it is satisfactory to know that Hargreaves
was spared the want which is the usual lot of inventors,
and although he did not build up a great fortune, he
was able to leave his wife and children in comfortable
circumstances.

Samuel   Samuel Crompton, the inventor of the mule, first saw
Crompton. light at Firwood, near Bolton, in the year 1753. He was
sixteen years of age when he learnt to spin upon Hargreaves's spinning jenny, and was barely twenty-one when
he started to make improvements, a task which occupied
his leisure moments for the next five years. " As he was
not a regular mechanic," wrote his friend and biographer,
Kennedy, " and possessed only such tools as he purchased
with his little earnings, acquired by labour at the loom or
jenny, and as he had also to learn the use of those simple
tools, we may be justly surprised that even in five years he
succeeded so far as to make his machine practically useful."
His work was carried on under the greatest difficulties, and
in after days he related some of the trials which had befallen
him. " Once when he was at work on the mule he heard
the rioters shouting at the destruction of a building at
' Folds ' (an adjoining hamlet), where there was a carding
engine. Fearing that they would come to the Hall-in-the-
Wood "—this was the name of a decayed mansion where
Crompton lived with his mother—" and destroy his mule,

he took it to pieces and put it into a skip which he hoisted through the ceiling into the attic " by a trap door which he had prepared, apparently in anticipation of a hostile intrusion. At last his patience and ingenuity were rewarded with success, but his triumph only brought with it fresh anxieties, for he was not allowed to enjoy the fruits of his skill in the privacy for which he craved. " He often said that what annoyed him most was that he could not get leave to enjoy his little invention to himself in his garret; for, the product of his machine obtaining a better price than other yarns of those times, a report soon got abroad that he had constructed a new machine for the purpose of improved spinning, and people from the neighbourhood for miles around came and climbed up at the windows to see him at his work. He erected a screen to prevent this, but the annoyance was so great that he could not proceed advantageously with his ingenious labour." He was too poor, or perhaps not enterprising enough, to purchase a patent, and too diffident to protect his invention from prying eyes. He resolved therefore to surrender it to the public. After all, he thought, " a man had a very insecure tenure of a property which another could carry away with his eyes "; and he was not strong enough to resist the importunity of his townsfolk, who promised him a generous reward if he would disclose the secret of his invention. Confiding in their liberal promises, he yielded in a weak moment to their solicitations, but no sooner was his machine in the hands of the manufacturers than he awoke to the cruel deception practised upon him. In exchange for a secret which was worth a fortune to its possessor, the inventor obtained the paltry sum of £106; and many of the manufacturers were so incredibly mean that they not only refused to pay the guinea—this was the highest subscription —or the half-guinea to which they had pledged themselves, but they had the effrontery to denounce Crompton as an impostor, and turn him from their doors when he asked them for payment. This shameful and treacherous conduct rankled permanently in Crompton's mind; an abiding sense of injustice filled his heart with resentment and clouded the rest of his years with gloom.

Crompton, like Edmund Cartwright, whose history we relate elsewhere, was never able to use his inventive genius as a lever with which to raise up great business enterprises. He was not fitted to battle with the world. His shy and retiring disposition was unsuited for the storm and stress of industrial life, and he resented the persecution to which his fame as an inventor subjected him. " To this day," he said, " though it is more than thirty years since my first machine was shown to the public, I am hunted and watched with as much never-ceasing care as if I was the most notorious villain that ever disgraced the human form; and I do affirm that if I were to go to a smithy to get a common nail made, if opportunity offered to the bystanders, they would examine it most minutely to see if it was anything but a nail." In these few words Crompton stands self-revealed; they throw a flood of light upon his shrinking, nervous temperament, explaining his failure to assume his proper station among the industrial captains of his age, and accounting for the striking difference between his own career and that of his fellow-townsman, Richard Arkwright. No greater contrast, indeed, can be conceived in the character and fortunes of men than the contrast between the inventor of the mule and the founder of the factory system. " Crompton's start in life was made from a much more favourable position than Arkwright's. A carefully nurtured only son, his early education was excellent, and during his long life he persevered in acquiring knowledge. He was a good mathematician . . . an accomplished musician." But he lacked " that practical knowledge of the world of men which is essentially necessary for success in any business. This rendered him quite unable to dispose of his yarn and muslins when he had made them, however great their intrinsic value. His naturally shy disposition, moreover, had been increased and his temper injured by cruel injustice. . . . When he attended the Manchester Exchange to sell his yarns or muslins and any rough-and-ready manufacturer ventured to offer him a less price than he had asked, he would invariably wrap up his samples, put them into his pocket, and quietly walk away. He was never either in want or in debt. . . . Utterly averse to speculation, he was well content with a moderate and regular profit." Arkwright, on the other hand, "was turned into the world without education, trained to a servile handicraft, and without a shilling of capital," but possessing " an indomitable energy of purpose, a brazened assurance, an unscrupulous hand to grasp and appropriate the ideas and immature inventions of others, a rude health, and an undaunted spirit for speculation."

After the lapse of thirty years (1780-1812) the friends of Crompton began to press his claims upon the attention of the public. A memorial was signed in his favour by most of the principal manufacturers of the kingdom and received the powerful support of Mr. Perceval, the Chancellor of the Exchequer. Crompton expected, as he deserved, a considerable reward, proportioned to the wealth which had accrued to the country from his ingenuity and perseverance; and the least sum that was considered adequate was £20,000. An evil destiny, however, continued to afflict the unfortunate inventor. " On the eleventh day of May Mr. Crompton was in the lobby of the House of Commons in conversation with Sir Robert Peel and Mr. Blackburne upon the subject of his claim, which was about to be brought forward, when one of these gentlemen remarked: ' Here comes Mr. Perceval.' The group was immediately joined by the Chancellor of the Exchequer, who addressed them with the remark: ' You will be glad to know that we mean to propose twenty thousand pounds for Crompton; do you think that will be satisfactory?' Mr. Crompton did not hear the reply, as from motives of delicacy he left the party and walked down a short stair leading out of the lobby; but before he left it he heard a great rush of people and exclamations that Mr. Perceval had been shot." The assassination of the Chancellor, the act of a madman, fatally impaired Crompton's prospects. Instead of £20,000 he received only £5,000, in spite of evidence that the mule was then giving employment to 70,000 spinners directly and to 150,000 weavers indirectly, and that the number of mule spindles was nearly 5,000,000. In contrast with

Crompton's reward.

the meanness with which it had responded to the claims of
the great inventor, one of the architects of England's
industrial greatness, Parliament in the same session granted
the sum of £50,000 to purchase freehold property as an
endowment for the heirs of the Earl (afterwards Duke) of
Wellington.

Descrip-
tion of the
mule.

Crompton died in 1827, but long before his death the
mule had displaced the water-frame and the jenny. His
invention combined the principles both of Arkwright's and
Hargreaves's machines:

> " The forces of Nature could no further go;
> To make a third she joined the former two."

On the one hand, it had the system of rollers which drew
out and lengthened the rovings; on the other hand, it had
the spindles which imparted the twist. The rovings as
they were drawn out from the bobbins passed through the
rollers to spindles placed on a spindle carriage. The
leading feature of the mule—" the great and important
invention of Crompton," as Kennedy termed it—was this
spindle carriage. Instead of the spindles being stationary,
as in the case of the jenny or the water-frame, they were
erected on a movable carriage or box which ran on wheels.
As the rollers gave out the roving from the bobbins, the
movable carriage—with the spindles in it rotating in order
to twist the thread—receded from the rollers, drawing out
and lengthening the thread. When the rollers had measured
out a sufficient amount of the roving they ceased to revolve
and held the roving fast, while the spindle carriage continued to recede to a distance of 4 to 5 feet. This stretched
the thread to the requisite degree of fineness and imparted
the necessary twist. In order to wind the thread upon the
spindles, the carriage was made to return to its original
position.

Improve-
ments in
the ma-
chine.

Many improvements were afterwards introduced into the
mule as practical experience of the machine brought to
light its deficiencies. " The art of spinning on Crompton's
machine," wrote Kennedy, " was tolerably well known
from the circumstance of the high wages that could be

obtained by those working on it, above the ordinary wages of other artisans, such as shoemakers, joiners, hat-makers, etc., who on that account left their previous em-ployment; and to them might be applied the fable of the town in a state of siege. For, if in the course of their working the machine, there was any little thing out of gear, each workman endeavoured to fill up the deficiency with some expedient suggested by his former trade; the smith suggested a piece of iron, the shoemaker a welt of leather, etc., all which had a good effect in improving the machine." The most important improvement was the work of Richard Roberts, who invented an automatic or self-acting mule (1825). The year in which water-power was applied to the mule was 1790.

The mule produced finer thread than either the jenny or the water-frame. Arkwright's machine in particular was not suited for the finer qualities of yarn, and the yarn was used only for warps. But the mule spun yarn for wefts as well as warps. Hirst, a Yorkshire manufacturer, claims to have been the first to introduce the use of mules into the woollen manufacture. At the present day woollen yarns are always spun on the mule; worsted yarns generally on some modification of the frame or throstle—namely, the " flyer," " cap," and " ring " spinning. Present-day use of the mule and frame.

The introduction of machinery into the manufacture of yarn removed the defects of hand spinning. For one thing machine-spun yarn was more uniform in quality; it was also firmer and stronger; the thread did not break so fre-quently. The weaver used only one-half the quantity of glue required for hand-spun yarn, which was " tenderer " and needed more glue to hold it together. Another result of machinery was to liberate the weaver from his dependency upon the hand-spinner. He was now able to draw upon an unlimited supply of material for his work. The yarn famine was brought to an end and scarcity yielded place to abundance. It was estimated that a jenny could keep two cloth looms at work, a mule perhaps ten looms, and a throstle about the same number. Now that an abundance of material was always at hand, the weaver was able to Advan-tages of machine-spun yarn.

carry on his work with more regularity throughout the year. The source upon which farmers had previously relied for labour in the harvest season—unemployed weavers—dried up, and it is significant to observe the complaints raised in some parts of the country that there was a general lack of labourers. A new problem was thus raised: instead of a shortage of spinners there was now a shortage of weavers, and the invention of machinery in the weaving process seemed imperatively demanded. This was the achievement of Edmund Cartwright.

Edmund Cart-wright.

Edmund Cartwright, the inventor of the power loom[1] and the combing machine, was born in 1743 in the county of Nottinghamshire and educated at Wakefield Grammar School. At fourteen years of age he entered the University of Oxford, where, in due course, he obtained his degree and took holy orders. His own wish to enter the navy was resisted by his parents, and he became instead a curate at Brampton near Chesterfield, and was afterwards presented to a living in Leicestershire. Here he lived a quiet, retired existence, ministering to the medical as well as to the spiritual needs of his parishioners, and employing his leisure moments in writing poems, some of which earned the praise of Sir Walter Scott. A curious chance of fate changed the current of his life and embarked him on an inventor's career. The story can best be told in his own words.

His account of his invention.

" Happening to be at Matlock in the summer of 1784 I fell in company with some gentlemen of Manchester, when the conversation turned on Arkwright's spinning machinery. One of the company observed that as soon as Arkwright's patent expired so many mills would be erected and so much cotton spun that hands could never be found to weave it. To this observation I replied that Arkwright must then set his wits to work to invent a weaving machine. This brought on a conversation on the subject, in which the Manchester gentlemen unanimously agreed that the thing was impracticable; and in defence of their opinion

[1] A loom worked by water power was invented about 1678 by M. de Gennes, but it does not appear to have come into use.

they adduced arguments which I certainly was incompetent to answer or even comprehend, being totally ignorant of the subject, having never at that time seen a person weave. I controverted, however, the impracticability of the thing by remarking that there had lately been exhibited in London an automatic figure which played at chess. ' Now you will not assert, gentlemen,' said I, ' that it is more difficult to construct a machine that shall weave than one which shall make all the variety of moves which are required in that complicated game.'

" Some little time afterwards, a particular circumstance recalling this conversation to my mind, it struck me that, as in plain weaving, according to the conception I then had of the business, there could only be three movements[1] which were to follow each other in succession, there would be little difficulty in producing and repeating them. Full of these ideas I immediately employed a carpenter and smith to carry them into effect. As soon as the machine was finished, I got a weaver to put in the warp, which was of such materials as sail-cloth is usually made of. To my great delight a piece of cloth, such as it was, was the produce. As I had never before turned my thoughts to anything mechanical either in theory or in practice, nor had ever seen a loom at work, or knew anything of its construction, you will readily suppose that my first loom was a most rude piece of machinery. The warp was placed perpendicularly, the reed fell with the weight of at least half a hundredweight, and the springs which threw the shuttle were strong enough to have thrown a Congreve rocket. In short, it required the strength of two powerful men to work the machine at a slow rate, and only for a short time. Considering in my simplicity that I had accomplished all that was required I then secured what I thought a most valuable property, by a patent dated April 4, 1785. This being done I then condescended to see how other people wove, and you will guess my astonishment when I compared their easy modes of operations with

---

[1] The three movements would be: opening the shed, throwing the shuttle, and beating the weft threads together.

mine. Availing myself, however, of what I then saw, I made a loom in its general principles nearly as they are now made.[1] But it was not till the year 1787 that I completed my invention."

Cartwright's faith in his machine was unbounded. With all an inventor's eager enthusiasm, he sought to turn his discovery to practical account. "May you weave your webs of gold," wrote the poet Crabbe to him, but the wish remained unfulfilled, and from the start misfortune dogged the inventor's steps. In 1785 he had become possessed of some property at Doncaster, and here he resolved to establish a weaving and spinning factory for the purpose of pursuing his mechanical experiments. The machine was at first worked by a bull, but afterwards the motive power was supplied by a steam-engine. A few years later (1791) an opportunity arose for the introduction of his loom into the cotton industry. A Manchester firm erected a factory large enough to house 500 power-looms, and a few looms were set to work as an experiment. "These looms worked exceedingly well; they wrought the work for half the amount of wages which they were then paying to hand weavers; the weavers in consequence threatened to destroy the mill, and the owners received anonymous letters to that effect." The threat was soon carried into execution, and the mill was burnt down. As a result Cartwright found himself ruined. "No other manufacturer ventured on repeating so hazardous an experiment"; and the exhaustion of his resources compelled him to close his own works at Doncaster. The fortitude of the inventor in the face of these unexampled disasters is revealed in the following lines, written after the destruction of the factory:

" With sails expanding to the gales of hope,
    My venturous bark pursued her leading star;
  Hers was a voyage of no common scope,
    A voyage of Discovery distant far !
  To bright Invention's intellectual clime,
    In search of useful Arts, 'twas mine to roam.

[1] It differed from the hand-loom in the substitution of mechanical contrivances for the weaver's hands and feet.

I reached the object of my views sublime,
 And richly freighted, bore my cargo home.
My friends expectant fill the crowded strand;
 But ere I gain the shore, what storms arise !
My vessel founders e'en in sight of land !
 And now a wreck upon the beach she lies !
With firm unshaken mind the wreck I see,
Nor think the doom of man should be reversed for me."

It was now too late, wrote his daughter in a memoir of her
father, to return to " that peaceful mode of life and those
literary pursuits in which he had passed the best and happiest
of his years." Undaunted by the setback to his fortunes,
he removed to London, and there carried on with unabated
ardour his mechanical researches. Among other things he
invented geometrical bricks, conceived the project of
making houses fireproof, and assisted Fulton in his invention of steamboats. His fertile genius, restless energy, and
remarkable versatility were displayed in the attention which
he paid even to small matters. " In the most common arts
of his life," his daughter tells us, " he could seldom abstain
from attempting some contrivance to reduce manual
labour." In his own house bread was made by a machine;
he invented a three-furrow plough, and received the gold
medal of the Board of Agriculture for an Essay on Manures,
and a silver medal for an Essay on the Culture of Potatoes.
His greatest achievement, after the invention of the power-
loom, was the construction of a combing machine about
which we shall speak presently.

Although Cartwright's discoveries were destined to confer His later
inestimable benefit upon the textile industries, the inventor career.
himself reaped only a harvest of disappointments. In 1801
he presented a petition to Parliament for the extension of
his patent rights, and in it he records how " hitherto the
labour of many anxious years, fruitful in benefit to the
public, hath brought him no other reward than barren
reputation, accompanied by ruined fortunes, a situation
bitterly aggravated by his having been obliged to behold
many scandalous invasions of his property without the
means of resistance." " The whole of his actual loss from
prosecuting his mechanical inventions," he said, " much

exceeds the sum of £30,000." The appeal was granted by
a special Act of Parliament, but the renewal of his patent
rights brought him no pecuniary gain. A few years later
(1809) a memorial was presented to the Government in
his favour by some influential citizens of Manchester, and
he received a grant of £10,000 " for the good service he
had rendered the public by his invention of weaving."
He was now sixty-six years of age, and with the money
bought a small farm in Kent, where he occupied the last
years of his life with experiments in agriculture, chemistry,
and mechanics; a " portly, dignified old gentleman of the
last generation " (so a friend of the family describes him),
" grave and polite, but full of humour and spirit." He
enjoyed the respect of his contemporaries and retained to
the last (1823) the sanguine temperament, buoyant spirits,
and restless activity of mind which had proved impervious
to the sharpest stings of adversity. He had resigned himself to the disappointment of his ambitious hopes—

> " To fame and to fortune adieu !
> The toils of ambition are o'er;
> Let folly these phantoms pursue,
> I now will be cheated no more "—

yet in his eightieth year he could write:

> " With mind unwearied still will I engage,
> In spite of failing vigour and of age,
> Nor quit the conflict till I quit the stage."

The trials of an inventor.   One reason for Cartwright's failure to convert his discoveries into a source of pecuniary profit was the imperfect
nature of his machines as they were first given to the world,
but another reason was the difficulty of protecting his
patents against infringement. The trials and disappointments of an inventor are expressed with humour by Cartwright himself in a letter written shortly before his death.
" A patent is a feeble protection against the rapacity,
piracy, and theft of too many of the manufacturing class.
There is scarcely an instance, I believe, of a patent being
granted for any invention of real value, against which
attempts have not been made to overthrow or evade it.

It might be supposed that whatever was confessedly original, and which had never been heard or thought of before, would have some chance to escape the attacks of the invader. No such thing. Were that eminent surgeon and anatomist, Mr. Carpue, who, it is said, has lately furnished some of his patients with supplementary noses, to discover a method of putting an additional pair of eyes into a man's head, and to take out a patent for the discovery, I should not be surprised if forty witnesses were to come forward to swear that it was not a new invention ' for that they had seen forty people with forty extra pairs of eyes in their heads forty years ago.' "

In his construction of a combing machine Cartwright seems to have been guided by the same principle which underlies the mechanism of the power-loom: to imitate as closely as possible the movements of the hand, but to substitute a mechanical force for manual labour. The principal operations involved in hand-combing, as we have seen above, were threefold: (1) filling the comb with wool; (2) combing out the " noil "; and (3) drawing off the sliver of " top." These operations were reproduced in Cartwright's combing machine. The wool was passed through an oscillating frame, which was governed by a crank action, over and into the teeth of a circular comb revolving horizontally. " As this comb slowly revolves it gradually becomes filled by a succession of tufts of wool lashed in from the frame, the fringe [or " beard "] of the tufts so held is carried round till it passes under the working comb, which also traverses by a crank motion across the face of the [holding] comb, inserting the points of its teeth into the fringe, and so—combing out the noil and refuse as the [holding] comb passes round—it brings the fringe in contact with the drawing-off rollers, which draw out the sliver of top, leaving the noil behind in the chambers of the comb; the sliver is then carried forward through the conducting rollers into the receiving can below." Cartwright's invention earned for him the title of the " new Bishop Blaize "— the patron saint of the wool-combers—and his machine was known as " Big Ben." In honour of " Big Ben " a song was composed by one of Cartwright's workmen:

Cartwright's combing machine.

" Come all ye master-combers, and hear of new Big Ben,
　He'll comb more wool in one day than fifty of your men,
　With their hand-combs and comb-pots and such old-
　　fashion'd ways;
　There'll be no more occasion for old Bishop Blaize."

The machine did not prove a satisfactory substitute for
hand-combing. It was introduced into Bradford in 1794,
where it was worked by a horse, but the experiment was
unsuccessful and was not repeated.

Cart-
wright's
successors.
The genius of Edmund Cartwright pointed the way, but
fifty years were to elapse before the combing machine
attained practical value and the requisite degree of perfection. Within a century of Cartwright's own invention
the number of patents taken out in connection with combing machines was nearly five hundred, and this affords
remarkable proof of the industry and zeal with which a
long line of inventors applied themselves to the problem.
It is possible here to mention only the achievements of
Heilmann, Donisthorpe, Lister, Holden, and Noble, but
we must not forget the host of fellow-workers whose patient
experiments rendered practicable the creative ideas of these
master-minds.

Josué
Heilmann.
Josué Heilmann was born in Alsace in the year 1796.
Smiles has related the story, for the truth of which we
have independent authority, how he first conceived the idea
enabling him to solve a problem which had baffled the
efforts of two generations. He was sitting by his hearth;
and, " meditating upon the hard fate of inventors and the
misfortunes in which their families so often become involved,
he found himself almost unconsciously watching his
daughters combing their long hair and drawing it out at
full length between their fingers. The thought suddenly
struck him that if he could successfully imitate in a machine
the process of combing out the longest hair, and forcing
back the short by reversing the action of the comb, it might
serve to extricate him from his difficulty." Acting upon
this inspiration, he was able to devise a fundamental improvement in the mechanism of the combing machine. To
understand the importance of Heilmann's achievement we

must first grasp the defects of the existing methods of hand-combing and the machines built on its principles.

"In the process of washing the staples of wool become The Nip machine. of course separated and the fibres crossed in all directions; when the comber, therefore, lashed the wool into the holding comb, the subsequent strain of working or drawing out would cause these crossed fibres to coil round the teeth of the holding comb and so ensure a firmer holding of the mass—and, indeed, it was necessary that it should be so held or the action of the working comb would draw it entirely out of the teeth—but the consequence was that when the operative came to draw out the end that had been worked, the other end became so firmly fixed that it could only be extracted by breaking a considerable portion of the long fibres; by this means the noil or refuse was greatly increased, and the most valuable part of the wool—*i.e.*, the top—in the same proportion diminished."

To avoid these evils Heilmann adopted the principle known as the Nip. "By means of two nipping instruments which closed upon the fleece as it was being fed into the machine, the point end was held in position till it was combed out by a revolving drum furnished with comb teeth; the cleaned end was then carried forward and taken hold of by another pair of nippers, till the other end had been treated in a similar manner. The same process was repeated again and again. By this gentle treatment the loss sustained under the old system was avoided."

Heilmann did not live to enjoy his triumph. His efforts to protect his patent rights against the depredations of unscrupulous manufacturers involved him in costly lawsuits, and when fortune at length smiled upon him he was already a stricken man. He died in 1848, but his last moments were not denied the consciousness that he had wrested out of the dark recesses of the Unknown the coveted secret of the wool-combing machine, an achievement which gives him an enduring place among the creators of modern industry.

While the Alsatian inventor was working out his ideas two English inventors, Donisthorpe and Lister, were striving

Donis-
thorpe and
Lister.

towards the same goal, and they reached independently
somewhat similar results. " Before Mr. Heilmann's patent
was heard of," Lister has affirmed, " we had succeeded in
mastering all the difficulties connected with the invention."
Donisthorpe was the first to conceive the project, and his
machine was the starting-point of Lister's subsequent
improvements. Afterwards the two men collaborated, and
the Nip machine (1851) was the product of their combined
investigations. Like other inventors, Lister did not
" achieve success at a bound." " In the year 1842," he
afterwards related, " I was a young man with comparatively
small means—being a fourth son—whatever brains I had.
I then turned my attention to wool-combing, and took my
first lesson from Mr. Donisthorpe. But then unfortunately
Mr. Donisthorpe, like all the earlier inventors of wool-
combing machinery—like the learned and clever Mr. Cartwright—had been ruined; somehow or other it happened
that they all got a white elephant which ate them up.
Being young and foolish I bought a white elephant myself;
I bought it from Mr. Donisthorpe, who was very anxious
to part with it. After I had trotted it about, asking every-
body to buy it, or accept it for nothing, and being at last
in danger of being eaten up by it, I set determinedly to
work to see if I could not bring the beast into order. The
fact was the machine was not in a fit state to present to
anybody—it would not work." Genius has been defined
as an infinite capacity for taking pains, and the first condition of a successful invention is immeasurable patience
and devotion to details. This devotion Lister displayed
in an abundant degree, and after many experiments he
tasted the sweets of success in designing a machine which
" would work." His reward was proportionate to the
merits of his achievement. His machine was widely
adopted, and for the use of each machine he obtained a
royalty of £1,000.

Lister's
machine.

" The three difficulties which Lister and Donisthorpe
had to overcome," Burnley has pointed out, " were: (1) to
comb perfectly; (2) to prevent ' clogging ' in the process;
and (3) to reduce the proportion of ' noil ' or waste in the

course of the operation. When they took the matter in hand there was no machine existing that answered all these requirements—but ultimately they arrived at the Nip machine in which the tuft of wool was drawn by a nipper " —a pair of curved metal jaws—" through a gill comb. They drew the wool through the teeth " of the great circle " horizontally, while Heilmann drew the teeth through the wool in a circle—*i.e.*, worked the ends of the wool by a circular carder." Heilmann's machine was adopted in Germany, and the patent rights for England were purchased by Lister in order to keep the field in England for his own machine.

Isaac Holden, another outstanding figure in the history of the worsted industry, was born in Scotland in 1807. *Isaac Holden.* In his boyhood he worked in a cotton factory, where he acquired a taste for industrial pursuits; but his father, imbued with his countrymen's passion for learning, was anxious that the boy should receive a good education, and eventually he became a schoolmaster. He did not remain long in this profession. He was thrilled with the romance of industry, and we are told that " as he read the accounts of the marvellous developments which invention was working in the field of industrial enterprise he was fired with an intense longing to take his part in the great mechanical achievements that were going forward." His opportunity came to him in the offer of a post as book-keeper in the firm of Townend Brothers of Allingworth, near Bradford, and he gladly embraced it. He was able now to indulge his natural bent for mechanical research, and he threw himself into his work with unsparing ardour and zeal. All his leisure was devoted to working out improvements in the machinery, and the good results which he achieved attracted the notice of his employers, who eventually raised him to the position of manager, and afterwards made him a partner in the firm. Ambitious to solve a problem which was taxing the ingenuity of his contemporaries to the utmost, Holden turned his attention to wool-combing, and in collaboration with Lister designed the combing machine known as the Square Motion.

The
Square
Motion.The principles of the Square Motion can best be described
in Holden's own words. The fault of earlier working combs
(the screw gill working comb) " was that the comb was
pushed away too slowly by the screw after it entered the
beard "—the beard is the fringe of the fibres of wool—
" close to the circular comb-head. The consequence was
that the comb was locked in the beard if it entered it near
the comb-head; and therefore, to avoid this, it was necessary
to strike into it at some distance, and even then to use
coarse and strong combs. The result was bad combing.
This evil, I felt certain, could be avoided by the mode of
working I conceived of—the Square Motion—viz., striking
a fine comb into the beard *near to the comb-head and at once
pushing it away from it* to avoid locking. The whole secret
of the invention lay in this discovery—the necessity of
pushing away quickly, so simple at first sight, but difficult
to conceive and appreciate at that early period; and though
so apparently simple it was the result of much continued
thought." This description serves to elucidate the two
cardinal principles of the Square Motion machine. (1) On
the one hand, the teeth of the working comb are made to
enter the fibres of wool at the exact point where the ends
of the fibres are held in position by the circular comb in order
to leave as little uncombed wool or noil as possible. (2) But,
on the other hand, no sooner are the teeth of the working
comb inserted in the teeth of the circular comb than they
are instantaneously withdrawn, in order to prevent the
locking of the combs and consequent breakage of the
fibres. It is claimed for the Square Motion machine that
" it is a perfect imitation of the mode of working of the
hand-comber, and the work it accomplishes resembles that
of the hand-comber. It produces the same polish, the same
curl or crochet, the same softness and loftiness, and the
same high spinning qualities, the length of fibre in top and
noil being well preserved."

James
Noble.One last invention needs to be mentioned. In 1853
James Noble, a working mechanic, took out a patent for
the machine which bears his name. It was designed on
novel principles and discarded the features of the Nip

machine, in which the combing was "largely done by mechanism external to the circle." Noble conceived the idea of two circles—a circular revolving comb carrying the wool, and a circular working comb inside the revolving comb. His machine was "a compact, circular structure in which the main circle stands at a height of about 2 feet from the ground. Inside this circle are two smaller ones, about a foot and a half in diameter, each touching the main circle at opposite points on the interior of its circumference. All rotate in one direction. The slivers of wool to be combed are rolled up in creels attached to the outer side of the great circle and travelling with it. They move up automatically in turn, and fall on to the pins of the circles at the points where the outer one touches the two inner ones. A brush, rising and falling rapidly, dabs the wool down among the two sets of pins, and there true combing begins." The Noble machine is in general use in England; the Square Motion machine in France and at the works of Holden in Bradford; and the Heilmann machine in Germany.

CHAPTER V

THE INTRODUCTION OF MACHINERY

Survival of the Domestic System in Yorkshire. IT is often assumed that the introduction of machinery forthwith created the factory system and extinguished the domestic system. This view needs to be very much qualified. The factory owners—for example, Benjamin Gott—undoubtedly made their appearance very early in the nineteenth century. They were recruited partly from the ranks of successful clothiers who bought machinery and started mills, but mainly from the class of merchants who were already responsible for the finishing processes,[1] and now turned manufacturers, taking over from the clothier all the earlier processes. None the less, the domestic system held its ground successfully among the "working clothiers" of the West Riding even beyond the middle of the nineteenth century, and as late as 1856 only about one-half of those engaged in the woollen industry in Yorkshire were employed in factories. The reasons for the survival of the domestic system in Yorkshire are twofold. In the first place, the adoption of the power-loom in the woollen industry was very gradual. In 1835 Yorkshire contained only 688 power-looms for woollen weaving, or less than one-fourth of the number used in worsted weaving. The slow introduction of the power-loom can be explained on technical grounds. The essential characteristic of woollen cloth is its felting property, which enables the fibres to be interlaced; and on this account woollen yarn must be spun more loosely. This made weaving a more difficult operation, since the threads were easily broken, and the power-loom, therefore, worked no faster than the hand-loom the shuttle flying about forty times a minute, whereas the worsted power-loom made 160 "picks" a minute. In

[1] See above, pp. 67, 79.

this technical peculiarity we may find one of the main
causes of the survival of the domestic system in the woollen
industry during the first half of the nineteenth century.
In the second place, the small clothiers showed considerable
powers of adaptation to circumstances.   In place of resisting
the new conditions of production, they turned them to their
own account.   The fly shuttle was adopted earlier in
Yorkshire than elsewhere; and, recognising the advantages
of machinery, the domestic manufacturers now combined
their resources in order to obtain machines for their own
use.   The numerous woollen mills scattered throughout the
West Riding were said to be chiefly owned by groups of
clothiers, holding in shares.   The following is a description
of these joint-stock woollen mills written by an inspector
of factories in 1843:

" The history of Joint-Stock Company Woollen Mills
exhibits a singular instance of energy amongst the smaller
capitalists of the manufacturing districts.   In the earlier
periods of the woollen manufacture, the wool was scribbled
and carded at home, then spun and woven, and afterwards
carried to the fulling mills to full, and then returned and
sold in the balk[1] state.   The next step was the employment
of power by asses, horses, and air, to scribble the wool
by their machinery, which soon, however, merged into
water-power, scribbling machines being added to the power
which fulled the cloth.   These fulling, and afterwards
fulling and scribbling, mills were everywhere situated on the
banks of streams, as the rivers Aire, Wharf, and Calder,
but particularly on the River Aire, the sites of many of
which are of very ancient date.   Leeds, Bradford, Shipley,
and the neighbourhood of Dewsbury are all places where
these ancient fulling mills were to be found.   When steam
became a moving power, and was employed in the woollen
manufacture, the mills were first erected in the neighbourhood of towns, and being a more available power than water
generally, and less liable to stoppages, the current of manufacture was directed to towns from the country districts.
One can easily imagine this on looking at the rapid strides

(margin note: Joint-Stock Woollen Mills.)

---

[1] Unfinished.

which were made in Yorkshire in a very short space of time—from about 1810 to 1830—and that the old fulling mills became not only inconvenient on account of the distances at which they were situated from the clothiers, but an absolute loss, owing to the loss of time which was occasioned by the transit of goods to and from the mill. It was customary, for instance, for carts to come as many as twelve miles into the clothing district for wool three times a week, which wool had to be brought first into the district from neighbouring towns; then it had to return, scribbled, to be spun and woven; then it had to be re-sent to the mill to be fulled, and then returned to be prepared for the market, and, lastly, to be sent to the market for sale. The inconvenience of all this need not be further pointed out, nor the difficulty of getting the work done within the specified time, especially for particular trades, which require goods to be shipped to a day; and hence the clothiers of certain country districts, such as Paisley, Idle, Ecclesfield, Botley, Dewsbury, etc., put their heads together, and subsequently their purses, to overcome these difficulties, and, by erecting mills at home, to scribble their own wool and full their own cloth without the cost of labour of so much carriage and dependence upon variable circumstances. The erection of the steam-engine in towns paved the way for their erection in the country, and as coal was near and plentiful, these difficulties were very readily overcome. The first company mill near Leeds was erected at Stanningley, about thirty years ago, by a few persons who ultimately got into difficulties and were dissolved. The second was commenced at Ecclesfield, the third at Paisley, and they have been continued to be erected until there are more company mills now than work can be found for. In the formation of a company mill a number of clothiers (for they must be clothiers to be partners) of small capital meet together and determine to become a company of so many partners, from ten to fifty, in shares generally of £25 each, each person taking as many shares as his capital will enable him. . . . With this subscribed capital deeds of partnership are drawn, land is bought, a mill erected,

and machinery put up. . . . The processes which are
carried on in these company mills are scribbling, carding,
slubbing, and fulling cloth, which are the preparatory
processes of the cloth manufacture, and the remaining
processes—viz., spinning, warping, weaving, and burling—
are done at home by members of the family or by persons
employed for that purpose." The wool was sent to the
mill to be scribbled and slubbed, then returned to the
clothier, in whose home it was spun on the jenny and woven
on the hand-loom, again sent to the mill to be fulled, and
afterwards sold in an unfinished state to the merchant,
who dyed and finished it ready for use.

Outside the ranks of the West Riding clothiers the intro- Advan-
duction of machinery in the woollen and worsted industries disadvan-
aroused violent opposition. "Who does not consider the tages of
employment of machinery," asked a writer in *The Union* ery.
Pilot, "one of the greatest evils that ever befell the
country? And who would not rejoice at a return to the
rude habits of industry which once characterised the country, and under whose sway Englishmen were healthy,
happy, and contented?" It would be a mistake to regard
this hostility as wholly unreasonable, although the benefits
of machinery were undoubtedly considerable. In the first
place, it effected a great economy of labour, cheapened the
price of commodities, stimulated the demand, and so
ultimately led to increased production and expansion of
trade. In the second place, it enabled work which was
often unpleasant and unhealthy to be done by motive
power instead of by hand. "I think the most beneficial
consequences have resulted from the introduction of
machinery, particularly to the scribblers. The scribblers
need to work in bodies, and very close together, and on
wool that from the oil and smell became quite obnoxious.
They were a poor, sickly, decrepit race of beings." Hand-
loom weaving itself was not necessarily an unhealthy occupation, although weavers prior to the introduction of the
fly shuttle were liable to breast disorders, but it was tedious
and laborious. In the third place, most of the work done
in the textile industries was already mechanical in character

even before the use of mechanical devices. The processes
of carding, combing, spinning, weaving, and dressing, consisted in the monotonous repetition of certain movements
of the hand, and afforded little or no scope for that expression of individuality which is the justification of true craftsmanship. And, finally, the creation of factories, if it
subjected the worker to a novel and strict discipline, had
its compensation in the shorter and more regular hours
which were ultimately imposed by the State,[1] and it was
preferable that the preparatory processes, at any rate,
should be carried on in large, airy buildings, as they were
later, rather than in crowded tenements, where the same
room had often to serve as workshop and living place. On
the other hand, the invention of machinery meant a great
displacement of labour. The apologists for machinery
contended at the time, and the argument has been repeated
ever since, that machinery creates in the long run a demand
for more labour than is, at the moment, displaced. The
expansion of industry, resulting from the cheapening of
production, causes many more hands to be employed than
when commodities are hand-made and relatively dear.
Thus Dyer, speaking of Paul's invention, bade the spinners
not to lose heart:

" Nor hence, ye nymphs, let anger cloud your brows;
  The more is wrought, the more is still requir'd."

In this connection it is fair to remember two things. In
the first place, the belief was widespread among the woollen
operatives that the sources of our wool-supply were strictly
limited,[2] and therefore that there was no possibility of a
great extension of the woollen manufacture, accompanied
by an increase in the amount of employment. The poten-
tialities of Australia as a wool-producing country were
practically unknown at the end of the eighteenth century,
although one or two men in England and Australia had a
vision of the future.[3] In the second place, it was no con-

---

[1] For this reason employers found it to their interest to let the
work be done at home as much as possible.

[2] See below, p. 191.

[3] Sir Joseph Banks, President of the Royal Society, and Captain
Macarthur. See below, p. 217.

solation to a man whose skill, his sole property, was rendered useless by a new machine, to be told that at some distant date there would be an increased amount of employment in his industry. A contemporary writer[1] correctly understood the position when he pointed out that " it is not sufficient to say everything will find its proper level, and if the people are deprived of one particular mode of employment they will find another." In some cases, no doubt, those who were displaced in one branch of industry were able to find employment in another. " When the scribbling machine was introduced there was a great clamour against it. The manufacturers told the scribblers that they should have much better employment, and they have been thrown into different employments, such as spinning. They used to earn eight or nine shillings a week in the noisome work; now they are dispersed on different parts of the manufacture, they earn seventeen, eighteen shillings, or a guinea a week; they are now clean and neat, and fit to associate with others in the neighbourhood. It is known to all the neighbourhood that there is a difference in their appearance and comfort." In other cases the introduction of machinery spelt disaster for the workers. Take, for example, Eden's account of the condition of a village in Wiltshire, Seend, in the year 1796: " As the chapelry consists almost entirely of dairy farms, and consequently affords very little employment in husbandry, except during the hay harvest, the labouring poor are very dependent on the neighbouring towns, where the cloth manufacture is carried on; but unfortunately, since the introduction of machinery which lately took place, hand-spinning has fallen into disuse, and for these two reasons the clothier no longer depends on the poor for the yarn which they formerly spun for him at their own homes, as he finds that fifty persons (to speak within compass), with the help of machines, will do as much work as five hundred without them; and the poor, from the great reduction in the price of spinning, scarcely have the heart to earn the little that is obtained by it." As regards hand-loom weavers they have been censured for clinging

---

[1] Anstie (1803).

to a dying industry instead of entering the factories, but the opportunities for employment in factories were more restricted than is commonly supposed. The machines were often tended by women and children, whose labour was cheaper and more docile, and it was not always easy for men to escape destitution by becoming factory hands even when they were willing to do so.

Adoption of mechanical inventions: (i.) The Fly Shuttle. We have now to describe the adoption of mechanical inventions in the woollen and worsted industries.

1. *The Fly Shuttle.*—The earliest of the textile inventions, the fly shuttle, was used by the West Riding clothiers in Kay's own lifetime,[1] but in the West Country its introduction was very gradual. Dyer, whose poem was published in 1757, assumes that two weavers are still necessary to work the broad loom.

> " If the broader mantle be the task
> He chooses some companion to his toil."

Adam Smith in *The Wealth of Nations*, published in 1776, noted " three very capital improvements " in the woollen industry—namely, the substitution of the spinning wheel for the rock and spindle, the use of fulling mills, and machines for facilitating the winding of yarn and the proper arrangement of the warp and woof before they were fixed on the loom—but he omits any mention of Kay's device. About 1793 a Gloucestershire clothier introduced spring shuttles, as the fly shuttles were sometimes called, into his factory. The weavers were greatly alarmed, fearing that they would be driven from their homes to work in factories. They therefore held a public meeting, attended by three or four thousand people, and appointed delegates to wait on the manufacturers. The latter induced the clothier to dispose of his spring looms, and he sold them to the weavers. " From that time we heard nothing more of it till about five years ago [*i.e.*, 1798] we applied to them [the weavers]

---

[1] In 1803 a Yorkshire clothier, asked if spring looms were used in Yorkshire, replied: " I never saw any other." Among worsted weavers in Yorkshire the fly shuttle was not at first in general use, as the thread was liable to break, but technical improvements in the loom (the invention of the false reed) and the use of mill-spun yarn brought about its adoption.

to give us more weaving. They said they could not supply
us for want of journeymen. The demand was so great in
consequence of this press for weavers, they had recourse
to the spring shuttle gladly themselves, and I believe it
is now become general throughout the country. We give
them the same price for weaving as we did in the old looms,
and the advantage we derive is having a greater quantity
of weaving done. At first when they were introduced we
suffered inconvenience. They were not masters of the art,
and the cloth was not so well wove, but we submitted to
that, and they are now masters of it, and do very well
with it."

An attempt to introduce the fly shuttle into Wiltshire
was made about 1792, for in that year Trowbridge was
reported to be " in a commotion not altogether subsided
arising from the weavers having taken a dislike to the late
improvements in machinery (particularly to the introduction of the spring shuttle) from an idea that their labour
would thereby be rendered in less request. The military
who had been called in to suppress the insurrection of the
weavers were still in the town." Ten years later the spring
loom had been adopted in Wiltshire, although it was not
yet in general use. In Somersetshire the fly shuttle is said
to have been introduced about 1801 " by a person who
had been in the North of England to work. He worked
with it only a few weeks on account of the riotous assemblage
of a mob who made him relinquish it." As late as 1822
a request was made that soldiers should be quartered at
Frome, " in order to prevent any disturbances during the
introduction of spring looms, which will now be generally
used here, as they have long been in Yorkshire, Gloucestershire, and Wiltshire."

2. *Spinning Machinery*. — While the West Country (ii.) Spin-
weavers were slowly reconciling themselves to improve- ning
Machinery
ments in the mode of weaving invented as far back as
1733, the preliminary processes of the woollen and worsted
industries were being revolutionised in the North. " If you
give out wool instead of warp and weft," said a Yorkshire
employer, " they won't manufacture it in the way they

used to at their own houses, but carry it to the slubbing engine to be scribbled, carded, and slubbed." In the last decade of 'he eighteenth century machinery was used in *scribbling*—a kind of preparatory carding intended to separate the fibres of the wool—in *carding* itself, and in *slubbing*—a process between carding and spinning, by which the wool slivers were joined together, drawn out into a continuous thread, and slightly twisted. The first machine in Yorkshire for spinning worsted yarn (the " frame ") was erected at Addingham as early as 1787.[1] A few years later (1794) it was introduced into Bradford, where it was accompanied by an attempt to erect a factory in the town. But the residents of the future metropolis of the worsted industry raised strenuous opposition on the ground that the steam-engine was a " smoky nuisance," and threatened the manufacturer with legal proceedings. " Take notice," they warned him, " that if you shall presume to erect any steam-engine for the manufacture of cotton or wool we shall, if the same be found a nuisance, seek such redress as the law shall give." This attempt to arrest the march of industrial progress was abortive; hand-spinning steadily lost ground, and the opening of the nine-teenth century was marked by the erection of a worsted mill at Bradford, where Arkwright's water-frame displaced the spindle and the wheel. The year 1810 is given as the date when hand-spinning began to be generally superseded in the worsted manufacture. The ease with which machine-spinning achieved its victory over hand-spinning may be explained on three grounds. Firstly, the spinners were women and children, who could offer no effective resistance to the introduction of machinery; secondly, the demand for women and children in the factories created fresh avenues of employment for them; thirdly, the weavers profited by the increased production of yarn and raised no opposition to the new methods. While worsted spinning was thus

[1] The first worsted factory with water-frames was erected in 1784 at Dolphin Holme in Lancashire. At first machinery was worked by horse or water power. But the use of steam followed shortly after. A steam cotton mill was erected at Papplewick in Nottinghamshire in 1785.

revolutionised in the North of England, it continued on the traditional lines in Norfolk, where the first yarn factory was not erected until 1834.

The factory system thus achieved a speedier victory in the worsted industry than in the woollen industry, where spinning was still carried on as a household occupation. The question naturally arises, Why did domestic spinning survive longer in the woollen than in the worsted branch ? The explanation may be sought for in the differences of economic organisation. The worsted trade in Yorkshire appears, from its inception, to have been more definitely capitalistic in character than the woollen trade, possibly because the introduction of the worsted manufacture into the North of England was due to the enterprise of capitalist pioneers.[1] The leaders of the industry, at any rate, had more command of capital than the domestic clothiers, and they specialised to a greater extent. The account-books of one of these early worsted men have been preserved for the years 1762-79. They show that he transacted business on a large scale, buying considerable quantities of wool, which he combed and dyed at home with hired assistants, and then put out to be spun over a wide area, the yarn being afterwards apparently sold; at his death his stock amounted to nearly £700 worth of raw wool, and over £800 worth of combed wool and yarn. The demand for worsted yarn outside Yorkshire may also have helped to stimulate specialisation in worsted spinning as a distinct trade. Whatever the reason, specialisation has remained even at the present day a feature of the worsted industry, the processes of combing, spinning, and weaving being usually, though not invariably, organised in different hands. In the woollen industry, on the other hand, the same firm generally both spins and weaves. The worsted business is also, as a rule, a much larger concern than the woollen

The woollen and worsted industries contrasted.

[1] See below, p. 240. The reasons usually assigned are (i) that the materials were more expensive and (ii) the work was less difficult; hence, " capital took control and operative skill became subservient." But the long wool used for " worsteds " was cheaper than the wool used for " woollens," and combing in particular was skilled work, the wool-combers earning higher wages than carders or weavers in the woollen industry.

business, and employs many more hands. Where an industry is thus highly specialised, and has control of considerable capital, the inducement to adopt the most efficient methods of production is correspondingly greater.

(iii.) The Power Loom.

3. *The Power-Loom.*—The conquest of hand-loom weaving by the power-loom was a much slower process than the conquest of spinning by the frame or mule. Apart from the hostility of the weavers, which made the introduction of steam-looms a venturesome undertaking, there were technical reasons for its tardy progress. In the case of the woollen industry, as we have already seen, the loose woollen thread was not suited to its operations so well as the worsted yarn, which was spun hard and tight. Yet even in the worsted industry—where the power-loom established its predominance earlier than in the other branch[1]—the adoption of steam-weaving was delayed on account of the necessity for frequent stoppages of the machine in order to " size " or " dress " the warp[2] as it unrolled from the yarn beam. This obstacle was only removed in 1803 when William Radcliffe, who had been assisted by a mechanic, Thomas Johnson, took out a patent for a dressing machine which starched the whole of the warp before it was bound upon the loom. Nor was the saving of labour at first considerable; as late as 1819 it was said that " one person cannot attend upon more than two power-looms, and it is still problematical whether this saving of labour counterbalances the expense of power and machinery." Again, the hand-loom weavers submitted to the fatal policy of " lowering the dyke "; they carried on an unequal contest with machinery, in which they maintained a precarious existence by submitting to repeated reductions of wages. The sacrifice they thus made retarded, although it could not avert, the ultimate extinction of the industry.

The first attempt to introduce the power-loom naturally

---

[1] Above, p. 176.
[2] " Sizing " means to saturate the warp with paste to strengthen it, and so enable it to bear the operation of weaving.

excited violent opposition. In 1822 a Bradford manu- Opposition
facturer " constructed a power-loom as secretly as possible power
to evade any attack which might be made to destroy it, loom.
and sent the obnoxious machine " to be worked at Shipley,
where he thought it would be safe. " But in this idea he
was mistaken, for it had scarcely been put in motion ere
the bellman was sent round to give notice in the neighbouring villages of its arrival. A great number of weavers
in a short time surrounded the mill, and threatened the
whole fabric with destruction if the power-loom were not
instantly removed. It was therefore immediately taken
down, and placed in a cart under a convoy of constables,
but the enraged weavers attacked and routed the constables, destroyed the loom, and dragged its roller and
warp in triumph through Baildon." A few years later the
experiment was repeated. Power-looms were set up at
Messrs. Horsfall's mill in Bradford, and popular resentment
again flared up in a determined effort to wreck the machines.
On May 1, 1826, a crowd of unemployed workmen number-
ing about two hundred and fifty assembled on Fairweather-
Green, near Bradford, and proceeded to the mill, where
they smashed the windows. Reinforced by another two
hundred men, they renewed the attack, but when the Riot
Act was read they scattered. Two days later a more
numerous body again assembled and attacked the mill,
but were unable to force an entrance. The Riot Act was
read once more, but the mob threw stones, and one of them
is said to have fired a pistol into the mill. Its defenders,
a small band of forty men, fired on the people, killed two
persons, a youth of eighteen and a boy of thirteen, and
wounded many others. The rioters, frustrated in their
purpose, soon afterwards dispersed. This was the most
serious outbreak which Bradford witnessed, and it was
followed by a general adoption of power-looms on the part
of the worsted manufacturers. The belated introduction
of the power-loom in the West Country will be seen from
the following table:[1]

[1] It will be observed that Norfolk is not represented by any power-
looms

TABLE SHOWING THE NUMBER OF POWER LOOMS USED
IN WOOLLEN AND WORSTED FACTORIES IN 1835.[1]

County.	Woollen.	Worsted.
Yorkshire	688[2]	2,856[2]
Lancashire	1142	—
Westmorland ..	8	—
Cheshire	8	—
Leicestershire ..	89[3]	—
Gloucestershire ..	4	—
Somersetshire ..	74[4]	—
Montgomeryshire ..	4	—
Northumberland ..	6	—

(iv.) The
Gig Mill
and Shear-
ing Frame.

4. *The Gig Mill and Shearing Frame.*—The introduction
of machinery into the dressing of cloth aroused dissension
as early as the fifteenth century.   A Statute of 1495 forbade
shearmen to use " instruments of iron " in place of " the
broad shears," and a Statute of 1551 prohibited " gig
mills " for raising the nap.   The latter prohibition does not
appear to have taken effect, for Charles I. found occasion
to issue a proclamation against them, and a *Report on the
Decay of the Cloth Industry,* dated 1640, alluding to the
frequent use of gig mills, " now called mozing[5] mills, for
avoiding the penalties of the law," states that these
" engines " still required to be suppressed in Gloucestershire " about Stroudwater."   A writer in 1803 remarks

---

[1] In 1856 the number of power-looms in the United Kingdom
was 14,453 in the woollen industry (an increase of 572 per cent.) and
38,956 in the worsted industry (an increase of 1,212 per cent.).
   [2] There were also 226 power-looms used for woollen and worsted,
and 307 for worsted and cotton.   Messrs. Horsfall and Co. had 378
worsted looms, the largest number of any Bradford manufacturer,
and the largest but one of any Yorkshire manufacturer.
   [3] Used for woollen and worsted.
   [4] " In strictness perhaps these can hardly be called power-looms.
Power is in them applied to part only of the operation of weaving :
the shuttle is thrown by hand, consequently each loom requires its
own separate attendant."   The number of workmen was therefore
not diminished.
   [5] Mozing = brushing.

that the gig mill had been employed in Gloucestershire and Wiltshire for dressing coarse white cloth "longer than anyone can remember," although no strict proof could be adduced to identify this machine—which contained a cylinder covered with teasles—with that mentioned in Edward VI.'s Statute. The saving of labour was said to be very considerable, a machine managed by one man and two boys doing the work of eighteen men and six boys. But the attempt to apply the gig mill to the dressing of fine white as well as medley[1] cloth excited violent opposition among the workmen in Wiltshire, and the manufacturers there were forced to send their cloth to be " gigged " in Gloucestershire, which contained public mills working for the clothiers on commission.. Their example was imitated by the manufacturers of Somersetshire, who refrained from using gig mills at home to avoid riots. In the West Riding, where most kinds of machinery were introduced more easily than elsewhere, the opposition was even more pro-tracted than in the West Country. At the end of the eighteenth century the gig mill, although not unknown in Yorkshire, was still very exceptional, and the majority of the cloths were dressed by hand on account of the hostility of the men. One mill (Bradley Mill) was partly burnt down by shearmen, and the Royal Exchange Insurance Company was warned " not to insure any factory where any machinery was in belonging to the cloth-workers." Mr. Law Atkinson, a clothier at Bradley Mill, stated in evidence in 1803 that " because we used gig mills, ours was considered as an unlawful shop by the shearmen. Hearing of a combination among the shearmen to prevent our hiring workmen, I called up the whole of them[2] and insisted on their hiring with us till Christmas or they should finish their work and leave us previous to the general period when trade becomes more brisk that we might know what to expect from them. The whole of them but three turned out, refusing to work after the gig mill—the number, I believe, being twenty-four or twenty-five. But finding work not so plentiful as they expected, all except two submitted to our terms, and agreed

[1] See above, p. 142.   [2] I.e., the men in his employment.

to hire for the remainder of the year. Although many of them have been beaten, knocked down, dragged by the hair of the head, and the men swore that they would gig them as they gigged at Bradley Mill, they have again hired with us for the present year."

The Lud-
dites.
Another Yorkshire manufacturer, Hirst, who wrote an account of his career as a clothier, declares that as late as 1810, " if a Yorkshire manufacturer went into a market with one from the West of England, and they had both a piece of cloth manufactured from the same wool, the latter would get a better price by nearly one-half," the West Country having machinery for finishing cloth which York- shire employers dared not introduce; and " it was impossible to produce so good a finishing by manual labour." When Hirst himself introduced gig mills, the journeymen croppers complained bitterly: " Their bitterness against me was so great at that time that I had to keep ten armed men every night to guard my premises. I never ventured out at night; and even when I went out at daytime, I always had a brace of loaded pistols in my pocket." The fury of the Luddite rioters in 1812 was directed primarily against gig mills and shearing frames. The Luddites " were regularly organised and trained. After demolishing the works of Mr. Foster of Horbury in Yorkshire, their leader ordered them into a field, and their numbers (each man having a number to conceal his name) being called over, he dismissed them by the word of command: ' The work is done, dis- perse !' The time occupied in the business of mustering, destruction, and dispersing did not exceed twenty minutes." A verse of the croppers' ballad ran:

> " Great Enoch[1] still shall lead the van,
> Stop him who dare ! Stop him who can !
> Press forward every gallant man
> With hatchet, pike and gun !
> Oh, the cropper lads for me,
> The gallant lads for me,
> Who with lusty stroke
> The shear frames broke,
> The cropper lads for me."

[1] " Enoch " was the name given to the big hammer employed in the work of destruction.

The hostility of the cloth-finishers was not confined to the gig mill. They objected also to the use of shearing frames for cutting the nap raised by the gig mill. The shearing frame contained several pairs of shears worked by power, and it effected a great economy of labour. Moreover, it was said to be impossible to cut cloth from end to end evenly by hand, whereas a machine administered regular strokes with " mathematical nicety." The Yorkshire shearmen were better organised than other classes of textile workers in the West Riding, and they maintained close relations with shearmen's clubs in other parts of the country. This no doubt explains the stiff fight they were able to put up against the introduction of machinery into their branch of industry. But the ultimate issue of the struggle was the complete downfall of the shearmen, who failed to prevent the displacement of manual processes by mechanical contrivances. Between 1806 and 1817 the number of gig mills in Yorkshire was said to have increased from 5 to 72; the number of shears worked by machinery from 100 to 1,462; and out of 3,378 shearmen no less than 1,170 were out of work while 1,445 were only partly employed.

The Yorkshire shearmen.

5. *Wool-Combing.*—The invention of the combing machine raised a storm of opposition. It was assailed especially on the ground that it " diminished labour to an alarming degree." Parliament was inundated with petitions from all parts of the country, the burden of the complaint being that fifty thousand workmen, with their wives and families, would be reduced to beggary. " One machine only, with the assistance of one person and four or five children, will perform as much labour as thirty men in the customary manual manner." The arguments advanced in support of machinery in cotton, silk, and linen, claimed the Barnstaple wool-combers, did not apply to the woollen industry, " for that almost any quantity of the raw materials can be procured to supply the manufacturers of the former, which by enlarging their trade still retains an equal or greater number of persons in employ, whereas but a specific quantity can be obtained of the latter." " In the business of wool-

(v.) Wool-combing.

combing," contended the Leicester wool-combers, " it is not possible to increase the raw material beyond the present quantity. . . . The growth of wool is definite, and never equals the ability of the wool-combers to manufacture "; there was, therefore, no possibility of an extension of trade and consequent increase in the amount of employment. Parliament appointed a Committee to investigate the grievances of the wool-combers, and evidence was given that a machine worked by water at Twerton, near Bath, combed the wool " nearly as well as if it was worked by hands in the old way." Cartwright responded with a counter-petition stating that, as the inventor of the machine mentioned in the wool-combers' petitions, he was " willing to concur in any plan for limiting him in the sale of his machinery to such number annually as to the House shall appear expedient," though he trusted " that an extension of his patent will not be considered unreasonable if the unlimited use of it is to be restrained." Another petition was presented by a worsted manufacturer in Nottinghamshire, William Toplis, who claimed to have invented a machine for combing wool " after great labour and study." He denied that the growth of wool suitable for combing was limited, and cited the cotton industry as an example of the increased trade and employment resulting from the introduction of machinery. After hearing the report of the Committee, Parliament gave leave to bring in a Bill " for the purpose of protecting wool-combers from being injured in their manufacture by the use of certain machines lately introduced for the combing of wool." This provoked a violent remonstrance from factory owners in Yorkshire and Nottinghamshire, who protested that it was " the general right of the subject, which the wisdom of the Legislature has for ages admitted, that he be at liberty to exercise his art or profession in that way which appears to be the most conducive to his interest, nor offends against the laws or the right of others; that of this interest he is himself in all instances the fittest judge." The doctrine here enunciated was historically false, and the opponents of the Bill were on safer ground when they used the argument of economy in the cost of production. The price of combing inferior wool was reduced by machinery from 2½d. or 3d. to 1d. per lb., and when the finer wool was also worked by a machine the price of combing was expected to be reduced from 6d. or more to 1d. or 1½d. per lb.[1] The opposition received the support of the Committee of Worsted Manufacturers in the North of England, and the House of Commons, yielding to the pressure thus brought to bear upon it, postponed the further consideration of the Bill until " this day six months." As a concession, the wool-combers were permitted to engage in other trades "in any town or place within this kingdom" without serving a fresh apprenticeship.

All periods of transition are apt to be periods of distress. The period of transition. As the old order yields place to the new, the instability of the social organism throws to the surface all that is most evil in its constitution. A harsh destiny soon overtakes those who are unable to adapt themselves with ease and rapidity to the changed condition of things, for the race is to the swift and the strong, and the weak and the feeble " go to the wall." In the case of the Industrial Revolution the evils of the transition from implements to machinery were aggravated by a protracted war, in which the energies of the country were diverted from the normal channels of industrial activity, and the free development of the

---

[1] A similar statement as to the saving effected by the use of a combing machine is made in *Observations on the different Breeds of Sheep and the State of Sheep-farming in some of the Principal Counties of England*, by Messrs. Redhead, Laing, and Marshall, Store Farmers (1792): " We called on the Rev. Mr. Cartwright at Doncaster who showed us his newly invented machine for combing wool; by which, when it becomes general, Mr. Cartwright calculates that there will arise a saving of expense to the British manufacturer of £20,700 per annum. The expense of combing a pack of wool in the ordinary way is £2 10s. 0d., and it costs about 10s. for charcoal. But by this machinery it is done for less than it costs in the ordinary way for charcoal alone, whilst at the same time the staple of the wool is infinitely better preserved and less broken. A number of manufacturers have already got these machines made under Mr. Cartwright's inspection, who receives 10s. of premium for every pack the machine combs or prepares for being spun. Mr. Cartwright has now given up his sacerdotal functions, and has devoted himself to his manufactures."

national resources was shackled by the unparalleled growth of the national debt, coupled with a fantastical fiscal system.   We relate in the following section the sufferings of the hand-loom weavers, the story of whose extinction constitutes the most melancholy chapter in the history of the textile industries, and the classic example of the triumph of " economic progress " at the expense of " social welfare."

The immediate effects of the Industrial Revolution.   The immediate effects of the Industrial Revolution upon the hand-loom weavers were beneficial.   They profited by the enormous output of yarn from the spinning factories, and as a result of the increased demand for their labour they reaped a harvest of high wages.   The muslin weavers of Bolton may be cited in illustration of their flourishing condition, though the prosperity of other weavers was much more subdued.   " The trade was that of a gentleman," said a witness before a Select Committee of the House of Commons in 1834.   " They brought home their work in top boots and ruffled shirts, carried a cane and in some instances took a coach."   Many weavers at that time, we are told, " used to walk about the streets with a five-pound Bank of England note spread out under their hat-bands; they would smoke none but long ' churchwarden ' pipes, and objected to the intrusion of any other handicraftsmen into the particular rooms in the public-houses which they frequented.   This prosperity did not continue, and few operatives endured greater privations than the hand-loom weavers of Bolton for the succeeding fifty years."

Causes of the distress of the hand-loom weaver.   Among the numerous factors responsible for the distress of the hand-loom weavers the most important was the drastic fall in wages.   John Fielden, an eminent philanthropist, informed the Committee of 1834: " It is allowed by all that the immediate cause of the distress has been unfair reduction of wages by a few manufacturers in the first instances, but of necessity adopted by others who had a strong aversion to it, whereby has resulted reduction after reduction and the present state of things."   The sweeping nature of these reductions may be gauged from a comparison of the average wages paid by a Bolton manufac-

turer over a period of thirty-five years for weaving a piece
of cloth—24 yards—the measure of a week's work:

								£	s.	d.
Between	1797	and	1803	the price paid was				1	6	8
,,	1804	,,	1810	,,		,,		1	0	0
,,	1811	,,	1817	,,		,,		0	14	7
,,	1818	,,	1824	,,		,,		0	8	9
,,	1825	,,	1831	,,		,,		0	6	4
,,	1832	,,	1833	,,		,,		0	5	6

In the first period a weaver could purchase with his wages
25 lbs. of flour, 35½ lbs. of oatmeal, 206½ lbs. of potatoes,
and 14 lbs. of meat—in all 281 lbs. of provisions. In
the fifth period he could only purchase 10 lbs. of flour,
14½ lbs. of oatmeal, 55 lbs. of potatoes, and 3½ lbs. of meat
—in all 83 lbs. of provisions. Thus his wages in money
declined nearly 80 per cent., and the reduction involved
a proportionate decline in his command over the necessaries
of life.

According to the Hand-loom Commissioners, whose Report
was published in 1840, the wages of worsted weavers in the
West Riding, working full time, seldom exceeded six or
seven shillings a week, but, as they rarely had full employment, their actual earnings fell below this amount.[1] In the
West of England wages were sometimes even less than in
the North. At Frome, in Somersetshire, one-third of the
weavers were said to earn three to five shillings for an
84 hours' week; about three-fifths earned three to seven
shillings; and the price of bread was 11d. the 4-lb. loaf.
At Trowbridge, in Wiltshire, the average earnings of each
loom was 3s. 6½d.; on the average there were two looms
to a family, so that two persons in a family earned between
them 7s. 1d. The average weekly earnings of master-
weavers and journeymen-weavers in Gloucestershire were
estimated at 8s. 1½d. and 5s. 7d. respectively. Not only
were wages low, they were also extremely irregular. " Those
who earn so little do not regularly get 5s. for each week,
but will perhaps earn £2 in a fortnight, and nothing for

marginal note: Drastic fall in wages.

---

[1] The weavers' weekly earnings at Mirfield, near Huddersfield,
were 5s. 6d.

six weeks after. The mode of earning £2 in two weeks is this: where two in a family can weave and have only one loom's work, one person will work all night and the other all day. This injures them in many ways. The employer finds his work done in a short time, and thinks his wages are still too high: he never asks ' why,' and is not told. Working by night consumes extra candles and fire, and takes off from the weaver's profit; the cloth is most probably not so well made as if wove by one person throughout, by a better light than that of a candle." Taken as a body weavers were said to be out of work one-third of their time, and while thus unemployed got into debt and were forced to buy inferior goods at a high price. The Weavers' Union estimated in 1828 that the minimum amount sufficient to keep a man, his wife, and three children was 15s. 8d. a week;[1] and as the earnings of the weavers fell considerably below this, the Commissioners reported that the condition of a pauper in the workhouse was superior to that of a weaver's family.

Condition of the weavers in Yorkshire.

Some striking evidence as to the condition of the hand-loom weavers in the neighbourhood of Huddersfield was given by Richard Oastler, the stalwart champion of factory legislation. " I remember one particular circumstance that struck me very forcibly, for it was the very day when I read the Speech of the King to this House, in which he said: ' The manufacturing districts are in a state of prosperity.' On that very day I met with several of those weavers who were ' manufacturing ' operatives, and I questioned them very closely, and I found that on that day when they were said to be in such a state of ' prosperity,' those men—and those women, too—were carrying burdens on their backs

---

[1] The following is a list, drawn up by the Weavers' Union in 1828, of the expenses of a man, his wife, and three children: Rent, 2s.; wood and coal, 1s. 3d.; candles, 3½d.; soap, 3½d.; starch, 1d.; ashes (for washing), 1d.; pins, needles, and worsted, 1½d.; man's shoes, 3d.; woman's shoes, 1½d.; three children's ditto, 3d.; man's bread, 1s. 5d.; cheese, 1 lb., 7d.; meat, 1 lb., 7d.; butter, ¼ lb., 3d.; sugar, 3½d.; coffee, 1d.; vegetables, 7d.; woman's bread, 1s. 2d.; butter, ¼ lb., 3d.; cheese, ½ lb., 4d.; sugar, ½ lb., 3½d.; meat, 6d.; tea, 3d.; vegetables, 6d.; bread for three children, 1s. 9d.; cheese, ¾ lb., 6d.; butter, ¾ lb., 9d.; sugar, ¾ lb., 5½d.; vegetables, 4½d.;—15s. 8d. No clothes except shoes are included in the list.

eight or nine miles to fetch their work, and then had to carry them back again, and they were making from 4s. 6d. to 5s. 2d. a week clear wages." In reply to the question: "How many hours a day do the weavers generally work?" he answered: "Those persons whom I have asked say from twelve to fourteen hours a day, but I am speaking of weavers in constant work. I very often find them going home without work at all. I met a lot of them the week before last, and there were only three in the lot who had work.

"There are scores and hundreds of families in the district that I am now alluding to, to whom a piece of flesh meat is a luxury; it does not form a regular article in their daily consumption; they generally live upon porridge and potatoes, and they do not know what it is, many of them, very many of them, to taste flesh meat from year's end to year's end, excepting somebody gives them some; and their children will sometimes run to Huddersfield and beg, and bring a piece in, and it is quite a luxury when a piece goes into their houses. But as to their clothing, they are clothed with rags; and their furniture is such as I am sure I cannot describe, but such as a convict ought not to have."

He added: "I have marked not only a visible declension in their circumstances, but in their spirits and in their manners altogether. I sometimes ask them when I am walking with them if they go to church or chapel, and I generally get this answer: 'We have naught to go in.' And I often ask them: 'Do you know whether you live in a Christian country or not?' and a great many do not know what I mean by the question; sometimes they say: 'Yes, we do live in a Christian country; they tell us so.'"

Oastler's statements are corroborated by an overwhelm- Evidence of Commissioners. ing mass of evidence. One of the Commissioners visited at Leeds "a great number of the houses and cellars of the weavers, and great indeed was the misery and wretchedness I then witnessed. Many of the cellars were completely destitute of any single thing which could be called furniture. The floors were mostly of stone, and were not infrequently wet. In some of these wretched tenements there was not even a bedstead." "I cannot recollect an instance but one," said an employer, "where any weaver of mine has bought a new jacket for many years. I have seen many houses with only two or three stools, and some I have seen without a stool or chair, with only a tea-chest to put their clothes in and to sit upon." "I have seen beds," asserted a woollen manufacturer, "that have not had a blanket; in general they lie upon straw." It was stated by a witness from Nuneaton that out of a population of 8,000, who were almost entirely dependent on hand-loom weaving, nearly 3,000 were receiving poor relief.

The following is an official summary of the evidence laid before the Select Committee of 1834: "A very great number of these weavers are unable to provide for themselves and their families a sufficiency of food of the plainest and cheapest kind; they are clothed in rags, and indisposed on this account to go to any place of worship or to send their children to the Sunday Schools; they have scarcely anything like furniture in their houses; their beds and bedding are of the most wretched description, and many of them sleep upon straw; notwithstanding their want of food, clothing, furniture, and bedding, they for the most part have full employment; their labour is excessive, not unfrequently sixteen hours a day; this state of destitution and excessive labour induces them to drink ardent spirits, to revive their drooping spirits and allay their sorrows, whereby their suffering is increased; their poverty and wretchedness cause many to embezzle and sell the materials entrusted to them to be worked up . . . thus destroying the morals of the weavers."

Immo-
bility of
labour.

In consequence of their poverty the weavers were obliged to take whatever wages the master chose to give them—and different masters paid different wages for the same sort of work, the difference being in some cases 50 per cent. Moreover, they dared not leave the employer who paid low wages, however grinding and oppressive his treatment, because they were often in debt to him, and therefore bound to his service in the same way as the mediæval villein was tied to his lord's estate. One weaver, for example, told how his wife lay ill, and " I had not so much as to make a dish of gruel for her." He borrowed a few shillings from the warehouse. " Soon after that there was better work sprung up in the town, but I could not leave for six months till I had paid it off." The masters made advances on the understanding that the loan should be repaid " by a small stoppage out of the weaver's wages every time he delivered in any finished work, which stoppage out of wages the weaver's poverty often induces him to intreat his master to postpone. The tie is thus prolonged, fresh loans are made before the previous ones are repaid, and the hold the low-paying master has on his weaver is thus increased." Another obstacle which hindered mobility of labour—that is, prevented the weaver from carrying his labour to the best market—was the loss of time and expense involved in a change of employers, for alterations in the weaving necessitated new gears and implements, which the poverty-stricken weaver could not afford.

The result of this state of affairs was that the workman, at the end of a life spent in hard toil, had nothing but destitution to which to look forward. " I am now at this moment," remarked a weaver, " within a twelve months of sixty years of age, and I calculate that within eight years I shall myself become a pauper. I am not capable, by my most strenuous exertions, to gain ground to the amount of a shilling, and when I am in health it requires all my exertions to keep soul and body together." A complete change seemed to have passed over the manufacturing population. " Having been absent from Europe ten years," said a medical officer, " I have had an opportunity of drawing a comparison as to the physical deterioration in the manufacturing districts, and nothing struck me with more horror than the deterioration in the appearance of the population. I have observed it not only in the manufacturing, but also in agricultural communities in this country; they seem to have lost their animation, their vivacity, their field-games, and their village sports; they have become a sordid, discontented, miserable, anxious, struggling people, without health or gaiety or happiness.

Deterioration of the people.

This has been in a great measure occasioned by the hours of labour being extended."[1]

Causes of the fall in wages: (i.) Competition of machinery.   The question arises, Why did the fall in wages affect worsted weavers more than other classes of artisans ? One reason is that the worsted weavers competed with machinery. The power-loom was introduced only gradually, but it set the pace; and the ability of the power-loom master to undersell the hand-loom master forced the latter to cut rates of payment. Machinery was thus the great " screw," and the ever-present menace of its introduction destroyed the power of resistance of the worsted weavers. The menace was not so great in the woollen manufacture, and the slow progress of steam-weaving in this branch of industry largely accounts for the fact that the wages of cloth weavers were considerably above those of worsted weavers.[2]

(ii.) Absence of organised resistance.   The worsted weavers were not organised in strong trade unions, and so could not offer the same effective opposition which enabled spinners in factories to defeat any attempt to lower wages. Dr. Gaskell explains the weakness of the trade-union movement among the weavers on the ground that they were " a far more moral and conscientious body of people than the factory labourers "; they toiled on in silence, " whilst the turbulent and demoralised town and country steam-spinner, whilst rolling in comparative wealth, has been committing outrages of the most wanton and vicious description." But the failure of the hand-loom weavers to combine in order to maintain a fit and proper standard of life was due to other causes. In the first place,

[1] Cf. *The Weavers' Complaint or A Bundle of Plain Facts. A Novel Poem by an Operative of Keighley*, 1834.

" The weavers, a set of poor souls,
    With clothes on their backs much like riddles for holes,
    With faces quite pale and eyes sunk in the head,
    As if the whole race were half famished for bread.

" Indeed, when these wretches you happen to meet,
    You think they are shadows you see in the street;
    For their thin water-porridge is all they can get,
    And even with that they are often hard set."

[2] Cloth weavers working full time could earn 15s. a week, though as they were rarely fully employed, their earnings were proportionately diminished.

they were scattered over the countryside; even in the towns they were isolated and had no " accurate knowledge of what was going on." This isolation of the weavers imposed an insuperable obstacle to the development of a vigorous trade-union movement; and the weakness of their bargaining power rendered them " a defenceless prey " in all their dealings with unscrupulous employers. On the other hand, the workers in a factory were concentrated under one roof, and were more easily brought to combine together, " and combinations have a wonderful tendency to keep up the price of wages." Manufacturers found it more difficult to reduce the wages of men working together in communication with each other, than to lower the wages of isolated outdoor weavers.

In the next place, the extreme poverty of the weavers hindered the growth of trade unionism. Their exiguous resources could not stand the strain of a weekly contribution to the trade union funds; and the very circumstances which made the existence of a strong union peculiarly necessary conspired to check its development. " If they give a half-penny out of their pockets," remarked a weaver, " they must work for it again," and the absence of any feeling of *esprit de corps* among them increased their disinclination to make the sacrifices imperatively demanded in the common interest. In the third place, the machine upon which the weaver worked was his own property; if it stood idle he alone suffered. The spinner worked upon the machines of his employer, and in the event of a strike the mill-owner, whose capital was invested in his machinery, also suffered from the inactivity of the men. Obviously, then, a strike had more chances of success among spinners than among weavers, and this fact was a contributory cause of the backward state of trade unionism among the hand-loom weavers.

Another important point is that the trade was easily acquired, and the facility with which it was learnt made hand-loom weaving " a receptacle for the destitute from all other classes." " It is the easiest learnt of all trades," declared one witness. " A lad of fourteen may acquire a

Marginal notes:
Weakness of the trade union movement.

(iii) The art of weaving easily acquired.

sufficient knowledge of it in six weeks. He can be taught it generally in his father's house, he is freed from the necessity of apprenticeship, and all its disagreeable things of being under a master seven years, the common term of other trades; when in the course of a few months he becomes a very good weaver." As the result of the inventions in spinning—the jenny, the water-frame, and the mule—the existing body of weavers was unable to cope with the abundance of yarn, and the high prices at first paid for weaving attracted labourers from every other occupation. The Industrial Revolution coincided with an agricultural revolution, the substitution of large-scale production for small-scale production, and the consequent disappearance of the class of small farmers and cottagers. The displacement of the rural population, which also suffered from the extinction of cottage spinning, reacted upon the towns, for the labourers flocked to the large industrial centres, and " a new race of hand-loom weavers " was created. " This body of men," wrote Dr. Gaskell, " was of a still lower grade in the social scale than the original weavers, had been earning a much less amount of wages, and had been accustomed to be mere labourers. The master-spinners therefore found them ready to work at an inferior price, and thus discovered an outlet for their extra quantity of yarn. This at once led to a great depreciation in the price of hand-loom labour, and was the beginning of that train of disasters which has finally terminated in reducing those who have kept it to a state of starvation."

Invasion of the urban labour market.
The invasion of the urban labour market by agricultural labourers had pernicious effects; it not only swelled the numbers of the weavers to excess, but exposed them to unfair competition, for the newcomers, accustomed to a low standard of living, were prepared to accept low rates of remuneration. Nor were farm labourers the only competitors of the town weavers. The worsted weavers of Yorkshire attributed their distressed state, among other factors, to the immigration of Irish workmen who were compelled by their poverty to crowd the English labour market—two-thirds of the stuff weavers in Leeds were

Irish. Thus the history of the hand-loom weavers, their one-time prosperity and their subsequent decline, illustrates the famous dictum: when two employers run after one man wages rise; when two men run after one employer wages fall. Yet if the weavers had been organised, they could have maintained more successfully the standard of life in spite of their increased numbers, but the weakness of their bargaining power made them the helpless victims of destiny. They competed against each other; they under-sold each other; and they accepted work at any price.

The efforts of the weavers to improve their situation were the most fatal which it is possible to conceive. In order to eke out their scanty resources they put their children at an early age to weaving, thus involving them in the meshes of the same remorseless destiny in which they were them-selves inextricably entangled. " As each child becomes successively capable of profitable employment, it is so employed—in many branches of hand-loom weaving—at the age of six, or even younger. Of course, this precocious employment is injurious to the intellectual and moral education of the child; in many cases altogether prevents it; and the family grows up a set of human machines, with no futurity but that of treading in their parents' steps, marrying before they are adult, and giving birth to an equally degraded progeny. Such a state of things produces a rapidly increasing population, confined by ignorance, by habit, and generally by poverty to their own occupation.'' The weavers had large families because every child was a prospective bread-winner, but the immediate benefit to the parents was more than counteracted by the evil results upon the race as a whole.

Fatal remedies.

The fate which overtook the hand-loom weavers even-tually befell the wool-combers, but the latter did not succumb without resistance. The most famous strike in their history broke out in 1825, the moving spirit being John Tester, the secretary of the Combers' Union. It lasted five months, and involved 20,000 men. The strikers enjoyed considerable sympathy in their efforts to raise wages, and received contributions from all parts of the

Extinction of hand-combing.

kingdom. After the manner of the old ballad-writers they issued a statement of the workmen's case in rude verses:

> " ' Lads, pray what's the matter ?
> Are you with the masters about to fight ?'
> ' Yes, sir, we are, and well we might,
> For, let us work hard as we will,
> We're ne'er the better for it still.' . . ."

The masters in order to smash the union declared a lock-out and closed down the mills. They even induced the mill-owners at Halifax, Keighley, and other centres to pledge themselves to discharge all combers and weavers in their employment who supported the Bradford Union with funds. The strike was remarkable for " the peaceable and orderly manner " in which it was carried on, and it is said that " not a single outrage or breach of peace " occurred during its course. Nevertheless the men failed to over-come the resistance of the masters, and the only result of this ruinous contest was to stimulate the introduction of machinery. The year 1825 marks the turning-point in the history of the hand-combers, whose condition now under-went rapid deterioration. Their sufferings were intense, they worked long hours in an over-heated atmosphere, and their toil was wretchedly remunerated. Their spasmodic efforts to alleviate their distress were ineffectual. They no longer held the whip-hand over the employers, who were able to utilise machinery which every day was increasing in efficiency; and the recognition of their weakness con-strained the hand-combers to adopt a humbler tone, which was in striking contrast to their proud and defiant attitude in the eighteenth century. In 1840 the Bradford Wool-combers' Association drew up a statement which has been justly described as " one of the most touching expositions of industrial despondency " ever issued. " Knowing the evil effects of turn-outs [strikes]," it ran, " we desire if possible to avoid them in future. We know that they can only be avoided by our masters uniting with us for the good of each, and all angry feelings or animosities which exist in the bosoms of the employers or employed being banished and each other's interests considered reciprocal. It must have been evident to every master who has reduced the wages of his workmen that, previous to the reduction, it was scarcely possible for any of his wool-combers to obtain an honest living by their own hand-labour. But now that the reduction has taken place, our sufferings are augmented and our lives have become miserable. We are compelled to work from fourteen to sixteen hours per day, and with all this sweat and toil we are not able to procure sufficient of the necessaries of life wherewith to subsist on." The hand-combers had clung to the conviction that Cartwright's machine would never prove workable, but the improvements made by Lister and Donisthorpe, which we have related in the previous chapter, gave the death-blow to their fond anticipations. The middle of the nineteenth century may be taken as the period at which hand-combing as an industrial process became to all intents and purposes an extinct industry.

The hand-loom weavers and the wool-combers were not the only artisans to suffer from the introduction of machinery. Those who worked the machines, particularly the children, often endured terrible hardships. As we turn over the leaves of the official *Reports on the Employment of Children in Factories*, abundant evidence of their sufferings confronts us on every page. A few concrete illustrations are worth any amount of general comments, and we will therefore glance at the statements taken down from the lips of the children themselves. One boy, employed in the carding-room of a mill at Leicester where the spinning of worsted yarn was carried on, related his experiences thus:

Children in factories.

" I am twelve years old. I have been in the mill twelve months. I attend to a drawing machine. We begin at six o'clock and stop at half-past seven. We don't stop work for breakfast. We do sometimes. This week we have not. We have generally about twelve hours and a half of it. I get 2s. 6d. a week. I have a father and mother, and give them what I earn. I have worked over-

hours for two or three weeks together about a fortnight
since. All the difference was, we worked breakfast-time
and tea-time, and did not go away till eight. We are paid
for such over-hours at the rate of twopence for three hours.
I have worked nine hours over in one week."

He was asked: " Do you work over-hours or not, just as
you like ?"—" No; them as works must work."

" Does your mother like you to work over-hours ?"—
" No; she don't like it. She never asked for me to be
excused. She knows it wouldn't be no use. I would rather
stay and do it than anybody should come in my place. I
should lose the money. I go to school of a Sunday sometimes. I went first about a month ago. I have been
every Sunday since. I can only read in the alphabet yet.
I mean to go regular. There is no reason why I should not.
I wants to be a scholar."

At Nottingham a witness, fourteen years of age, said:
" I have worked in Milnes's factory two years. We go at
half-past five; give over at half-past nine. We sometimes
stay till twelve. I asked to come away one night lately,
at eight o'clock, being ill. I was told if I went I must not
come again." His father added: " It's killing him by
inches; he falls asleep over his food at night. I saw an
account of such things in the newspaper, and thought how
true it was of my own children."

A lad employed in a worsted factory at Bradford stated:
" I first began to work before I was five years of age. It
was a worsted mill. We used to begin at six o'clock in the
morning and go on till eight o'clock; sometimes nine. My
legs are now bent as you see." (The knees, reported the
Commissioner, were bent dreadfully. The height of the
boy, who was fifteen, was 3 feet 9 inches). " Got my knees
bent with standing so long. Have asked my father and
mother to let me stop away; they said they could not do
with me laiking at home, there was so many of us laiking
from not being old enough."

Another boy started life at a worsted mill near Halifax.
" I was hardly five when I went; I went in petticoats; got
a shilling a week when I'd been about a month. We used

to begin at six and I have wrought there while seven, and
eight, and nine o'clock at night."

One of the chief evils connected with the employment of Long
children was the long hours of labour. " Our hours were hours of
from six in the morning till eight at night. I have worked
till eleven busy times, and twelve. The children used to
fall asleep, and we had so much trouble with them. It
was very difficult to keep them awake till eight." Night
work was common. " We used to come at half-past eight
at night," said a girl fifteen years of age, " and work all
night till the rest of the girls came in the morning. They
would come at seven, I think. Sometimes we worked on
till half-past eight the next night after we had been working
all the night before. We worked on meal hours except at
dinner, but were not paid for them. The pieceners[1] would
work too. They used to go to sleep, poor things! when
they had over-hours in the night."

There were many complaints of ill-treatment. " Kind Ill-treat-
words are God-sends in many factories, and oaths and blows ment.
the usual order of the day." A little Scottish lassie, aged
thirteen, told how " when she was a child, too little to put
on her ain clathes, the onlooker used to beat her till she
screamed again." It is fair to remark that those responsible
for the brutal treatment of children were not the masters,
but a section of the workpeople themselves, the slubbers,
under whom the children worked. However, the masters
are not to be exonerated from blame, since it was part
of their duty to ensure that their young employees were
protected from violence.

One result of the long hours was that the children em- Lack of
ployed in factories were robbed of sufficient sleep. " A sleep.
great majority of the children," stated one of the Commissioners sent by the Government to investigate factory
conditions, " live from half a mile to perhaps a mile and
a half, and in some instances further, from the place at
which they work. The time, therefore, which is necessary

---

[1] The pieceners were employed in a spinning mill to keep frames
filled with rovings, and to join together ends of threads when they
broke in spinning. Formerly also they used to piece the cardings
together.

to walk this distance must be taken into account as labour
to a child, and that too of a distressing kind in winter-time
to those who are very poorly clothed, and are without
shoes and stockings, which is the case in numerous instances.
A fine is imposed if the party be not at work in time, and
that too—in a great number of mills—bearing a most
unjust proportion to the time lost. This severity produces
a corresponding anxiety in both young and old to be at
the mill in proper time, and in consequence children, as well
as adults, are often called from their rest much sooner
than is necessary in order to ensure their being at the mill
when the bell rings. They have to dress, and in many
instances to put up the food which they require for the
day, all of which takes up time, and which is so much
abstracted from the needful hours of sleep. I have seen
children, who have been thus too early called, sitting
together in the ash-pit of the fires of the boilers placing
their bare feet in the warm ashes, and sleeping with their
heads upon each other's shoulders until the bell rang, at
which time they were expected to go to work."

Effects on the children. The long hours of labour, combined with an insufficiency
of sleep, produced the inevitable effects: first, fatigue,
sleepiness, and pain; later, deterioration of the physical
constitution, deformity, disease, and deficient moral and
intellectual instruction. " I can have no hesitation in
stating my belief from what I saw myself," wrote a Commissioner, " that a large mass of deformity has been produced at Bradford by the factory system. The effect of
long and continuous work upon the frame and limbs is not
indicated by actual deformity alone; a more common
indication of it is found in a stunted growth, relaxed
muscle, and slender conformation. There remains no
doubt upon my mind that, under the system pursued in
many of the factories, the children of the labouring classes
stand in need of, and ought to have, legislative protection
against the conspiracy insensibly formed between their
masters and parents to tax them with a degree of toil
beyond their strength. I have found undoubted instances
of children five years old sent to work thirteen hours a

day; and frequently of children nine, ten, and eleven con-
signed to labour for· fourteen and fifteen hours." In a
factory at Nottingham " we have distinct information that
the clearing children are kept to their work constantly
during a period of sixteen hours." In view of this evidence
it is not surprising to find the opinion prevalent that the
factory children in England were worse off than the slaves
in the West Indies.

The earnings of young children were scanty in the extreme
and afforded " an advantage to the parent trivial indeed
compared with the injury inflicted on the child." Those
who were six years old sometimes earned a bare sixpence a
week, and the average wage of those ten years old was under
two shillings in some districts. *Earnings of children.*

In recommending factory legislation for the protection of
children the Commissioners were careful to dissociate themselves from " the pernicious notion," as they termed it,
" of the necessity of legislative interference to restrict
hours of adult labour." The employment of children
stood in a separate category because they were not " free
agents able to protect themselves," as adult artisans were
wrongly presumed to be. Cobden, for example, wrote in
a letter to a friend: " As respects the right and justice by
which young persons ought to be protected from excessive
labour, my mind has ever been decided, and I will not argue
the matter for a moment with political economy; it is a
question for the medical, and not the economical, profession.
Nor does it require the aid of science to inform us that the
tender germ of childhood is unfitted for that period of
labour which even persons of mature age shrink from as
excessive. In my opinion, and I hope to see the day when
such a feeling is universal, no child ought to be put to work
in a mill at all so early as the age of thirteen years." On
this ground Parliament was induced to relax its system of
laissez-faire in favour of a limited measure of industrial
control designed in the interests of the weakest section of
the community. The Factory Act of 1833[1] prohibited *Factory legislation*

[1] An Act on behalf of parish apprentices had been passed in 1802,
but was evaded by employing children without an apprenticeship.

night-work—between 8.30 p.m. and 5.30 a.m.—for all persons under eighteen in any woollen or worsted factory; no one under nine was to be employed at all; no one between the ages of nine and thirteen was to be employed more than nine hours in one day or forty-eight hours a week; no one under eighteen was to be employed more than twelve hours a day or sixty-nine hours a week. One hour and a half were allowed for meals, and factory inspectors were appointed to enforce these regulations. The Factory Act of 1844 restricted women's labour to twelve hours a day, and the Act of 1847 prescribed for women and young persons a maximum of ten hours.

Influence of the classical economists.

We have now to examine the attitude of the State towards the problems created by the introduction of machinery into the woollen industry. Its policy may be summed up in a single phrase: *Laissez-faire* (Let well alone). Throughout the eighteenth century, as we have seen above,[1] the State had been moving steadily in the direction of *laissez-faire* ; but it was the new form of capitalism created by the factory system, coupled with the influence of the economic experts, which finally secured the triumph in the sphere of industry and commerce of *laissez-faire* principles. The factory-owners, anxious to buy their labour as cheaply as possible and to capture the trade of foreign markets, were naturally opposed in the main to State control. Their arguments in favour of full industrial freedom were reinforced by the authority of the classical economists, a body of thinkers who drew their inspiration from Adam Smith, but derived their methods and principles from Ricardo. The destinies of England were largely in the hands of these economists during the first half of the nineteenth century, and they exercised the greatest influence in the councils of the nation. Their theories of society were elevated to the dignity of natural laws whose workings no human legislator could hope to arrest or evade, and when they proclaimed the supreme value of individual liberty, their doctrine was accepted without questioning by the majority of their

[1] Above, p. 114.

educated contemporaries.[1] The great mass of textile workers, on the other hand, saw in State intervention their only hope of salvation, and they appealed to the Statute Book which still enshrined in its pages the economic system of an earlier age. It would be a mistake to condemn their attitude as one of impracticable conservatism: the responsibility must rest, rather, with those who discarded the traditional safeguards bequeathed from the past for the protection of the working classes, but failed to devise fresh ones. The conflict between the exponents of the new economic creed and the old was fought out in the opening years of the nineteenth century.

The system of assessment of wages had been abolished— in so far as the woollen industry was concerned—in 1757, but the apprenticeship clauses of the Statute of Apprentices, though actually obsolete, were still technically in force. The weavers now had recourse to the old Elizabethan Statute in order to protect themselves from the competition of cheap labour; they raised a fund for the purpose, and employed attorneys to bring actions on their behalf against illegal workmen who had not been properly trained. Attempts were made at the same time to enforce the Act of Edward VI. prohibiting the use of gig mills, and the Act of Philip and Mary limiting the number of looms.[2] The agitation on behalf of the latter Act was intended to serve the interests of the West Country weavers, whose independence as " housekeepers and heads of families " was menaced by the growing practice of employing weavers on " shop " looms—that is, looms owned by the clothiers and worked on their premises. But the small Yorkshire clothiers also demanded that the northern counties, which were excluded from the Act of Philip and Mary, should be brought within its scope in order to check the growth of the factory system and preserve from extinction the domestic system.

Agitation for the enforcement of the old laws.

[1] One of the Hand-loom Commissioners, alluding in his Report (1840) to the weavers' demand that they should not be allowed to work more than twelve hours a day, remarked: " Such remedies as these are so contrary to the principles of political economy that I scarcely need make any further comments on them."

[2] Above, pp. 50, 188.

The clothiers thereupon appealed to Parliament for protection, and demanded the repeal of all restrictive legislation. The Government, however, was divided in its counsels. The writer of a letter[1] to Lord Grenville gives an interesting account of the situation. " A new trace of dissension in the Cabinet has appeared within the last two days, which I will not let pass without mentioning it to you. It seems that the informers and attorneys have lately left the clergy to fasten upon the clothiers; they have rummaged out obsolete but existing laws, in which they have found large penalties for manufacturing cloth except with certain threads and of certain breadths; penalties for employing any persons not having served a regular apprenticeship; forfeiture of all unshorn cloth exported from this country, such as our Bath greatcoats and such like; in short a formidable list of breaches of laws, some as old as Edward VI., and so entirely disregarded that the execution of them would attach upon all the dealers in fine cloth, and some of those who deal in coarse also. Regular notice, however, having been given by the attorneys of their pursuing these penalties and confiscations in regular course, the clothiers at the meeting of Parliament stated their case to Addington [the Prime Minister] who promised them immediately an Act of Suspension of the above laws until a new detailed law should pass upon good consideration of the subject. It was not till to-day that I heard to my utter surprise that such a Bill of Suspension had been silently brought in by Vansittart, had actually passed our House without the smallest notice of the nature of this Bill; a Bill which, after all, whether actually justifiable or not, could only be justified by a satisfactory statement of the necessity of the case, and such evidence upon it as ought to warrant so strong and extraordinary a measure. This Bill, however, such as it was, went up to the Lords," but the Chancellor, and Lord Pelham, the Home Secretary, expressing in private their entire dissent from such a mode of proceedings, " Lord Walsingham did not move yesterday for the third reading, and the matter so stands at sixes

[1] December, 1802.

and sevens; the clothiers, alarmed at this check after the dependence which they had placed upon this promise of Addington's, and Addington not knowing how to prevail over the difficulties which are made by the Chancellor and Pelham both as to a Suspending Bill being an unconstitutional measure and as to the indecency of any such important measure being taken without evidence. The best that the clothiers can hope is that the Lords will recommit the Bill in order to receive evidence, and then the Commons will be put in the disgraceful state of having done with their eyes shut what the Lords can hardly be brought to do upon evidence and enquiry. . . . I am assured that this perversity of the Lords . . . has created a serious ferment among the ministers." Two days later the same writer reported that " to my utter astonishment the Chancellor, who is the natural guardian of the law, and whose opinions were pledged against the principle of suspension, did not say one syllable upon that part of the subject; and he was very washy and very unmeaning in that which he did say." Pelham, on the other hand, " was more direct and manly in his objections to the measure being pursued without sufficient evidence." It seemed for a time as though the measure would be defeated, and in their jubilation weavers paraded the streets, and the bells were set ringing; but their triumph was shortlived.   In spite of numerous petitions the Suspension Bill became law in 1803, and year by year a Suspending Act was passed until 1809, when the whole code of restric- *Emancipation of the woollen manufacturers.* tive legislation relating to the assize and " true making " of cloths, compulsory apprenticeship, limitation of looms, and the prohibition of gig mills—the heritage of Tudor statesmanship—was swept away in obedience to the demand of the woollen manufacturers for complete industrial freedom.   A few years later (1814) a memorable debate took place in Parliament, when the exponents of the new economic doctrines seized the occasion to fling scorn upon the old-fashioned principles which had held sway in the sixteenth century.   " The reign of Queen Elizabeth," it was proclaimed, " though glorious, was not one in which sound principles of commerce were known."   " If the law, as it now stood, were put into force," declared one member, " it would have the effect of imposing the strongest possible fetters upon ingenuity and industry." Another speaker wished to see every man have the liberty of employing his hands and genius in the best way he could for his own advantage and for the benefit of the country. This no man was at liberty to do so long as the present law remained in force. The present law was necessarily broken every day. It was clear that the judges always wished to evade it when they could do so. He knew a case of two men who were prosecuted under the Act for sawing a piece of wood; another, of a good and bad baker in the same town, where the bad baker, finding that the good baker had not served a regular apprenticeship, had him turned out, and got liberty to poison all his neighbours with his bad bread. He quoted the opinion of Lord Mansfield that " it was against the natural rights of man and contrary to the common law rights of the land." An opponent of the Bill, on the other hand, contended that its enactment would operate seriously to the prejudice of our manufactures, both in regard to skill and reputation. " Indeed, such had been found the effect of the partial repeal of the Statute of Elizabeth with respect to the woollen manufacture. For although the Yorkshire tag had formerly been a sufficient recommendation upon the Continent, yet since the repeal alluded to our pieces of woollen manufactures were examined yard by yard before they were purchased." There were, in fact, strong arguments on both sides. On the one hand, it seemed unfair that trained workmen who had served a seven years' apprenticeship should be exposed to the competition of those who had served no apprenticeship; and the effects on the moral and social discipline of the young were bound to be injurious. On the other hand, compulsory apprenticeship prevented a workman, when trade was slack, seeking employment in another industry, and it handicapped men of ability who could not afford the premiums, or who did not need a long term of servitude in which to learn their craft.

In the application of *laissez-faire* doctrines to industry

there was no novelty; in their application to commerce there was unmistakably a new departure. For two centuries it had been a leading principle of English trade policy to prevent the export of wool, and as late as 1788 the penalties had been made more stringent. But the new school of statesmen, whose views were moulded by the teachings of Adam Smith, wished to break down artificial commercial barriers and establish free trade, and they lent a willing ear to the demand of the wool-growers that, as they were not allowed to export their wool to foreign markets, they ought to have the monopoly of the home market. The manufacturers were therefore offered the choice of the free export of British wool or a heavy duty on imported wool.[1] Both alternatives were equally distasteful to them. The manufacturers persisted in their belief that " should foreigners be able to procure English wool to mix with that of their own growth, the exportation of woollen goods from this country would immediately cease." Nevertheless they could not reconcile themselves to a duty on imported wool, of which they now used large quantities. In the Middle Ages English wool had been considered the finest in the world, and as late as 1557 an Italian wrote that " the wool is so fine that the Spanish wools cannot be compared to it."[2] At the end of the seventeenth century, the position was reversed, and English writers were constrained to admit that " we must submit to Spain in the utmost curiosity of fineness." The reasons for the deterioration in the quality of English wool were much disputed. The graziers contended that it was due to the wool laws, which made it less profitable to grow fine wool, but the deterioration was more commonly attributed to enclosures and the breeding of larger sheep in place of the " ancient small breed of English sheep." " So long as Englishmen are fond of fat mutton, they must not expect to grow fine wool." Experiments were tried in the hope of producing

[1] In 1802 a duty of 5s. 3d. had been laid on imported wool, and in 1813 it was raised to 6s. 8d.

[2] Spanish wool had been imported into England as early as the beginning of the fourteenth century.

wool in the British Isles as fine as the wool of Spain, and
George III. imported from Spain several rams and ewes
of the famous Negretti breed. In addition sheep of the
Merino breed were introduced into England, but the agri-
culturists were disappointed in their efforts to produce wool
equal in fineness to Spanish or Saxon wool, and they therefore pressed upon the Government the taxation of foreign
wool. " The increase in the growth of wool of the Spanish
race upon the Continent, particularly in France, Germany,
and Hungary, calls imperiously," they declared, " for some
Parliamentary interference to protect our wool-growers
from being driven out of our own market." A proposal of
this kind was mooted in 1816, but Parliament decided that
it was not expedient " to make any alterations in the laws
relating to the trade in wool." However, in 1819 the Chancellor of the Exchequer felt himself strong enough to propose
a duty of 6d. per pound on foreign wool, and with the support
of the landed interest the tax was imposed. The Government soon offered to repeal the tax if no opposition were
made to the export of British wool, and the manufacturers,
impaled on the horns of a dilemma, yielded to force of
circumstances (1824).[1] The following year the duty on
foreign cloth imported into England was reduced from
50 to 15 per cent. In thus withdrawing its protection from
the woollen industry the State abandoned the most tenacious
doctrine of its former economic creed.

Sources of
the wool-
supply.
This complete reversal of our commercial policy was
accompanied by, and indeed was largely the result of,
changes in the sources of our wool-supply. We have
already remarked that English manufacturers were becoming increasingly dependent upon foreign wool. In the
year 1766 we imported (in round figures) nearly 2 million
pounds of wool; in 1790 about 2½ millions; in 1800 the
amount was 8½ millions; in 1814 this quantity was nearly
doubled; in 1818, an exceptional year, the amount was
over 26 millions. During the next few years the import
figures fluctuated considerably—in 1825 they actually

[1] A duty of 1d. per lb. was imposed on the import of foreign wool
and the export of British wool.

exceeded 44 millions; in 1840 they were nearly 50 millions; in 1850 about 72½ millions; and in 1907 the quantity of wool imported and retained in the United Kingdom was no less than 393½ millions. The sources from which the imported supplies were obtained are worth noticing. At first the main source was Spain and the Canaries, which in 1802 sent us 5½ million pounds, and in 1818 over 8¾ millions. This was the high-water mark of the Spanish supply, which in 1820 fell to 3½ millions, in 1830 to 1½ millions, in 1840 to 1¼ millions, and in 1850 to less than ½ million. Another source was Germany, from which in 1815 we imported 3 million pounds, in 1820 over 5 millions, and in 1830 over 26 millions; but in 1840 the figure fell to 22 millions, and in 1850 to 9 millions. The most important source of the wool-supply in the nineteenth century was neither Spain nor Germany, but Australia. When the first fleet sailed from England for New South Wales in 1787, it took in some sheep at the Cape of Good Hope; these sheep were of the Spanish breed, sent originally from Holland to the Cape. The early experiences of the colonists did not prove encouraging. "In 1788 the Governor had the mortification to learn that five ewes and a lamb had been destroyed at a farm, supposed to have been killed by dogs belonging to the natives. This, to the happy inhabitants of Great Britain, may appear a circumstance too trivial to record, but to the founders of a new colony it would be of magnitude sufficient to be by them deemed a public calamity." The number of sheep mounted up from 29 in 1788 to 526 in 1793, 2,457 in 1797, and 10,157 in 1803. Captain John Macarthur endeavoured to interest the mother-country in the prospects of Australia as a wool-producing country, and brought home specimens of wool from Port Jackson. In 1820 we imported from Australia 100,000 pounds of wool; ten years later this quantity had increased twenty-fold, and twenty years later a hundredfold; in 1850 the amount was almost 40 million pounds.

Meanwhile the export trade in British wool had been growing, though at a slower rate. In 1820 about 35,000 pounds were exported; in 1826 about 143,000; in

1828 about 1,700,000; in 1832 the amount exceeded 4 millions; in 1850 it reached 12 millions; and in 1907 it was nearly 38 millions. The manufacturers had prophesied that the export of English wool would extinguish the export trade in cloth. Never was a prophecy more signally falsified. Owing to the perfection of our machinery and the skill of the manufacturers, who were now forced to rely upon their own native ingenuity, our foreign trade was not destroyed. The statistics of the woollen exports need not be given in detail; it is sufficient to remark that the declared value of woollen manufactured goods exported from Great Britain averaged from 1814 to 1820, £8,000,000; in 1907 their value (including Irish exports) was £19,200,000. This increase of 140 per cent. was achieved in spite of the competition of the cotton industry, the value of the cotton yarns and manufactures exported from the United Kingdom in 1907 exceeding £95,000,000. The total value of the output of woollen and worsted factories in the United Kingdom in 1907 was £70,331,000; the estimated total consumption of sheep's and lambs' wool was 490 million pounds (including shoddy, mohair, etc., the total estimated quantity was 741·3 million pounds); and the number of persons employed was 257,017.[1] In the cotton industry the total value of the output of the cotton factories was £176,940,000, and the number of persons employed was 572,869.

The policy of the State in the nineteenth century has thus been the exact reverse of its policy in the eighteenth century. In the earlier period it favoured the principle of *laissez-faire* in industry and the principle of *mercantilism* in commerce. It gave a free hand to the woollen manufacturers in their relations with labour and in the internal economy of the industry, permitting the Tudor industrial code to fall into disuse, and finally sweeping it away in 1809; on the other hand, it protected the manufacturers from the competition of their rivals abroad. In the later

---

[1] Males under eighteen years of age—21,953; females ditto—89,485. Males over eighteen—34,087; females ditto—111,492. These figures are taken from the returns received under the Census of Production Act 1906.

period the State has favoured *laissez-faire* in commerce and protection in industry; it has established free trade and deprived the woollen industry of the protection it had for many centuries enjoyed; on the other hand, it has instituted new safeguards for the protection of the working classes. This remarkable reversal of policy was due to a growing recognition of the fact that the pursuit of wealth is not the highest goal of human effort, and that maximum production can be purchased too dearly if it is achieved at the expense of the health and happiness of the community. Accordingly the State has been compelled to revive, under new conditions, the old principle of safeguarding the social and economic welfare of the workers. Naturally the new legislation differs from the old, which—however necessary at a time when the nation had to be schooled to obedience—is no longer suited to the altered needs of the present age. In respect of certain commodities, elaborate legislation is still necessary to prevent adulteration and fraud, but in the woollen industry manufacturers are now free to make cloth " as long and as short as a man will," to use any material they please, and to employ any kind of machinery. On the other hand, factory laws prohibiting child labour and regulating hours of work provide conditions of employment which are an advance even upon the Tudor conception of social welfare. And the proposal to establish a minimum wage will extend the sphere of State intervention in a new and wholesome direction.[1]

[1] Certain developments in the woollen and worsted industries during the nineteenth century must be briefly noticed. One is the introduction of cotton warps into the weaving of worsted stuffs. This has enabled lighter fabrics to be produced to meet changes in fashion. Another is the use of alpaca (imported from Peru and Chili) and mohair (drawn from Turkish and South African sources), in the worsted trade. A third is the growth of the shoddy manufacture in the woollen industry. The last few years have also witnessed a marked development of trade unionism among textile workers. The general condition of the woollen and worsted industries, as they existed in 1906, is described in detail in J. H. Clapham, *The Woollen and Worsted Industries*.

CHAPTER VI

THE GEOGRAPHICAL DISTRIBUTION OF THE WOOLLEN
AND WORSTED INDUSTRIES

Centres of the woollen industry in early times.

THE purpose of the present chapter is to show in what parts of the country the woollen and worsted industries have flourished at different periods of English history. The chief centres of the cloth trade in the twelfth century were London, Oxford, Lincoln, Huntingdon, Nottingham, Winchester, and York: all these towns contained gilds of weavers. Other important places were Northampton, Leicester, and Stamford, the last of which seemed likely at one time to become the seat of a University and to rival the supremacy of Oxford and Cambridge. In Suffolk the most important centre was Bury St. Edmunds, where the fullers were bidden by the cellarer of the Abbey to " furnish cloth for his salt, otherwise he would prohibit them the use of the waters and would seize the webs he found there." Cloth-dealers, dyers, and weavers are also mentioned at Ipswich, and textile workers at Blackbourne. In Essex cloth-makers from Bruges are said to have settled early in the fourteenth century; and at Colchester the cloth industry already engaged the main energies of its inhabitants. Oxford held the leading position in its own county, but Woodstock could also boast a weaver, dyer, and tailor, while weavers figure early in the list of burgesses at Wallingford in Berkshire. St. Albans in Hertfordshire contained a street named " Fullerstrete," and the Abbot of the monastery, according to the account given by Walsingham, demanded that all cloth, and especially coarse cloth, must be fulled at his mill. The townsmen disputed this claim and set up hand-mills in their own houses (1274). The Abbot, " unwilling to tolerate so great an injury," sent his officers to distrain upon the townsmen, and they seized a

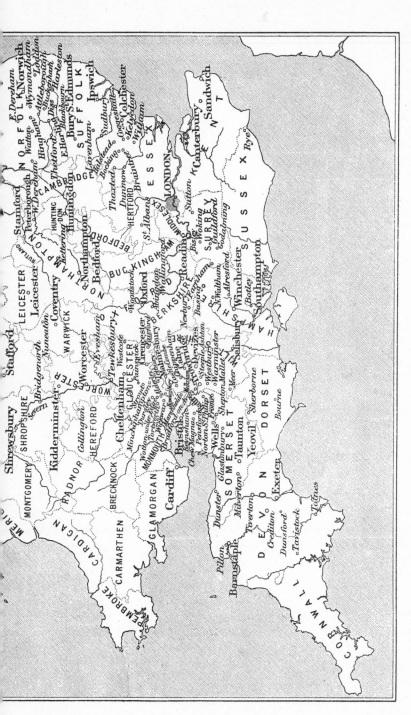

MAP ILLUSTRATING THE GEOGRAPHICAL DISTRIBUTION OF THE WOOLLEN AND WORSTED INDUSTRIES.

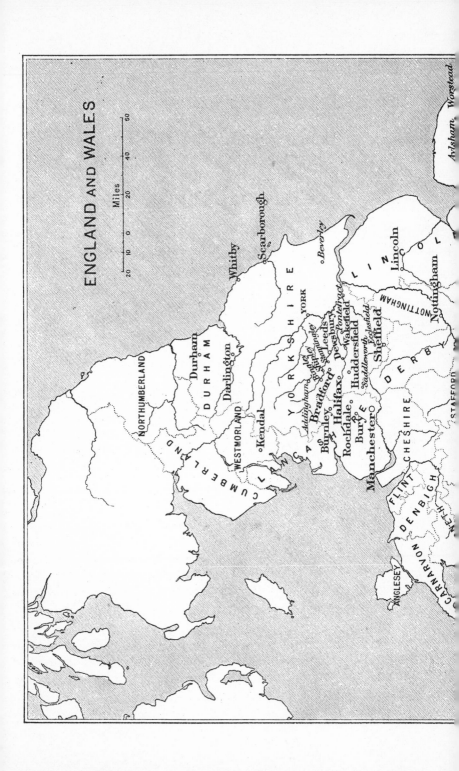

ENGLAND AND WALES

Miles
20 10 0   10   20   40   50

NORTHUMBERLAND

Durham
DURHAM
Darlington

Whitby

Scarborough

CUMBERLAND

WESTMORLAND

Kendal

L

YORKSHIRE

YORK

Beverley

Addingham
Keighley
Shipley
Bingley
Bradford
Burnley
Halifax
Rochdale
Bury
Manchester

Dewsbury
Leeds
Pontefract
Wakefield
Huddersfield
Saddleworth
Holmfield

Lincoln

L   I   N   C   O   L   N

Sheffield

DERB

CHESHIRE

STAFFORD

NOTTINGHAM

Nottingham

FLINT

DENBIGH

NETH.

CARNARVON

ANGLESEY

Aylsham Worstead

russet cloth worth 30s. belonging to Henry de Porta. The townsmen sought redress in a court of law, taxing themselves to meet the legal expenses. When Queen Eleanor visited the monastery, the townsmen were eager to lay their grievance before her, but the Abbot brought the Queen into the monastery by a secret way. However the townsmen, accompanied by a great multitude of women, " whose attack was formidable since it is difficult to restrain successfully the anger of women," forced their way in, and the Queen censured the Abbot for keeping the people away from her. When the case was tried at court the townsmen lost their suit and were forced to submit. In the West of England the cloth trade had rapidly developed. One-fifth of the townsfolk of Bristol were connected with the woollen industry, and part of the High Street was called the Drapery. Cirencester contained a Dyers' Street, Tewkesbury a Fullers' Street, and there are indications of a cloth trade at Cardiff, Worcester, Evesham, and Bridgnorth. Even in the North of England the woollen industry had gained a footing. The existence of a cloth manufacture in Lancashire is shown by the presence of fulling mills at Manchester and other places, while in the county of Durham we find dyers at Darlington. In Yorkshire the chief centre of the cloth trade was the capital of the county, but York did not possess the sole monopoly of cloth-making, for other Yorkshire towns, including Beverley and Scarborough, also manufactured cloth. The woollen industry soon spread through the West Riding, and Leeds, Wakefield, Halifax, and Bradford were connected with it at an early period. Even Whitby contained textile workers, and Sheffield had its weaver and fullers, one of whom was a woman. This shows that the textile manufactures were growing up in country places as well as in towns; indeed, as early as 1264 the industrial rivalry of town and country manifested itself in an ordinance of the Leicester authorities forbidding craftsmen to weave the cloth of neighbouring villages unless they were short of work. There are signs that the woollen industry was spreading also in the villages of Gloucestershire, Somersetshire, Hampshire, and Surrey:

thus there were fullers at Clively and Hawkesbury, weavers at Cheltenham and Dunster, and fulling mills at Waltham, Sutton, Alresford, and Woking. The manufacture of worsted was associated at first, not with Norwich, afterwards its most famous centre, but with Worstead and Aylsham in Norfolk. The accounts of the City Chamberlain of Norwich for 1301 include " presents sent to the justices of the lord king and others his ministers, as in cloth, wine, oats, cloths of Worstead, and cloths of Aylsham out of courtesy of the whole community." It is evident, then, that worsted cloth had gained a reputation before the coming of Flemish artisans under Edward III. Norwich itself had not yet become the seat of a worsted industry, but traded in leather and leather goods, although an old chronicler explains the easy capture of the city by rebels in 1194 on the ground that the men of Norwich " for the most part were weavers," and " knew not how to bear arms in knightly wise." Whether this is true or not, part of the inhabitants were engaged in the finishing processes such as fulling and dyeing.

The chief cloth-making areas in the fifteenth century.

In the fifteenth century the principal cloth-making areas of England were the West Country, East Anglia, and Yorkshire. About the year 1470 Somersetshire, Gloucestershire, and Wiltshire were producing one-third of the woollen cloth made in this country, East Anglia a quarter, and Yorkshire an eighth. In the list of textile counties Suffolk ranked first, Somersetshire second, Yorkshire third, Gloucestershire fourth, and Wiltshire fifth. These five counties were responsible for three-fifths of the entire output of cloth, excluding the coarsest varieties. Norfolk (including Norwich) occupies a very low position in the list —it produced less than one-sixth of the cloth made in Suffolk or Yorkshire—because the figures on which the above estimate is based leave out the worsted industry.[1]

In early times the towns were the centres of the cloth manufacture, but in the course of centuries the woollen industry overflowed from the towns into the suburbs and country districts, where it ran its course free from any

[1] See Bibliographical Note.

impediment or restraint. This trend of the cloth trade away from the ancient boroughs to new industrial centres was in part, no doubt, prompted by the desire to evade the control of the craft gilds and escape financial obligations, but it was ultimately due to the rapid expansion of the woollen manufacture. Nevertheless, the corporate towns did not surrender their privileged position without a struggle. They endeavoured as much as possible to retain in their own hands the sole right to manufacture cloth, and they invoked in support of their claims the charters bestowed upon them by the Crown in the twelfth century, which gave them a practical monopoly within a large area. In early times their monopoly was not seriously contested, and Norwich, York, and other important centres remained the emporium to which the cloth-makers settled in the vicinity brought their cloth for sale. Moreover, the town clothier often became the employer of country weavers, who worked for him in their cottage homes. In the eyes of the clothiers the system had a twofold advantage: it enabled them to obtain cheap labour and to evade the regulations of the gild authorities. But it provoked the jealousy of the urban craftsman, whose opportunities for employment were proportionately diminished, and it started the industrial conflict of town and country, which existed as early as the thirteenth century.[1] In order to crush the rivalry of rural artisans, and to protect their industrial population from "foreign" competition, the corporate towns ordered their citizens not to give employment to country-folk. At Worcester, for example, the burgesses were forbidden to " put out any wool " to strangers " in hurting of the said city or in hindering of the poor commonalty of the same, where there be persons enough to dye, card, or spin, weave or cloth-walk [full] within the city," and the prohibition was repeated in other towns, which would not allow woollen cloth to be woven in country districts.

In the sixteenth century the rivalry of urban and rural craftsmen gradually receded into the background; instead

Rivalry of urban and rural craftsmen.

---

[1] *Cf.* above, p. 221.

there grew up a rivalry of town and country clothiers.
The villages now ceased to depend upon the towns for
industrial employment; and, owing to the rapid extension
of the woollen manufacture in rural districts, the control
over it began to slip from the grasp of the older boroughs.
In Suffolk, for example, Bury St. Edmunds, Ipswich, and
Sudbury no longer remained the only centres of the cloth
trade, and the weaving industry became established in
villages like Lavenham. If we follow in the wake of
Leland's *Itinerary*, which gives an account of his travels
in the years 1535-1543, we can trace in certain counties of
England both the decay of the older towns and the rise of
the new country " townlets," which owed their prosperity
to the spread of the textile industries. At Beverley, once
famous for its cloth, the woollen manufacture was " much
decayed." Bridgnorth in Shropshire formerly " stood by
clothing, and that now decayed there the town sorely
decayed therewith." Coventry had risen " by the making
of cloth and caps, that now decaying the glory of the city
decayeth." On the other hand, in Somersetshire, Gloucestershire, and Wiltshire numerous " clothing towns " and
" clothing villages " are enumerated: Frome, Pensford, Chew
Magna, and Norton St. Philip in Somersetshire; Alderley,
Wotton, Dursley, Tortworth, and Wickwar in Gloucestershire; Bradford, Devizes, Steeple Ashton, and Westbury
in Wiltshire. Of all these places Leland tells how one is
" well occupied with clothiers," and how another " standeth
most by clothing "; and his list could easily be extended from
other sources. A similar movement can be discerned in
the West Riding of Yorkshire. The aulnager's rolls[1] for
the county at the end of the fourteenth century show
that weaving was carried on in country districts near York,
but was not yet organised on any large scale in the remoter
parts of Yorkshire. In the sixteenth century,[2] however,
the prosperity of the corporate towns in Yorkshire began

[1] See above, p. 113.
[2] And even earlier. In 1395, York paid over £53 in subsidy on
cloth—more than three times the amount paid by the West Riding
the following year. Eighty years later it paid only £15, about half
the amount paid by the West Riding.

to wane, and their place was usurped by their younger rivals. Leland, whose evidence we have already cited for Beverley, specially mentions Wakefield as a town whose " whole profit standeth by coarse drapery." In 1561 the authorities of York complained of the decayed fortunes of their city. " The cause of the decay of the weavers and looms for woollen cloth within the city as I do understand and learn is the lack of cloth-making in the city as was in old time accustomed, which is now increased and used in the towns of Halifax, Leeds, and Wakefield: for that not only the commodity of the water-mills is there nigh at hand, but also the poor folk as spinners, carders, and other necessary workfolk for the weaving, may there beside their hand-labour have rye, fire (wood), and other relief good cheap, which is in this city very dear and wanting." But it was not only the presence of water-mills and the cheapness of provisions which attracted artisans into the rural districts; even more important was the absence or at any rate the difficulty of supervision. In the villages the weaving industry was left to a large extent unregulated, a circumstance which contributed to the disadvantages to which the older towns were exposed. In Yorkshire, for example, the country weavers made cloth " with woof of flocks," a practice afterwards prohibited by Parliament. The oppressive ordinances of craft gilds concerning the fees of apprentices and admission to mastership must have operated in the same direction. Under Henry VIII. an attempt was made to redress the balance by an Act (1543) which gave to York a monopoly of the manufacture of coverlets and conferred upon its gild of coverlet-makers power of search throughout the country. The ostensible purpose of the Act is explained in the following passage: " Now of late divers and sundry evil disposed persons, apprentices, not expert in the same occupation, withdrawing themselves out of the city of York into the county of York and other places thereabouts, and also divers other persons inhabiting in villages and towns within the said county and nigh to the same; intermeddling with the same craft or occupation, having little experience therein, not being bound to the said rules and ordinances, do daily make coverlets and covering neither of good stuff, nor of good assize, length, or breadth . . . to the great impoverishing of the inhabitants of the said city."

Attempts
to confine
the
woollen
industry
to urban
centres.
The struggle between the established seats of industry and villages which were growing into towns constitutes one of the main economic movements of the sixteenth century.   The former sought by means of legislative action to check the spread of industry, and to repress the activities of the new industrial centres that were springing up around them.   In 1534 an Act was passed on behalf of Worcestershire of which the capital town, together with four other towns in the county, found their prosperity menaced by the growing competition of the country districts. " In time past," recites the Statute, these five Worcestershire towns were " well and substantially inhabited, occupied, maintained, and upholden by the reason of the making of woollen cloth, and the poor people daily set awork, until now within few years past divers persons inhabiting and dwelling in the hamlets, thorpes, and villages adjoining to the said city, borough, and towns, for their private wealth, singular advantages and commodities, nothing regarding the maintenance and upholding of the said city, do exercise the misteries of cloth-making in the country." It was now ordered that no cloth should be made in the county except in the above five towns.   The Act would seem to have been effective, for Leland wrote that " the wealth of Worcester standeth most by draping, and no town of England at the present time maketh so many cloths yearly as this town doth."   In Mary's reign a renewed effort was made to revive the prosperity of the corporate and market towns.   The celebrated Weavers Act (1555) extended to most parts of the kingdom the principle embodied in the Acts relating to Worcester and York.   Henceforth " no person whatsoever, which heretofore hath not used or exercised the feat, mistery, or art of cloth-making, shall make or weave any kind of broad white woollen cloths but only in a city, borough, town corporate, or market town, or else in such place or places where such cloths

have been used to be commonly made by the space of ten years." This legislation throws a remarkable light upon the efforts of the Tudor Government to control the economic life of the country and determine the direction of its industrial development. At the end of Mary's reign another Act was passed, the preamble of which shows the nature of the exodus which was taking place from the towns to the villages. " Divers ancient cities hath been in times past well and substantially inhabited, at which time also tillage was well maintained," but " divers years past such persons as do use the feat or mistery of cloth-making do daily plant themselves in villages and towns, being no cities, boroughs, and towns corporate," and " draw with them out of cities all sorts of artificers." to the decay of the old towns; and moreover, " the weavers and workmen of clothiers when they have been traded up in the trade of cloth-making and weaving three and four years do forsake their masters, and do become clothiers and occupiers for themselves without stock, skill, or knowledge." The preamble is again followed by a prohibition against the manufacture of cloth except in market or corporate towns.[1] None the less the Tudor monarchy was powerless to divert the tide of economic change which was transforming mediæval conditions and for good or evil ushering in the modern world. At the opening of the seventeenth century the Venetian Secretary in London wrote that broad cloth " and especially kersies are made all over the kingdom in the small hamlets and villages, and not in the big towns only."

The distribution of the woollen industry under the Early Fuller's list. Stuarts is roughly indicated in Fuller's list:

" East : (1) Norfolk, Norwich fustians;
   (2) Suffolk, Sudbury baize;
   (3) Essex, Colchester says and serges;
   (4) Kent, Kentish broad cloths.
 West : (1) Devonshire, kersies;
   (2) Gloucestershire, cloth;
   (3) Worcestershire, cloth;
   (4) Wales, Welsh friezes.

[1] This Act was repealed in 1624.

North: (1) Westmorland, Kendal cloth;
      (2) Lancashire, Manchester cotton;
      (3) Yorkshire, Halifax cloths.
South: (1) Somersetshire, Taunton serges;
      (2) Hampshire, cloth;
      (3) Berkshire, cloth;
      (4) Sussex, cloth."

" Observe we here," adds Fuller, " that mid-England—Northamptonshire, Lincolnshire, and Cambridge—having most of wool, have least of clothing therein."

Distribution of the woollen industry in the eighteenth century. The main source of information for the eighteenth century is Defoe's *Tour of Great Britain*, which covers the years 1724-1727. In addition there are occasional notices in the works of Arthur Young, Eden, and various topographical writers. The natural starting-point of an industrial itinerary is Norfolk, which is described by Defoe in the following terms:

Norfolk. " When we come into Norfolk we see a face of diligence spread over the whole country; the vast manufactures carried on (in chief) by the Norwich weavers employs all the country round in spinning yarn for them; besides many thousand packs of yarn which they receive from other countries,[1] even from as far as Yorkshire and Westmorland.

" This [eastern] side of Norfolk is very populous and thronged with great and spacious market towns more and larger than any other part of England so far from London, except Devonshire and the West Riding of Yorkshire; for example, between the frontiers of Suffolk and the city of Norwich on this side, which is not above twenty-two miles in breadth, are the following towns, viz.: Thetford, Hingham, Harleston, Dis, West Deerham, East Deerham, Harling, Attleboro', Watton, Bucknam, Windham, Loddon, etc.

" Most of these towns are very populous and large; but that which is most remarkable is that the whole country round them is so interspersed with villages, and those villages so large and so full of people, that they are equal

---

[1] *I.e.*, counties.

to market towns in other countries; in a word they render this eastern part of Norfolk exceeding full of inhabitants. . . .

" This throng of villages continues through all the east part of the country, which is of the greatest extent and where the manufacture is chiefly carried on. . . . Put it all together the county of Norfolk has the most people in the least tract of land of any county in England except about London and Exeter and the West Riding of Yorkshire." And, adds Defoe, " the manufacturers assured me that there was not in all the eastern and middle part of Norfolk any hand unemployed, if they would work, and that the very children after four or five years of age could every one earn their own bread."

Of this busy hive of industry the thriving centre was Norwich, once the metropolis of East Anglia and the greatest manufacturing town in England. " Norwich is the capital of all the county and the centre of all the trades and manufactures which I have just mentioned; an ancient, large, rich, and populous city. If a stranger was only to ride through or view the city of Norwich for a day, he would have much more reason to think there was a town without inhabitants, but, on the contrary, if he was to view the city either on a Sabbath Day or on any public occasion, he would wonder where all the people could dwell, the multitude is so great. But the case is this: the inhabitants being all busy at their manufactures dwell in their garrets at their looms and in their combing shops, so they call them, twisting mills, and other work-houses, almost all the works they are employed in being done within doors."

According to a calculation made by " an eminent weaver of Norwich," the number of workers engaged in the stuff-weaving manufacture of Norwich was 120,000. This estimate seems exaggerated, since Arthur Young, who asserts that the manufactures of Norwich had increased threefold between 1700 and 1770, gives the number of hands employed by the Norwich looms in 1770 as only 72,000. Those engaged in the manufacture did not all live in the city itself, but were employed in spinning yarn for the looms of Norwich. The staple manufactures were

16

worsted stuffs, crapes, and camblets, made from the long-stapled wool of Lincolnshire and Leicestershire. The wool produced in Norfolk itself was not used at home, but was sent to Yorkshire, where it was carded and spun into cloth.

Suffolk.   The county of Suffolk was associated with the woollen industry from remote times. As early as the twelfth century Bury St. Edmunds contained fullers and house-wives spinning on the distaff, and in the fifteenth century the weavers were organised in a craft gild equipped with numerous ordinances regulating their economic concerns. In the sixteenth century Suffolk profited by the settlement of aliens who reinvigorated its decaying industries, but at Bury St. Edmunds itself the cloth manufacture died out almost completely. Its place was taken by Sudbury, " an exceeding dirty (so Arthur Young describes it) but a great manufacturing town." Defoe tells us that it was very populous and very poor. " They have a great manufacture of says and perpetuana's; and multitudes of poor people are employed in working them; but the number of the poor is almost ready to eat up the rich." The manufacture of bays and says was also carried on at Lavenham and Hen-ningham. Nevertheless the mass of the population of Suffolk was occupied in the preliminary branches of the worsted industry, wool-combing and yarn-making, for the manufacturers of Norfolk and other counties, and in particular the weavers of Norwich drew from Suffolk their supplies of yarn.

Essex.   The most important town in Essex was Colchester, renowned for the manufacture of bays and says. Other places associated with the bay trade were Bocking, Brain-tree, which was "exceedingly full of manufacturers," Coggeshall, Dunmow, Kelvedon, Thaxted, and Wittham, while the whole county was employed in spinning wool for this industry. During the Civil War, when Colchester was besieged by the Parliamentarians under Fairfax, the bay-makers were allowed to hold a market outside the town once a week, and even oftener, for the sale of their goods. This incident, almost unique in the annals of war, reveals the estimation in which the woollen industry was held at this period. " Many thousands of people in and about Colchester," we learn from a Parliamentary petition dated 1701, " are employed in the woollen manufacture; for the managing whereof great quantities of wool are weekly bought at London, Buckinghamshire, and other inland counties, and brought to Colchester, and are weekly carried to spinners, many whereof live thirty miles off." The bay-makers were organised in an ancient society known as the Dutch Bay Hall, the name of which betrays its origin. It dated from the sixteenth century, when Colchester received a great influx of immigrants, who introduced into the town the new draperies. The strangers followed the process already adopted at Sandwich and other places for the " true and upright making and ensealing of bays and says." They obtained possession of a hall, and " chose amongst themselves twelve men of the discreetest and best skill to attend at the hall at certain hours of the day to view the bays and other stuffs brought unto them." The cloth was inspected twice before it was stamped, first as it came from the looms, a second time after it was fulled. Various seals were affixed to it, indicating the place of its manufacture, the number of threads in the warp, and the quality and breadth of the cloth. Originally the bay trade was free to all who had served their apprenticeship to any branch of the woollen manufacture, but in 1707 the governors of the Dutch Bay Hall framed a by-law excluding from the manufacture of bays all who had not served seven years in the bay trade. The by-law was condemned by Parliament, in spite of the defence that the market was over-stocked with bays, and that the apprentices of a bay-maker often paid a premium of forty to fifty pounds.

Norfolk, Suffolk, and Essex were " famed for industry," ^{Cambridge-} but another part of East Anglia, Cambridgeshire, had " no ^{shire.} manufacture at all, nor are the poor, except the husbandmen, famed for anything so much as idleness and sloth, to their scandal be it spoken." This unfavourable estimate may be qualified by the fact that the county possessed the greatest commercial mart in the whole kingdom—Stourbridge Fair, near Cambridge. A part of the fair, known as the Duddery, was set apart for dealers in the cloth trade; and the booths, or tents, which were grouped together in the form of a square, were so immense that they gave the impression of another Blackwell Hall.

Stour-
bridge
Fair.

" In this Duddery, as I have been informed, there have been sold one hundred thousand pounds' worth of woollen manufactures in less than a week's time, besides the prodigious trade carried on here by wholesale men from London and all parts of England," taking orders from their customers. It was " frequent for the London wholesale men to carry back orders from their dealers for ten thousand pounds' worth of goods a man, and some much more."

" Here are clothiers from Halifax, Leeds, Wakefield, and Huddersfield, in Yorkshire, and from Rochdale, Bury, etc., in Lancashire, with vast quantities of Yorkshire cloths, kersies, pennistons, cottons, etc., with all sorts of Manchester ware, fustians, and things made of cotton-wool.

" I saw one warehouse . . . belonging to a dealer in Norwich stuffs only, who, they said, had there above twenty thousand [pounds] value in those goods and no other.   Western goods had their share also."

Great quantities of wool were also sold, especially the wool raised in Lincolnshire, where the longest staple was found.   Hence the buyers were chiefly drawn from the manufacturers of Norfolk, Suffolk, and Essex, whose trade demanded the long or combed wool.

Kent.

In the early Middle Ages the economic condition of Kent was in advance of most other English counties.   Owing to its proximity to the French coast it was the high-road of commerce, and the free circulation of money proved a powerful dissolvent of those economic practices which in other parts of England survived for many centuries. Lambard, in his *Perambulation of Kent*, written in 1576, declared that the artificers of Kent excelled as makers of coloured woollen cloths, and that from them was " drawn both sufficient store to furnish the wear of the best sort of our own nation at home, and great plenty also to be transported to other foreign countries abroad."   In the sixteenth century Kent received a large incursion of alien

weavers, particularly at Sandwich, and Fuller in the next
century declared that " clothing is as vigorously applied
here as in any other place; and Kentish cloth at the present
keepeth up the credit thereof as high as ever before."
None the less the county was unable to maintain its position
among the manufacturing districts of England, and under
the Hanoverians it was numbered with Sussex, Surrey and
Hampshire, Leicestershire, Northamptonshire and Lincolnshire, among the counties which were not employed " in
any considerable woollen manufacture."

We now turn to the West Country, the seat of the broad The West
cloth manufacture, upon which the fame of English industry Country.
rested down to the era of the Industrial Revolution. At
Painswick, on the way towards Stroud, as a traveller wrote
in 1681, " you begin to enter *the land of the clothiers*, who
in these bourns building fair houses because of the con-
veniency of water, so useful for their trade, do extend their
country some miles."   The heart of the West Country was
" the low, flat country full of rivers and towns and infinitely populous," comprising part of the three counties
of Somersetshire, Wiltshire, and Gloucestershire, and
stretching from Cirencester in the north to Sherborne in
the south, and from Devizes in the east to Bristol in the
west. This tract of country extended " about fifty miles
in length where longest, and twenty miles in breadth where
narrowest," and it contained innumerable market towns
whose inhabitants were engaged in the woollen manufacture. " The River Avon waters this whole fruitful vale,
and the water seems particularly qualified for the use of
clothiers—for dyeing the best colours, and for fulling and
dressing the cloth—so that the clothiers generally plant
themselves upon this river."

Among the manufacturing counties of England, Glouces- Gloucestershire held a foremost place: " famous not for the finest tershire.
cloths only, but for dyeing those cloths of the finest scarlets
and other grain colours that are anywhere in England."
She owed her pre-eminence, in part, to the number of sheep
covering the downs and plains of Dorsetshire, Wiltshire,
and Hampshire—although, as the home-grown supply

proved insufficient for her needs, she came to draw upon the Midland counties of Northampton, Leicester, and Lincoln, and even upon Ireland and Spain—and in part also to the " excellent water " of the Stroud, which was said to have a peculiar quality for dyeing scarlets.[1] Among the chief centres of the Gloucestershire woollen industry Defoe enumerates Cirencester, " populous and rich, full of clothiers," and Tetbury, Marshfield, Minchinghampton, and Fairford. " These towns are interspersed with a very great number of villages, I had almost said, innumerable villages, hamlets, and scattered houses in which, generally speaking, the spinning work of all this manufacture is performed by the poor people; the master-clothiers, who generally live in the greater towns, sending out the wool weekly to their houses by their servants and horses, and at the same time bringing back the yarn which they have spun." The county was thus covered, in Leland's picturesque phrase, with a network of " clothing towns " and " clothing villages."

Wiltshire. Wiltshire ranked with Gloucestershire and Somersetshire as one of the great industrial districts of the West Country. The most important town in the county was Bradford; other centres were Calne, Castlecombe, Chippenham, Devizes, Malmesbury, Meer, Trowbridge, Warminster, and Westbury.

Somerset-shire. The low-lying parts of Somersetshire were covered with grazing cattle, the rest of the county was occupied with the woollen manufacture, " and the best and most profitable part of it," namely:

Taunton: Serges, druggets, and several other kinds of stuffs.

Wells, Shepton Mallet, Glastonbury, etc.: Knitting of stockings, principally for the Spanish trade.

Bristol and many towns on the Somersetshire side: Druggets, cantaloons, and other stuffs.

Frome, " Philip's Norton," and all the country bordering upon Wiltshire: Fine Spanish medley cloths (cloths dyed in the wool), " with which all the gentlemen and persons of any fashion in England are clothed," large quantities also being sent abroad.

[1] Fuller, writing in the seventeenth century, states that the clothiers of Gloucestershire enjoyed a double advantage. "First,

Even in Fuller's day Taunton serges were " eminent in their kind, being a fashionable wearing as lighter than cloth, yet thicker than many other stuffs. When Dionysius sacrilegiously plundered Jove's statue of his golden coat (pretending it too cold for winter and too hot for summer), he bestowed such a vestment upon him as to fit both seasons." Taunton is described by Defoe as " a large, wealthy, and exceedingly populous town." " One of the chief manufacturers of the town told us that there was at that time so good a trade in the town that they had then 1,100 looms going for the weaving of sagathies, du-roys, and such kind of stuffs which are made there." Defoe adds that there was not a child in the town or surrounding villages above five years old, " but if it was not neglected by its parents and untaught, could earn its own bread." Another important town was Frome; at the end of the eighteenth century it was " the chief residence of the clothiers in these parts, whose trade in this county amounts to £200,000 per annum, some making 3,000 cloths a year." Frome was regarded as the centre of the cloth industry in this part of Somersetshire, but its population did not amount to 6,000, and its appearance was not prepossessing. " This town is very ancient," wrote Eden, " and has been the seat of the woollen manufacture for centuries; yet the external appearance of the town does not indicate that wealth which is usually attendant on commerce; the houses are very different from the elegant dwellings that are to be found in the Yorkshire manufacturing towns or their neighbourhood; the streets are narrow, unpaved, and dirty." Even Bath was at one time the seat of a woollen manufacture; it was famed for the woollen article known as Bath beaver; and at the Restoration the single parish of St. Michael is said to have contained no less than sixty broad looms. A short distance from Bath was Twerton,

plenty of the best wool growing therein on Cotswolds Hills; so that whereas clothiers in some counties fetch their wool far off with great cost, it is here but the removing it from the backs of the sheep into their work-houses. Secondly, they have the benefit of an ex-cellent water for colouring their cloth, being the sweet rivulet of Stroud."

where cloth was manufactured at the end of the eighteenth century, the machinery being worked by water-power.

Devon-
shire. The county of Devon was " the largest and most populous in England, Yorkshire excepted." It was " so full of great towns, and those towns so full of people, and those people so universally employed in trade and manufactures that not only it cannot be equalled in England, but perhaps not in Europe." Its original industry was the manufacture of kersies, and Devonshire kersies were the boast of Devonshire writers. " Here are made the best and finest of the kingdom, which obtaineth to the inhabitants wealth, to the merchants traffic, and glory to the nation." After the Revolution kersies were displaced by mixed worsted serges, the warp of which was made with worsted yarn and the weft with yarn of a softer twist.

Among the centres of the Devonshire cloth industry, which included Crediton, Totnes, Barnstaple, Pilton, and Tavistock, two held pride of place—Exeter and Tiverton.

Exeter. Exeter was the greatest manufacturing town in the county. Fuller wrote that clothing was " plied in this city with great industry and judgment. It is hardly to be believed, what credible persons attest for truth, that the return for serges alone in this city amounteth weekly to £3,000." The city was famed especially for its serge market. " The serge market held here every week is well worth a stranger's seeing, and next to the brigg-market at Leeds in Yorkshire is the greatest in England. The people assured me that at this market is generally sold from sixty to seventy to eighty and sometimes one hundred thousand pounds' value in serges in a week." At the end of the eighteenth century " almost every other man you met wore an apron of emerald green serge, girded and tied with a scarlet woollen band— they all belonged to the ' Guild of Incorporated Weavers, Fullers, and Shearmen,' who were alone permitted to exer-

Tiverton. cise their craft." Tiverton ranked second in importance to Exeter alone. A royal brief, issued by James I. in 1612 after the great fire at Tiverton, states that the inhabitants " through their great trade in clothing kept always in work eight thousand men, women, and children." " The said town hath lately been accounted the chiefest market town in all the west parts of England," and two thousand pounds " at least " were expended every week throughout the year in cloth, wool, and yarn. The prosperity of the town was maintained during the first quarter of the eighteenth century; fifteen hundred looms were daily at work, and more than seven hundred wool-combers were in constant employment. The end of the century witnessed a marked decline; the number of looms was reduced by one-half, and the number of wool-combers by one-third.[1]

While the woollen industry was carried on in every part of the country, in contrast with the cotton industry, which has always been, in the main, associated with a single county, certain parts of the kingdom became pre-eminent as the " manufacturing districts " of England *par excellence*. These " manufacturing districts " were East Anglia, the West Country, and Yorkshire. We have already devoted attention to East Anglia and the West Country, and it therefore remains to give some account of Yorkshire. "The manufacturing districts" of England.

The history of the West Riding is remarkable in many ways. The records of its woollen industry stretch back to remotest times, but for centuries the Yorkshire cloth manufacture was in a backward condition. Yorkshire was not immune from the lethargy[2] which made the North of England, with its primitive social and economic system, so marked a contrast to the South, with its advanced civilisation, its flourishing industry and commerce, its organised urban centres, and its rich and abundant vitality. But in the eighteenth century the dormant energies of the North were quickened to new life. A fresh impulse seems to have communicated itself to its people, who began to turn to advantage the vast potential resources of which they were possessed. Their thrifty and hardy character, their resourcefulness and adaptability, were immense assets in the The West Riding.

---

[1] Cloth was also manufactured in Cornwall and in the sixteenth century was exported abroad.

[2] At the end of the fifteenth century Yorkshire—in spite of its extent—produced only one-third of the cloth made in Somersetshire, Gloucestershire, and Wiltshire, and only one-half of the cloth made in East Anglia. The quality was also greatly inferior.

task which they now took upon themselves to wrest from Norwich and the Stroud Valley their industrial supremacy over the rest of England. The Industrial Revolution assured them the final victory in this struggle largely on account of the comparative ease with which machinery was introduced into the North of England.

Growth of Yorkshire towns. In the Middle Ages the greatest centre of the weaving industry in the North was York—at the end of the fourteenth century the number of weavers in the city who paid the tax on cloth was more than double the number of the weavers in the rest of the county. Beverley was also renowned for its cloth, and the West Riding was connected with the woollen industry as early as the thirteenth and fourteenth centuries: there were dyers at Wakefield before 1250, cloth-workers at Halifax and Bradford, fullers at Leeds. The conditions under which the clothing towns struggled into existence are set before us in a Statute of Queen Mary (1555). " Forasmuch as the parish of Halifax and other places thereunto adjoining, being planted in the great waste and moors where the fertility of ground is not apt to bring forth any corn nor good grass, but in rare places and by exceeding and great industry of the inhabitants; and the same inhabitants altogether do live by cloth-making, and the greater part of them neither getteth corn nor [are] able to keep a horse to carry wool, nor yet to buy much wool at once, but hath ever used only to repair to the town of Halifax and some other nigh thereunto, and there to buy from the wool-driver some a stone, some two, and some three or four, according to their ability, and to carry the same to their houses some three, four, and six miles off, upon their heads and backs, and so to make and convert the same either into yarn or cloth, and to sell the same, and so to buy more wool of the wool-driver. By means of which industry the barren ground in those parts be now much inhabited and above 500 households there newly increased within these forty years past."

Although large quantities of Yorkshire cloth were exported abroad, the general level of the industry as regards quality and skill was a low one.[1] The manufacturers gained an evil notoriety for their use of lambs' wool, flocks, and other prohibited materials; and legislation was powerless to turn them from their malpractices. Henry VIII. appointed a Commission, which sat at Leeds and afterwards at Pontefract, to punish the offenders, but the Commissioners found it impossible to obtain evidence upon which to base convictions. "Sir John Nevyll, John Pullayn, and I sat at Leeds among divers of the cloth-makers, but by all the policy we could devise could not obtain proof against the great number of the offenders." The estimation in which Yorkshire cloth was held a century later may be gauged from Fuller's castigation: "As I am glad to hear the plenty of a coarser kind of cloth is made in this county, at Halifax, Leeds, and elsewhere, whereby the meaner sort are much employed, and the middle sort enriched; so I am sorry for the general complaints made thereof: insomuch that it is become a general by-word ' to shrink as northern cloths ' (a giant to the eye and dwarf in the use thereof) to signify such who fail their friends in deepest distress, depending on their assistance. Sad that the sheep, the emblem of Innocence, should unwillingly cover so much craft under the wool thereof, and sadder that fullers, commended in Scriptures for making cloth white, should justly be condemned for making their own consciences black by such fraudulent practices."

After the Restoration a corporation of clothiers was erected (1662) within the West Riding on the ground that "divers abuses and deceits have of late years been had and used in the manufacture of broad woollen cloth made within the West Riding, and the spinning and deceitful working thereof." It was composed of all the Justices of the Peace of the West Riding, together with two Masters, ten wardens, twelve assistants, and the commonalty, "all which Masters, wardens, and assistants are to be of the ablest and best experienced clothiers within the West

Character of the Yorkshire trade.

The West Riding Corporation.

---

[1] The superiority of the West Country cloth as compared with that of Yorkshire was variously attributed to (1) more careful sorting of wool; (2) better dyeing; (3) better finishing (see p. 190); and (4) greater specialisation (see p. 38).

Riding" and elected by "the free clothiers." It was vested with the power of making by-laws and ordinances "for the better spinning, working, making, fulling, and milling of woollen cloth, as in their judgments and discretions may tend to the good credit and advancement of the trade," and to punish clothiers for the infringement of their regulations.

The worsted industry in Yorkshire.   The staple industry of Yorkshire in early times was the manufacture of a coarse cloth called "kersey." A new page in the history of the county was opened up with the introduction of the worsted trade. The date usually assigned to this event is the end of the seventeenth century.[1] The fact that Yorkshire exported yarn to Norwich may well have suggested to Yorkshire men the possibility of working up the yarn at home and entering into competition with Norfolk manufacturers, and the fact that labour was apparently cheaper in the North made the experiment feasible. The progress of the industry was at first slow, but it brought the West Riding into rivalry with Norfolk, which had formerly enjoyed almost the sole monopoly of the worsted trade; and in 1727 Defoe enumerates shalloons (worsted cloth) along with broad woollen cloth and narrow woollen cloth (kersies), as "the three articles of that country's labour." The competition of Yorkshire with other centres of industry began to attract attention early in the eighteenth century. A writer in 1741 remarked: "Though some towns have sunk in trade, others have advanced. For I remember, in my time, the rise of some towns, and the fall of others in that [woollen] manufactory—viz., Sudbury, and, I think, Farnham, were famous for making shalloons, as was also Newbury. Then Kettering, a little market town in Northamptonshire, from manufacturing 20 or 30 pieces of dyed serges weekly fell into making shalloons, rivalled the towns above mentioned, and sent to London market upwards of 1,000 pieces per week. Yorkshire hath rivalled them since by under-working them, and very much decreased their trade, as also lowered their

[1] An attempt to establish the worsted industry at York was made in the reign of James I.

prices; they have also robbed the West and East; for I am told they not only make long Ells, but Bays in imitation of Bocking Bays, and sell them much cheaper for the reasons aforesaid."

The *Letter Books of Joseph Holroyd and Sam Hill* afford vivid glimpses of the difficulties with which the early worsted makers of Yorkshire had to contend. In one of the letters to an agent abroad we see the manufacturer's anxiety to open up a market even at a sacrifice. " I am studying," Hill writes (1737) in reference to a consignment of shalloons, " to outdo all England with the sort *Sam Hill*, and be assured if quality and price will do it ye shall have the command in your own hand, or it shall be because it is not in my power, but must earnestly beg of ye to let yon go for as small profit now till they be known." Another letter shows his readiness to imitate his competitors in the trade. " There is another thing you will do well to teach me—viz., if the Broad must be sold in imitation of those made in other parts of England, as you formerly mentioned to me, then I think you should have the Lists and the Head Ends made as like them as possible, which if you describe I shall imitate as near as I can, but if you cannot describe them right you had best send a pattern." In spite of occasional moments of despondency, he did not lose confidence in himself. " I like to make them and fancy I shall in time do it well. . . . The narrow shalloons of the mark *Sam Hill* are, I think, such goods as I may say are not to be outdone in England by any man, let him be who he will." And his confidence was not without justification. The success which attended the efforts of Yorkshire capitalists to develop the worsted industry is shown by the fact that the worsted cloth made in the West Riding in 1772 equalled in value the cloth made in Norwich. Nevertheless their success was not achieved at the expense of the Norwich trade, since the latter was growing at the same time; moreover, the Norwich weavers were engaged in the production of the finer qualities of worsted, while the Yorkshire men made the middle and lower qualities. Nor was it due to the use of any machinery, which at this date had not been adopted in the worsted industry, even the fly shuttle being more suitable at first for the making of broad woollen cloth.

Centres of the Yorkshire trade. In the eighteenth century a group of five towns were the centres of " that vast clothing trade by which the wealth and opulence of this part of the country has been raised to what it now is." These five towns were Leeds, Halifax, Wakefield, Huddersfield, and Bradford. Leeds, " a large, wealthy, and populous town," was described by Thoresby in 1714 as " deservedly celebrated both at home and in the most distant trading parts of Europe for the woollen manufacture." It was famous for its cloth market, which has been described in another chapter.[1] The staple manufacture was broad cloth, although stuffs were also made. " Of the prosperity of Leeds," observes Eden, " the high price both of land and water, the many new streets in the town, and the manufactories and villas in the neighbourhood, erected and erecting, are a very convincing proof." In 1775 the number of inhabitants was estimated at 17,000; a quarter of a century later, this figure was nearly doubled; and all classes were connected, in a greater or less degree, with the woollen industry. Halifax, as early as the reign of Elizabeth, was " a very famous town." According to Camden, the cloth manufacture was first established here " about seventy years ago "—that is, in the sixteenth century; and Defoe places its origin about the year 1480. These dates, however, are incorrect, for clothmakers existed in Halifax in the twelfth century, and in the last quarter of the fifteenth century it was next to York in importance as a clothing town. The weavers of Halifax were mainly stuff weavers, and the town drove a great trade in kersies and shalloons, tammies, callimancoes, and russets. The inhabitants of Halifax preserved the right of beheading cloth-stealers and other thieves down to 1650, and a verse of the Beggars' Litany ran:

" From Hell, Hull, and Halifax,
Good Lord, deliver us !"

---

[1] Above, p. 79.

Wakefield was renowned for its cloth market, which ranked
second only to Leeds. It was also famed for cheapness of
living. "A right honest man," observed Leland, "shall
fare well for twopence a meal." The town specialised in
cloth-finishing, and here cloth was brought to be dyed and
to undergo the final processes of cloth-working. Huddersfield was "another large clothing place," but Bradford,
destined in the nineteenth century to become the metropolis
of the worsted industry, had not yet acquired the prominence which it afterwards enjoyed. The inhabitants were
supposed to number about five thousand, and two-thirds of
the population were employed in the manufacture of callimancoes, russets, and other materials. The town's reputation for fraudulent work may be gauged from a verse in
a Methodist hymn:

> " On Bradford likewise look Thou down
>   Where Satan keeps his seat."

The woollen industry was not confined in Yorkshire to Defoe's description
the large towns. The greater part of the domestic clothiers of the West
lived in villages or hamlets scattered over a district measur- Riding.
ing twenty to thirty miles in length and twelve to fifteen
miles in breadth. Their dispersed state was regarded by
contemporaries as "highly favourable to their morals and
happiness"; and it was one of the criticisms against the
factory system that it concentrated great masses of the
industrial population within restricted urban areas. The
classical description of the West Riding, with its continuous
line of villages growing one into the other and linked up
by innumerable hamlets and detached houses, is contained
in Defoe's *Tour of Great Britain*:

" From Blackstone Edge to Halifax is eight miles; and
all the way, except from Sorby to Halifax, is thus up hill
and down; so that, I suppose, we mounted up to the clouds,
and descended to the water-level, about eight times in that
little part of the journey.

" But now I must observe to you that after having
passed the second hill and come down into the valley again,

and so still the nearer we came to Halifax, we found the houses thicker and the villages greater in every bottom; and not only so, but the sides of the hills, which were very steep every way, were spread with houses, and that very thick; for the land being divided into small enclosures— that is to say, from two acres to six or seven acres each, seldom more—every three or four pieces of land had a house belonging to it.

" Such has been the bounty of nature to this county that two things essential to the [clothing trade] as well as to the ease of the people are found here, and that in a situation which I never saw the like of in any part of England; and, I believe, the like is not to be seen so contrived in any part of the world—I mean, coals and running water upon the tops of the highest hills. This seems to have been directed by the wise hand of Providence for the very purpose which is now served by it, namely, the manufactures which otherwise could not be carried on; neither indeed could one-fifth of the inhabitants be supported without them, for the land could not maintain them.

" After we had mounted the third hill we found the country, in short, one continued village, though mountainous every way as before; hardly a house standing out of a speaking distance from another; and, the day clearing up and the sun shining, we could see that almost at every house there was a tenter, and almost on every tenter a piece of cloth, or kersey, or shalloon, for they are the three articles of that country's labour.

" Wherever we passed any house we found a little rill or gutter of running water; and at every considerable house was a manufactory or work-house, and, as they could not do their business without water, the little streams were so parted and guided by gutters or pipes that none of those houses were without a river running into and through their work-houses.

" Again, as the dyeing-houses, scouring shops, and places where they used this water, emitted the water again tinged with the drugs of the dyeing vat and with the oil, the soap, the tallow, and other ingredients used by the clothiers in dressing and scouring, etc.," the lands through which it runs are enriched and made fertile by it to an extent hardly to be imagined.

" Then, as every clothier must necessarily keep a horse, perhaps two, to fetch home his wool and his provisions from the market, to carry his yarn to the spinners, his manufacture to the fulling mill, and when finished to the market to be sold, and the like; so every manufacturer generally keeps a cow or two or more for his family. And this employs the pieces of enclosed land about his house, for they scarce sow corn enough for their cocks and hens.

" Among the manufacturers' houses are likewise scattered an infinite number of cottages or small dwellings in which dwell the workmen which are employed, the women and children all of whom are always busy carding, spinning, etc., so that no hands being unemployed, all can gain their bread even from the youngest to the ancient; hardly anything above four years old, but its hands are sufficient to itself.

" This is the reason also why we saw so few people without doors; but if we knocked at the door of any of the master manufacturers, we presently saw a house full of lusty fellows, some at the dye-vat, some dressing the cloths, some in the loom, some one thing, some another, all hard at work and full employed upon the manufacture. . . . This is one of the most populous parts of Britain, London and the adjacent parts excepted."

We must not omit to mention some other important centres of the woollen industry: Worcester, Coventry, Newbury, Reading, Shrewsbury, Bristol, Kendal, and Rochdale. Worcester was one of the five Worcestershire towns on whose behalf an Act was passed in the reign of Henry VIII., ordering that no cloth should be made in the county except in these five towns. The Act evidently arrested the decay of Worcester, for we have the testimony of Leland, a few years later, that no town in England " made so many cloths yearly as this town doth." None the less its prosperity was short-lived, as we learn from

Other centres of the woollen industry.

an oration pronounced on the occasion of Queen Elizabeth's visit in 1575: " This city of long time so increased in wealth, substance, and beautiful buildings, and became so fortunate in the trade of clothing, as by the only means thereof, in good and fresh memory of man, there were here used and maintained for the said trade of clothing three hundred and fourscore great looms, whereby 8,000 persons were well maintained in wealth and ability, besides masters and their children "; whereas now the number of looms was reduced to eight score, " and thereby above 5,000 persons that were well-wrought and relieved " were unemployed.   At the end of the reign " the trade of clothing " had been so effectually restored that " 6,000 persons were employed in the trade in Worcester, and above twice that number in carding, spinning, etc., in the neighbouring towns and villages "; and the historian of Worcester[1] affirms that in the seventeenth century its manufacture of broad cloth was the most considerable of any town in England. Certainly as late as 1724 the town still carried on " a great share of the clothing trade," and was famous for making some of the best broadcloth in England.   " It is almost incredible," remarked a traveller a few years later, " the number of hands employed here and in the adjacent villages, in carding, spinning, and weaving."   Its subsequent decline was due to causes the operation of which was not confined to Worcester, but was general throughout the West Country.[2] Another centre of the cloth trade in Worcestershire was Kidderminster, which was described in a charter of 1636 as a place " of great commerce for working and making of cloths; and by reason thereof, and by the daily confluence of many thither, it is very populous."

Coventry, " a large and populous city " where " the timber houses project forward and towards one another till in the narrow streets they are ready to touch one another at the top," drove a great trade in tammies.   But Newbury, " an ancient clothing town," famed for its association with the great clothier, John Winchcombe, was now stripped of its former glories, its woollen industry having " much

[1] Green, writing in 1796.   [2] See below, p. 251.

declined " in the early part of the eighteenth century. Reading was once "a very considerable clothing town," and, according to the evidence of its municipal records, covering the period 1432-1602, contained a very large number of clothiers, but in the time of Defoe it retained only " a remnant " of its woollen manufacture. The decay of the cloth trade here was attributed by the historian of Reading to the Civil War, which appears to have left no slight traces upon the economic development of the country. Shrewsbury carried on a great manufacture of white broad cloth, and the fame of Bristol cloth under the Tudors is reflected in Skelton's description of a gay dress: " Her kyrtle was of Bristowe red." Kendal in Westmorland obtained a reputation for the manufacture of Kendal cottons, a coarse narrow cloth made not from cotton, but from Westmorland wool. Camden spoke of the town as " the glory of wool-making, excelling in industry," and Fuller declared that Kendal cottons were " famous all over England." Another centre in the North of England was Knutsford, which carried on a worsted manufacture. Of the Lancashire towns formerly connected with the woollen industry particular interest attaches to Rochdale, which still remains the principal centre of the Lancashire woollen manufacture. In 1778 it was described as " famous for manufactories of cloth, kersies, and shalloon. Every considerable house is a manufactory and is supplied with a rivulet or little stream, without which the business cannot be carried on. . . . The women and children all employed here, not a beggar or idle person being to be seen." In former days Manchester, now the metropolis of the cotton industry, was also a seat of the woollen manufacture. "It excels," wrote Camden in 1590, " the towns immediately around it in handsomeness, populousness, woollen manufacture, church, and college, but did much more excel them in the last age by the glory of its woollen cloths, which they call Manchester cottons."

The Industrial Revolution had the most remarkable
effects upon the geographical distribution of the woollen
and worsted industries. Instead of being carried on in
every part of the country, in innumerable towns, villages,
and hamlets, as in former centuries, they are now concentrated mainly in the West Riding of Yorkshire. In East
Anglia, once its chief seat, the worsted industry is practically
extinct; Devon still boasts a few mills, and Gloucestershire,
Wiltshire, and Somersetshire, the ancient centre of the
broad cloth trade, still manufacture the finest woollen
cloths, but over all these districts may be written the
epitaph " Ichabod." This migration of industry was the
outcome of various factors, and it would be a mistake to
regard the introduction of machinery as the only explanation of the growth of the West Riding. The expansion of
industry in the North was, as we saw above,[1] anterior to the
advent of the factory system. The number of pieces of
broad cloth manufactured in the West Riding grew (in
round figures) from 26,000 in 1726 to 60,000 in 1750, and
to 172,000 in 1790; while the quantity of narrow cloth
increased in fifty years (1740-90) from 58,000 pieces to
140,000; yet down to 1790 the use of machinery was still
confined to the preparatory processes. The early Yorkshire clothiers were therefore not without justification when
they boasted—even before the days of machinery—that,
" in spite of fate," the woollen manufactures would " come
into these northern counties."

We may examine first the reasons for the decay of
Norwich as the greatest centre of the worsted industry.
According to Arthur Young, the trade of Norwich was
trebled between 1700 and 1770, notwithstanding the even
more rapid progress of Yorkshire during the same period.[2]
It is evident that the growth of commerce made it possible
for the trade of Norwich to expand *pari passu* with the
trade of the West Riding. We may also infer that, as
yet, there was no considerable migration from the eastern
to the northern counties—although Morant asserted (in
1748) that the trade of Colchester had " removed in a great

---

[1] Above, pp. 241-2.   [2] See above, p. 241.

measure into the western and northern parts of this kingdom, where provisions are cheaper, the poor more easily
satisfied, and coals are very plentiful." After 1818, however, the worsted industry of Norwich declined not only
relatively in comparison with the West Riding, but abso-
lutely. Arthur Young tells us that 12,000 looms were
employed in Norwich in 1770. In 1818 there were said
to be 10,000 in Norwich and its vicinity, and in 1839,
according to the Hand-loom Commissioners, there were
only 5,075, of which 1,021 were unemployed. The decline
of Norwich is often explained on the ground that Yorkshire
had certain natural advantages—namely, coal and iron;
but Norwich had one great asset in its favour—the reputation of its fabrics due to the ingenuity of its manufacturers,
coupled with the inherited skill of its weavers; and after
all, coal and iron could have been imported,[1] if the manufacturers had shown an enterprising spirit. A yarn factory
was indeed started in 1834, but by this time Yorkshire had
forged completely ahead.

Among the factors responsible for the decay of the Reasons
Norwich trade three may be singled out for mention. In decay.
the first place, the Norwich manufacturers displayed great
ingenuity in the invention and introduction of new fabrics,
and in this way endeavoured to overcome the ruinous
effects of the American and French wars upon their trade,
but their fabrics were soon imitated in Yorkshire, " made
in an inferior manner " (as it was alleged) " and substituted
at a cheaper rate." Thus, in the last years of the eighteenth
century the mainstay of the Norwich trade was the manufacture of camblets, made entirely of worsted, for the East
India Company. After the Company lost its monopoly of
trade with India (1813) and China (1833), the Yorkshire
manufacturers were allowed to export to Eastern markets
an inferior imitation which did their Norwich rivals " very
great injury." It was the cheapness of Yorkshire cloth,
combined with a very colourable imitation of the original,
which enabled the West Riding to gain command over the
market at home and abroad. Changes in fashion also told

[1] See p. 251, n. 1.

in favour of the Yorkshire manufacturers, who introduced light stuffs made with cotton warps, supplies of which were close at hand. In the second place, the Norwich manufacturers failed to keep pace with the North in regard to machinery, on account, it was said, of " the existence of a violent and odiously virulent party spirit." " No man of either political party could introduce machinery into this city," it was reported as late as 1840, " but he would in all probability, at some election contest, be held up as an obnoxious individual, and his property and perhaps his life endangered thereby." As a result Norwich in 1839 contained but a handful of power-looms in one of its mills; whereas four years before, according to the returns made by the factory inspectors, Yorkshire contained 2,856 worsted power-looms, and 533 power-looms used partly for worsted and partly for woollen or cotton. Ten years later Norfolk counted 428 power-looms, but by this time Yorkshire had 30,850. The difficulty of competing with the Yorkshire manufacturers in these circumstances proved insuperable, especially since the Norwich weavers, owing to their superior organisation, resisted reductions of wages with more success than their Yorkshire fellows. In the third place, the failure to introduce machinery in spinning was probably not unconnected with the fact that the Norwich worsted industry did not depend on local supplies of yarn, and therefore the manufacturers had not the same inducement in promoting the new methods of spinning. The first yarn factory was not set up until 1834, and it was then too late to overcome the advantages which Yorkshire now possessed: the possession of coal and iron in close proximity; the practical monopolisation of the combing processes, against which it was impossible to compete without the erection of costly machinery; and, finally, the existence of a large foreign demand for Yorkshire yarn, which made the outlay of capital in the North a profitable venture. For these various reasons Yorkshire had in 1850 no less than 746,000 spindles—forty times the number in Norfolk.

We have seen that the migration of industry from East Anglia to the West Riding was not due primarily, as is commonly supposed, to the possession of iron and coal Decline of industry in the West Country. fields, though these were important factors in the situation. It was the inability of the old-established seats of industry to adapt themselves to the altered economic conditions, which enabled their younger and more enterprising rival to outstrip them in the race for industrial pre-eminence. Just as the older English boroughs proved unable in the sixteenth century to retain their control of industry because their economic organisation failed to keep pace with the industrial needs of the time, so in the nineteenth century industry migrated to those districts which showed the greatest power of adaptation to the new industrial order. The reasons for the fatal delay in the introduction of machinery in the eastern and western counties of England were twofold: firstly, the conservatism of the workers, who claimed a vested interest in the industry, and were able to prevent, or at any rate retard, the use of machines which destroyed this vested interest; and secondly, the want of enterprise and energy on the part of the manufacturers, who lacked the stimulus which the proximity of the Lancashire cotton industry supplied to Yorkshire manufacturers to discard the traditional organisation of the woollen industry, and develop it—with the aid of machinery—on the lines of the factory system. "While the men of Leeds and Huddersfield," wrote a Hand-loom Commissioner in 1839, "were constantly in their mills and taking their meals at the same hours as their workpeople, the clothiers of Gloucestershire, some of them, were indulging in the habits and mixing with the 'gentle blood' of the land." We must now examine more closely the decline of industry in the West Country in order to see whether the evidence supports the view we expressed above as to the causes of the decline.

The West Country had water-power in abundance as Evidence of the decline. well as easy access to the coalfields;[1] yet neither one nor the other served to prevent the gradual decay of its woollen manufacture. Worcester, for example, boasted its streams, it was close to the Staffordshire coalfields, and a navigable

---

[1] Coal, of course, was cheaper in Yorkshire: it was said to be half the price in Gloucestershire.

river led to the Bristol Channel, yet the Worcester clothiers let their opportunities pass by and weakly succumbed. The Hand-loom Commissioner, who investigated the condition of the hand-loom weavers in the West Country, states that " twenty-three years ago (*i.e.*, in 1816) the great clothing district " of Somersetshire, Wiltshire, Devonshire, and Dorsetshire, " was in its most flourishing condition," but Collinson, the historian of Somersetshire, writing in 1791, gives repeated evidence of an earlier decline. Of Keynsham he says: " There was formerly a considerable woollen manufacture carried on here, but it is now entirely dropt." Pensford " has dreadfully decayed, and now, bereft of the benefit of trade, many of the houses are fallen into ruins." At Milverton " there was formerly a considerable manufacture of serges and druggets, which of late years is much declined." Yeovil had " formerly a large manufacture of woollen cloth, but now the principal one is of leather gloves." As regards Taunton, we are told that the woollen manufacture here " of late years has decayed "; and a later writer adds that " there is not at present (1821), it is believed, more than ten or twelve looms employed, and not above six or eight persons as wool-combers."

Somerset-shire.

A pamphlet written in 1800 attributed this decline of the West Country to the fact that " Yorkshire manufacturers can with much greater facility introduce machinery than we can in the West of England. The opposition that we generally meet with in introducing machinery is so great that until the Yorkshire manufacturers have stolen the article away from us, we are almost afraid to introduce it." We have already seen the difficulties which attended the introduction of the fly shuttle into the West Country,[1] and the spinning jenny received an equally hostile reception, provoking riots at Shepton Mallet in Somersetshire in 1776. In each case the opposition afterwards died down, but the delay enabled Yorkshire to reap the firstfruits of the new inventions and to consolidate her position. A clothier at Shepton Mallet has given evidence of the difficulties which he experienced in adopting improved methods. " I have

[1] Above, pp. 182-3.

upon introducing machinery been obliged to apply to
Government for military protection. I would introduce
machines that I do not now make use of, but for the great
opposition I know I must meet with from the labouring
manufacturers." In 1835 Somersetshire contained seventy-
four power-looms, but these " in strictness perhaps can
hardly be called power-looms. Power is in them applied
to part only of the operation of weaving; the shuttle is
thrown by hand, consequently each loom requires its own
separate attendant."

Some of the Gloucestershire manufacturers were more Glouces-
successful in overcoming the opposition to machinery. tershire.
One writer tells us that " in the county of Gloucester fifty
years ago (*i.e.*, 1750) the clothing business flourished to a
very great extent, but afterwards migrated in a considerable degree to Yorkshire, where the price of labour was
less, the necessaries of life cheaper, and actual wealth had
not produced indolence. In consequence of this decline the
populous parishes of Bisley, Horsley, Stroud, and others in
those enchanting vales, fell into decay, and almost wholly
into beggary. I cannot forget the colonies of mendicants
which, thirty years ago, poured from them into the adjacent
towns on the Cotswold Hills. If you asked a beggar from
the first of those parishes whence he came, it was common,
even to a proverb, for him to answer: ' From Bisley—God
help !' Not many years have elapsed since the manufacturers of this county introduced into it the most perfect
machinery. Immediately all difference of local expense
was lost. Trade has been carried to a greater degree than
before; the inhabitants are employed; and an air of neat-
ness and comfort has succeeded to the most squalid
wretchedness."

While little opposition to machinery seems to have Wiltshire.
been experienced in Gloucestershire—at any rate until
the attempted introduction of the shearing frame —
in Wiltshire machinery was " more imperfect from the
blind prejudice of the workmen who have attempted to
oppose its introduction by force." The cloth-finishers
strenuously resisted the application of the gig mill to fine

cloth,[1] but the spinners, who were women and children, could not have prevented the erection of spinning machinery. Hence the failure to introduce spinning machinery in Wiltshire must be explained, not on the ground of the opposition which it might have been expected to excite, but because a large part of Wiltshire supplied its yarn to manufacturing districts in other counties. When, therefore, the latter began to establish their own factories, the Wiltshire industry received a fatal blow, and the spinners engaged in it were thrown out of employment.

Extent of the Migration of Industry. The extent of the migration of industry from the eastern and western counties to the West Riding is seen in the following table, showing the growth of population in the chief manufacturing areas:

Counties.	Population.		
	1700.	1801.	1851.
West Riding	242,139	572,168	1,325,495
Gloucestershire ..	157,348	250,723	458,805
Wiltshire	152,372	183,820	254,221
Norfolk	245,842	273,479	442,714

One feature of this migration was the growth of large towns as the result of the concentration of workmen in factories. The population of Leeds expanded from 53,000 at the beginning of the nineteenth century to 172,000 half a century later, and Bradford increased from 13,000 to 103,000. This unexampled growth of large urban centres brought in its train grave social problems. The accommodation provided for the new inhabitants was wretched in the extreme, and the Government ultimately found it necessary to appoint a Commission to enquire into the state of the towns. The Report of the Commissioners gave the following account of the sanitary conditions existing at Leeds in 1845: " By far the most unhealthy localities of Leeds are close squares of houses, or yards as they are called, which have been erected for the accommodation of working people. Some

[1] Above, p. 189.

of these, though situated in comparatively high ground, are airless from the enclosed structure, and being wholly unprovided with any form of under-drainage, or convenience, or arrangements for cleansing, are one mass of damp and filth. In some instances I found cellars or under-rooms, with from two to six inches of water standing over the floors. . . . The ashes, garbage, and filth of all kinds are thrown from the doors and windows of the house upon the surface of the streets and courts. . . . The feelings of the people are blunted to all seeming decency, and from the constantly contaminated state of the atmosphere, a vast amount of ill-health prevails, leading to listlessness, and inducing a desire for spirits and opiates; the combined influence of the whole condition causing much loss of time, increasing poverty, and terminating the existence of many in premature death."

In the course of the nineteenth century the state of the towns was gradually improved, but the progressive amelioration of the social and economic condition of textile workers is a duty still laid upon those who have inherited the ancient and proud traditions of the English woollen and worsted industries.

APPENDICES

APPENDIX I

ESTIMATES OF THE COST OF MANUFACTURING A PIECE OF CLOTH

THE first estimate is for the seventeenth century. It is contained in Sir Matthew Hale, *A Discourse touching Provision for the Poor*, p. 15 (published in 1683).

" The ordinary process and time and charge of making a common coarse medley cloth of our Gloucester wool at this day is:

I. " In every such cloth of about 32 yards long there is ninety pounds of wool, which will cost at this day, at 12d. per pound, £4 10s., viz., ordinary in a grey cloth.

	£	s.	d.
54 lb. of abb, 34 lb. of warp, 2 lb. of mixture	4	10	0

II. " The charge of making this cloth:

	£	s.	d.
1. Parting and picking	0	3	0
2. Colouring	0	16	0
3. Breaking and spinning the abb, at 2¼d. per lb.	1	7	9
4. Breaking and spinning the warp at 5d. per lb.	0	18	6
5. Cards and oil	1	0	0
6. Weaving, spooling, and warping	1	1	3
7. Milling (fulling) and burling	0	12	0
8. Shearing and dressing	0	18	0
9. Drawing	0	1	6
10. Carriage and factorage	0	7	0
[Cost of wool]	4	10	0
So the whole charges come to	£11	15	0

" Out of which, deducting the materials of wool and cards and oil, viz., £5 10s., there remains entirely for the expense of work [to the] amount [of], £6 5s. It is true, at this day, this cloth yields not above £12 to be sold, which is only 5s. profit; but when trade is quicker, it may yield £13 or more.

III. " The people that are employed in bringing about this cloth to be ready, are 14, viz., 3 weavers and spoolers, 2 breakers, 6 spinners, 1 fuller and burler, 1 shearman, 1 parter and picker: the weavers supply the office of spooler and warper.

IV. " These will bring about the first cloth in about 2 months' space; but being continued in a constant tract, the cloth will be brought about in 3 weeks' time; for all the other workmen are at work and fit the cloth for the weaver in that space, that he is weaving the first cloth.

V. " Consequently this one loom thus employed all the year round, allowing 2 months to the first cloth, and 3 weeks to every other, will make 14 returns the first year of cloth ready for sale, and 16 returns every year after.

VI. " Consequently that which this [loom] yields for bare wages to these 14 poor workmen for the first year is £87 10s., and for the following years is £97; and by this computation it is easy to see what every workman can gain a week being full employed."

TABLES SHOWING THE TIME REQUIRED BY AN INDIVIDUAL TO MAKE A PIECE OF SUPERFINE BROADCLOTH AND THE COST OF LABOUR. (*Parliamentary Papers*, 1840, vol. xxiii, p. 439 *et seq.*)

(A) From 1781 to 1796.

Nature of Employment.	Quantity.	Persons Employed.	Time.	Cost for a Piece.	Weekly Earnings.
			Hrs. Min.	£ s. d.	£ s. d.
1. Cleansing the wool	80 lbs.	1 man	3 22	0 0 9	0 12 0
2. Picking	80 ,,	1 woman	101 2	0 8 5¼	0 4 6
3. Scribbling by hand	75 ,,	1 man	96 0	0 11 8	0 8 0
4. Spinning warp	26 ,,	1 woman and 1 child	260 0	1 12 6	{ woman 0 7 2 / child 0 2 6 }
5. Spinning abb	44 ,,	1 woman and 2 children	352 0	1 9 4	{ woman 0 6 1 / 2 children 0 4 0 }
6. Spooling warp	26 ,,	1 old woman	52 0	0 2 2	0 3 0
7. Warping	26 ,,	1 woman	12 0	0 0 8½	0 4 0
8. Reeling abb	44 ,,	1 child	12 0	0 0 6	0 3 0
9. Weaving	1 piece, 34 ells	2 men and 1 child	364 0	2 15 6	{ master 0 12 3¾ / journeyman 0 3 6 / child 0 2 0 / sizing 0 0 9 }
10. Scouring	,,	1 man and 1 boy	3 0	0 0 6	(not known)
11. Burling	,,	1 woman	32 0	0 3 0	0 3 6
12. Felting	,,	1 man and 1 boy	10 0	0 8 0	boy 0 7 0
					The weekly earnings not known. Hours of labour uncertain: if paid by the week .. 1 4 0
13. Raising the nap	,,	1 man	88 0	0 14 2	0 11 0
14. Shearing	,,	1 man	72 0	0 10 0	0 10 0
15. Pressing and finishing	,,	1 man	2 0	0 1 0	0 10 0
Total				£8 18 2¼	

NOTE.—The weaver, out of his earnings, had to pay house-rent, and all the expenses of the wear and tear of loom and tackle.

(B) From 1796 to 1805.

Machinery was introduced in this period for scribbling, carding, and spinning. The fly shuttle also came into use.

Nature of Employment.	Quantity.	Persons Employed.	Time. Hrs. Min.	Cost for a Piece. £ s. d.	Weekly Earnings. £ s. d.
1. Cleansing the wool	80 lbs.	1 man	3 22	0 0 9	0 12 2
2. Picking	80 ,,	1 woman	101 2	0 10 2¼	0 5 0
3. Scribbling by machine	75 ,,	1 child	14 0	0 0 7	0 3 0
4. Carding by machine	75 ,,	1 child	13 21	0 0 7	0 3 0
5. Slubbing by machine	25 ,,	1 man and 2 children	7 4	0 2 7¼	{ man 0 19 4 / each child 0 2 6 }
6. Spinning warp	25 ,,	1 woman	38 17	0 11 1	0 14 4½
7. Spinning abb	50 ,,	1 man and 2 children	34 17	0 11 5½	{ man 0 19 6 / each child 0 2 0 }
8. Reeling abb	50 ,,	1 child	12 0	0 0 6	
9. Spooling by machinery	25 ,,	1 woman	24 0	0 1 6¼	
10. Warping round bar	25 ,,	1 woman	10 0	0 0 8½	
11. Weaving by spring shuttle	1 piece, 34 ells	1 man and 1 child	252 0	2 11 6	{ man 1 2 0 / child 0 2 6 / sizing 0 1 6 } (not known)
12. Scouring	,,	1 man and 1 boy	3 0	0 0 6	boy 0 6 0
13. Burling	,,	1 woman	32 0	0 3 0	0 7 0
14. Felting	,,	1 man and 1 boy	12 0	0 8 0	The weekly earnings not known. Hours of labour uncertain: if paid by the week .. 1 4 0
15. Raising the nap	,,	1 man and 1 boy	12 0	0 3 8	{ man 0 15 0 / boy 0 7 0 }
16. Shearing	,,	1 man	88 0	0 14 9	0 12 0
17. Pressing and finishing	,,	1 man	2 0	0 1 0	0 12 0
Total				£6 3 5	

(C) *From 1805 to 1820.*

Machinery was introduced in this period for shearing the cloth. One man now sheared a piece of cloth in 18 hours; the cost was 3s. 9d., and his weekly earnings were 15s. The cost for labour was thus reduced to £5 15s. 5d.

(D) *The year 1828.*

The Mule was introduced for spinning warp and abb. One man and one child spun 75 lbs. of wool with two mules in 12 hours at the cost of 1s. 9d.; the man's weekly earnings were 15s. and the child's 3s. A new operation, boiling the cloth, was also introduced. It occupied a man 1 hour and cost 2d. Further, a new machine enabled a man to shear the cloth in 6 hours at a cost of 1s. 3d.; his weekly earnings were 15s.

The cost of labour was reduced to £4 7s. 3½d., or 50 per cent. of the cost in the first period, and the time occupied was reduced to a quarter.

APPENDIX II

BIBLIOGRAPHICAL NOTE

THE materials for the history of the English woollen and worsted industries are drawn from numerous sources, which can be classified as follows. (I have given an account of the mediæval sources in the *Transactions of the Royal Historical Society*, Third Series, vol. x.)

I.—OFFICIAL RECORDS.

The most important for the Middle Ages are the *Statutes of the Realm, Rolls of Parliament, Patent Rolls, Close Rolls, Pipe Rolls,* Rymer's *Fœdera*. Occasional references will also be found in *Domesday Book, Hundred Rolls, Charter Rolls, Fine Rolls, Chancery Rolls, Reports of the Historical Manuscripts Commission*. The most important for the modern period (in addition to the *Statutes* and the *Hist. MSS. Comm.*) are the *Materials for the History of Henry VII., Letters and Papers of Henry VIII., Domestic State Papers, Acts of the Privy Council, Acts of the Interregnum, Journals of the House of Commons, Journals of the House of Lords, Venetian State Papers, Court of Requests,* Crawford's *Proclamations.* For the nineteenth century there is an invaluable series of Parliamentary Papers: *Reports on the Woollen Manufacture* (especially the Reports of 1803 and 1806), on the *Wool Trade*, on *Apprenticeship*, on *Artisans*, on *Trade Unionism*, on *Hand-loom Weavers*, on *Employment of Children in Factories*, on *The State of Large Towns*. Useful statistical material is contained in the *Accounts and Papers*.

II.—CHRONICLES.

Adam Murimuth, *Annales Monastici, De Antiquis Legibus Liber,* Fabyan, Jocelyn, Holinshed, Walter of Hemingburgh.

III.—TOWN RECORDS.

These are an invaluable depository of materials. Beverley (Leach, *Town Documents*). Bristol (Bickley, *Little Red Book*). Cardiff (Matthews, *Records*). Colchester (Benham, *Red Paper Book*). Coventry (Harris, *Leet Book*). Gloucester (Stevenson, *Corporation Records*). Leicester (Bateson, *Records*). London (Sharpe, *Letter Books ;* Riley, *Liber Albus, Liber Custumarum, Memorials*). Northampton (Markham, *Records*). Norwich (Hudson and Tingey, *Records*). Nottingham (Stevenson, *Records*). Oxford (Turner, *Records*). Reading (Guilding, *Records*). Southampton (Studer, *Oak Book ;* Gidden, *Letters Patent ;* Wallis Chapman, *Black Book*). York (Sellers, *Memorandum Book*).

18

IV.—TOWN (INCLUDING GILDS) AND COUNTY HISTORIES.

Abram (*History of Blackburn*). E. Baines (*History of Lancashire*). T. Baines (*Yorkshire Past and Present*). Ballard (*Chronicles of Woodstock*). Blomefield (*Norfolk*). Boyce (*Memoirs of Tiverton*). Coates (*History of Reading*). Collinson (*History of Somersetshire*). Cromwell (*History of Colchester*). Davies (*Records of York*). Drake (*Eboracum*). Dunsford (*Tiverton*). Eyton (*Antiquities of Shropshire*). Farrer (*Early Yorkshire Charters*). Fox (*Guild of Weavers in Bristol ; Merchant Taylors of Bristol*). Green (*History of Worcester*). Hall (*Ancient Charters of Sheffield ; Charters relating to Sheffield*). Harding (*History of Tiverton*). Harland (*Mamecestre*). Herbert (*Twelve Great Livery Companies*). Hibbert (*English Gilds*). Hudson (*Leet Jurisdiction in Norwich*). Johnson (*Drapers of London*). Latimer (*Merchant Venturers' Society, Bristol*). *History of Newbury and its Environs.* Noake (*Worcester*). Polwhele (*History of Cornwall*). Poulson (*Beverley*). Powell (*A Suffolk Hundred*). Risdon (*Description of Devon*). Rudder (*History of Cirencester*). Seyer (*Memoirs of Bristol*). Smith (*English Gilds*). Thoresby (*Topography of Leeds*). Toulmin (*History of Taunton*). *Victoria County Histories.* Warner (*History of Bath*). Watson (*History of Halifax*). Westcote (*View of Devonshire*). Wodderspoon (*Memorials of Ipswich*).

V.—TRANSACTIONS OF SOCIETIES, ETC.

Antiquaries of Scotland (*Proceedings*). *Archæological Journal. Bradford Chamber of Commerce* (*Reports*). *British Archæological Association. Bristol and Gloucestershire Archæological Society. Devonshire Association* (*Transactions*). *Economic Journal. English Historical Review. Gaelic Society of Inverness. London and Middlesex Archæological Society. Notes and Queries. Oxford Historical Society. Somerset Quarter Sessions Records. Somersetshire Archæological Society. Statistical Journal. Sussex Archæological Collections. Suffolk Institute. Ulster Journal. Wiltshire Archæological Magazine.* (With these may be grouped the eighteenth-century publications— the *British Merchant*, the *Gentleman's Magazine*, the *London Journal*, the *Manufacturer*, the *Pamphleteer*, and the *Weaver*.)

VI.—LITERARY AND MISCELLANEOUS SOURCES (FOR TOPO-
GRAPHICAL AND GENERAL ECONOMIC DETAILS).

Aikin (*Description of the Country round Manchester*). Ashby (*Poems*, ed. Bateson). Bakewell (*Observations on the Influence of Soil and Climate upon Wool*). Bamfard (*Dialect of South Lancashire*). *Black Book of the Admiralty.* Burnet (*History of the Reformation*, ed. Pocock). Camden (*Britannia*). Chamberlayne (*Anglia Notitia*). Chaucer (*Canterbury Tales*). Coke (*Second Part of the Institutes*). Collinge (*The Weaver's Pocket-Book*). Defoe (*Tour through Great Britain*, ed. 1724). Delony (*Works*, ed. Mann). Dryden (*King Arthur*). Eden (*State of the Poor*). *English Economic History, Select Documents* (ed. Bland, Brown, and Tawney). Fuller (*Church*

History, Worthies of England). Gaskell (*Artisans and Machinery ; Manufacturing Population of England*). Glyde (*New Suffolk Garland*). Hale (*Primitive Organisation of Mankind ; A Discourse touching Provision for the Poor*). Halliwell (*Norfolk Anthology*). Haslam (*The Handloom Weaver's Daughter*). Hazlitt (*Fugitive Poetical Tracts*). *Italian Relation of England* (Camden Soc. Pub.). Kingsford (*English Historical Literature in the Fifteenth Century*). Lambard (*Perambulation of Kent*). Langland (*Piers Plowman*). Leland (*Itinerary*, ed. Smith). *Letter Books of Holroyd and Hill* (ed. Heaton). Macpherson (*Annals of Commerce*). Madox (*History of the Exchequer*). May (*Declaration of the Estate of Clothing*). Misselden (*Circle of Commerce*). Moens (*Dutch Church at Colchester ; Walloon Church of Norwich*). Ogle (*Royal Letters addressed to Oxford*). Pauli (*Drei volkswirthschaftliche Denkschriften*). Pennant (*Tour in Scotland and Voyage to the Hebrides*). *Political Poems and Songs* (ed. Wright). Postlethwayt (*Dictionary of Trade and Commerce*). *Records of a Scottish Cloth Manufactory at New Mills, Haddingtonshire* (ed. Scott). *Report of the Highland Society of Scotland on Shetland Wool* (Appendix IV.). *Ricart's Kalendar* (ed. L. T. Smith). *Select Charters of Trading Companies* (Selden Soc. Pub.). Sharpe (*Calendar of Wills*). Smith (*Memoirs of Wool*). Smith, A. (*Wealth of Nations*, ed. Cannan). Stow (*Survey of London*, ed. Kingsford). Swift, J. (*Journal to Stella*, ed. Aitken). Taylor, W. C. (*Tour in the Manufacturing Districts of Lancashire*). *Winner and Waster* (ed. Gollancz). Yarranton (*England's Improvement*). Young (*Six Months' Tour*).

VII.—PAMPHLETS.

There exists, for the seventeenth and eighteenth centuries, an extensive pamphlet literature, to be found especially in the British Museum, the Bodleian Library, and the Goldsmiths' Library (London University). An enumeration of their titles would occupy considerable space and must therefore be omitted, but references to these pamphlets will be given in the second volume of the *Economic History of England*. The pamphlet, in the form of a play, referred to in the text (p. 53) is *The Beaux Merchant, A Comedy, By a Clothier* (? J. Blanch). The date is 1714.

VIII.—PROCESSES AND INVENTIONS.

(Some of the works mentioned above are also useful for this section.)

Baines (*Cotton Industry*). Barlow (*History and Principles of Weaving*). Beck (*The Draper's Dictionary*). Burnley (*History of Wool and Wool-Combing*). Cartwright (*Memoir of Edmund Cartwright*). Clapham (*Woollen and Worsted Industries*). Dobson (*Evolution of the Spinning Machine*). *Dictionary of National Biography*. Duncan (*Essays on the Art of Weaving*). Dyer (*The Fleece*). Espinasse (*Lancashire Worthies*). French (*Life and Times of Crompton*, with an Appendix by R. Cole). Gray (*Treatise on Spinning*

Machinery). Guest (*Compendious History of the Cotton Manufacture*). Hirst (*History of the Woollen Trade for the Last Sixty Years*). Kennedy (*Brief Memoir of Crompton* in *Memoirs of the Literary and Philosophical Society of Manchester*, 2nd Ser., V.). Luccock (*Wool*). Radcliffe (*Origin of Power-Loom Weaving*). Smiles (*Huguenots*). Watts (*The Young Man's Looking-Glass*). Woodcroft (*Brief Biographies of Inventors*). Wright (*Volume of Vocabularies*, containing the *Dictionary of John de Garlande*).

IX.—MODERN AUTHORITIES.

Abram (*Social England in the Fifteenth Century*). Ashley (*English Economic History: Woollen Industry*). Atton and Holland (*The King's Customs*). Baines (*The Woollen Trade of Yorkshire* in *Yorkshire Past and Present*). Beer (*Commercial Policy of England toward the American Colonies*). Bischoff (*History of the Woollen and Worsted Manufactures*). Bonwick (*Romance of the Wool Trade*). Bowley (*Wages in the United Kingdom*). Brentano (*History and Development of Gilds*). Burn (*History of the Foreign Refugees*). Clapham (Articles in the *Economic Journal*, 1906 and 1910). Clark (*Working Life of Women in the Seventeenth Century*). Lohmann (*Der englischen Woll-industrie*). Cunningham (*Alien Immigrants ; Growth of English Industry*). Duchesne (*L'Evolution de l'Industrie de la Laine*). Dunlop (*English Apprenticeship*). Gras (*Early English Customs System*). Green (*Town Life in the Fifteenth Century*). Hammond (*Town Labourer ; Skilled Labourer*). Heaton (*Yorkshire Woollen and Worsted Industries* [contains a map showing probable distribution of the woollen industry in 1470, and the colloquial poem quoted in the text, p. 72]; *Tricks of the Trade*, in Thoresby Soc., xxii., part 3 [contains an account of the Russian legend (see text, p. 120)]; *The Leeds White Cloth Hall*, in Thoresby Soc., xxii.). Holyoake (*The Co-operative Movement*). Hutchins and Harrison (*Factory Legislation*). James (*History of Bradford ; History of the Worsted Manufacture*). Leonard (*English Poor Relief*). Lipson (*Economic History of England*). Mantoux (*La Révolution Industrielle*). McCulloch (*Dictionary of Commerce*). Porter (*Progress of the Nation*). Pryce (*Memorials of the Canynges' Family*). Rogers (*History of Agriculture and Prices*). Salzmann (*English Industries of the Middle Ages*). Samuel Brothers (*Wool and Worsted Manufactures*). Scott (*Joint-Stock Companies*). Schanz (*Englische Handelspolitik*). Smart (*Economic Annals of the Nineteenth Century*). Swift (*James the First of Aragon*). Taylor, R. W. C. (*History of the Factory System*). Toynbee (*Industrial Revolution*). Unwin (*Finance and Trade under Edward III. ; Industrial Organisation*). Ure (*Dictionary of Art, Manufactures*). Webb (*History of Trade Unionism ; Industrial Democracy*). Wright (*Homes of Other Days ; History of Domestic Manners*).

INDEX

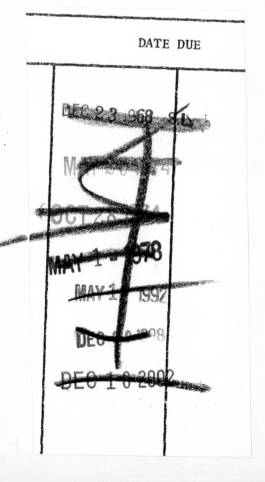